Class in Education

Access to economic resources is becoming the defining issue of the twenty-first century. Inequity is stark and pervasive. Consequently, from the daily papers to the academic presses, the once marginalized concept of "class" is gaining widespread attention. *Class in Education* argues that the "class" of much contemporary social and educational theory does not go far enough in its analyses. The authors suggest that, as a result, it cannot enable the production of knowledges, pedagogies, and subjectivities needed to change inequitable access to economic resources and the many socio-cultural inequities that this fosters.

In many contemporary articulations the term "class" shies away from explaining that it is the production relations of capitalism that cause economic inequity and therefore must be changed. Instead, it focuses on describing and changing various cultural attributes of groups and individuals, often in order to produce "updated" subjects better suited to compete with one another in circumstances of sharpening economic inequity. *Class in Education* intervenes in this trend, which quietly sustains and extends the tenets of neoliberalism into the daily lives of teachers and students, chief among which is the premise that a society based on free-market competition among individuals is not only singularly necessary but also pre-eminently natural. This volume of essays argues for the necessity and effectiveness of a materialist rather than a culturalist understanding of class.

Across a range of issues – from racism to reading, school-level curricula to educational policy – the essays in *Class in Education* argue for and demonstrate in their arguments that a materialist understanding of class has the explanatory power to analyze the structure of owning and power in social relations, and therefore to point to ways to abolish exploitation of human beings and restructure society in a more egalitarian way.

Deborah Kelsh is Associate Professor in the Department of Teacher Education at The College of Saint Rose in Albany, New York, US.

Dave Hill is Professor of Education Policy at the University of Northampton, UK.

Sheila Macrine is Associate Professor in the Curriculum and Teaching Department at Montclair State University in New Jersey, US.

Class in Education

Knowledge, pedagogy, subjectivity

Edited by Deborah Kelsh, Dave Hill
and Sheila Macrine

LONDON AND NEW YORK

First published 2010
by Routledge
2 Park Square, Milton Park, Abingdon, Oxon OX14 4RN

Simultaneously published in the USA and Canada
by Routledge
711 Third Avenue, New York, NY 10017

Routledge is an imprint of the Taylor & Francis Group, an informa business

Typeset in Garamond by Pindar NZ, Auckland, New Zealand

British Library Cataloguing in Publication Data
A catalogue record for this book is available from the British Library

Library of Congress Cataloging in Publication Data
Class in education : knowledge, pedagogy, subjectivity / edited by Deborah
Kelsh, Dave Hill, and Sheila Macrine.
    p. cm.
  Includes bibliographical references and index.
  1. Educational sociology. 2. Critical pedagogy. 3. Educational
equalization. 4. Social classes—Economic aspects. I. Kelsh, Deborah. II.
Hill, Dave, 1945- III. Macrine, Sheila L.
  LC189.C545 2010
    306.43s—dc22   2009009253

ISBN 13: 978-0-415-45027-0 (hbk)
ISBN 13: 978-0-203-87093-8 (ebk)
ISBN 13: 978-0-415-84660-8 (pbk)

Contents

Figures

Contributors

Grant Banfield teaches educational sociology and qualitative approaches to research in the School of Education at Flinders University, Adelaide. His intellectual interests lie in the application of Marxism and critical realist philosophy to the problems of education, schooling and "critical" pedagogy in contemporary capitalist society. Grant's research interests center on contributing to the development of emancipatory social science and practice directed towards the realization of an ecologically sane and truly human future.

Mike Cole is Research Professor in Education and Equality, and Head of Research at Bishop Grosseteste University College Lincoln, UK. He has published widely in the area of education and equality, racism, and Marxism and educational theory. He is the author of *Marxism and Educational Theory: origins and issues*, (2008), the editor of *Professional Attributes and Practice for Student Teachers*, 4th Edition (2008), and *Education, Equality and Human Rights: issues of gender, "race," sexuality, disability and social class*, 2nd edition, all published by Routledge.

Teresa L. Ebert's writings include *Ludic Feminism and After* and *The Task of Cultural Critique*. She is co-author (with Mas'ud Zavarzadeh) of *Class in Culture* and co-editor of two volumes in the Transformation series on Marxism and postmodernity and on Marxism, queer theory and gender. The essay on "hypohumanities" in this book is an excerpt from the book she has co-written, titled *Hypohumanities*.

Robert Faivre teaches a range of courses for the English Division at Adirondack Community College, State University of New York (US), where he is a Professor. His interests are in the intersections of reading and class, and he is working on a book that develops a materialist theory of reading.

Dave Hill is Professor of Education Policy at the University of Northampton, UK, and Chief Editor, *Journal for Critical Education Policy Studies*, at www.jceps.com. He heads the independent e-Institute for Education Policy Studies, at www.ieps.org.uk. He is the Series Editor for Education and Neoliberalism, and for Education and Marxism, both published by Routledge. He lectures worldwide on Marxism and Education and on Radical/Socialist education.

Deborah Kelsh is an Associate Professor in the Department of Teacher Education at The College of Saint Rose in Albany, New York (US). Her scholarship focuses on the question of class in relation to the production of knowledge and pedagogy. She has publications in several journals, including *The Red Critique* and *Cultural Logic*, and a chapter in *Feminism and Composition Studies* (1998). She is working on a book on materialist pedagogy.

Ravi Kumar teaches sociology in the Department of Sociology, Jamia Millia Islamia University, New Delhi. He has experience working with the students' movement and other grassroots movements in backward regions of India. His publications include *The Politics of Imperialism and Counterstrategies* (co-edited, Delhi: Aakar Books, 2004); *The Crisis of Elementary Education in India* (edited, Sage, 2006); and *Global Neoliberalism and Education and its Consequences* (co-edited, Routledge: New York, 2008).

Peter McLaren, Ph.D., is a Professor at the Graduate School of Education and Information Studies, University of California, Los Angeles. He is the author, co-author, editor and co-editor of approximately 40 books and monographs. Several hundred of his articles, chapters, interviews, reviews, commentaries and columns have appeared in dozens of scholarly journals and professional magazines since the publication of his first book, *Cries from the Corridor*, in 1980. His work has been translated into 17 languages. He lectures internationally and is a member of the Industrial Workers of the World.

Sheila Macrine, Ph.D., is an Associate Professor in the Curriculum and Teaching Department at Montclair State University in New Jersey (US). Her scholarly interests focus on connecting the cultural, institutional and personal contexts of pedagogy, particularly as they relate to the social imagination and progressive democratic education. She writes about the relationships among the complex social issues of difference (race, class, gender and disability, etc.) within urban schools and the political economy of schooling within the broader context of post-industrial capitalism.

Alpesh Maisuria is a Senior Lecturer at the University of Wolverhampton, UK. He teaches across a range of Education Studies modules. His specialization is the sociology of education, particularly the analysis of "race" through social class, adopting and developing a classical Marxist perspective. Alpesh has also published papers exploring the private sector's involvement in education. He has recently explored the "war on terror" and its linkages to capitalist relations of production, particularly exploring Critical Race Theory and the Marxist concept of racialization.

Enver Motala was a lawyer for the independent trade union movement during the apartheid era and also played a significant role in the anti-apartheid education movement. After the first democratic elections, he was appointed the Deputy Director-General of Education in the province of Gauteng. He is presently an associate of the Education Policy Consortium for whom he has coordinated research projects on democracy, human rights and social justice in education in South Africa. He has also done similar work for the Nelson Mandela Foundation.

Greg Queen is a social studies teacher at Fitzgerald High School in Warren, Michigan. He is co-editor of *The Rouge Forum News* and has made numerous presentations at professional meetings, including the National Council for the Social Studies and Michigan Council for the Social Studies. He is the lead author of "'I Participate, You Participate, We Participate…': Notes on Building a K-16 Movement for Democracy and Social Justice," published in *Workplace: A Journal for Academic Labor* (www.workplace-gsc.com).

E. Wayne Ross is Professor in the Department of Curriculum Studies at the University of British Columbia in Vancouver, Canada. He is the author of numerous publications on curriculum theory, politics of education, and critical pedagogy. His edited books include *Battleground Schools: an encyclopedia of conflict and controversy* (Greenwood, co-edited with Sandra Mathison), *Neoliberalism and Education Reform* (Hampton Press, co-edited with Rich Gibson) and *Democratic Social Education* (RoutledgeFalmer, co-edited with David Hursh). He is a former daycare and secondary school teacher and a co-founder of The Rouge Forum (www.rougeforum.org).

E. San Juan, Jr. heads the Philippines Cultural Studies Center, Storrs, CT (US). He is Emeritus Professor of English, Comparative Literature, and Ethnic Studies at various universities. He was a fellow at the W.E.B. Du Bois Institute, Harvard University, in Spring 2009. His recent books are *In the Wake of Terror* (Lexington) and *US Imperialism and Revolution in the Philippines* (Palgrave).

Salim Vally is a member of the Faculty of Education, University of Johannesburg, South Africa. He was a regional executive member of the high school South African Students Movement until its banning in 1977. He is the spokesperson of the Anti-War Coalition and the Palestine Solidarity Committee, serves on the boards of various non-governmental and professional organizations, and is an active member of various social movements. Vally is also the coordinator of the Education Rights Project which works with communities in many townships and informal settlements around the country.

Mas'ud Zavarzadeh is author of several books including *Seeing Films Politically*. His new book, *Totality and the Post*, will be published early next year.

Foreword

E. San Juan, Jr.

With the collapse of the Soviet Union in 1989, the ruling classes of the industrialized world celebrated the end of class struggle and the proverbial immortality of the capitalist world-system. But scarcely had its first decade ended when disaster struck. Behind the illusion of a permanent market utopia lurked internal decay, a precipitous meltdown. September 11, 2001 was just a portent of the impending breakdown. With the slide of the US and the world economy into an unprecedented impasse, a crisis reminiscent of the 1929 Wall Street crash, but much more all-encompassing given the "flat world" of globalized finance capital, we are faced with a lesson that should have been learned when Marx and Engels invoked the "specter" of revolution in their 1848 *Manifesto* – the lesson of class struggle as the necessary framework for understanding world history and its laws of motion. It is one we need today in order to grapple with and make sense of the contradictory currents and tendencies traversing our daily lives, for which this book is a timely heuristic and guide.

The contemporary situation is indeed even worse than in 1929, or since World War II (as Kevin Phillips observes [2008]). In her lead essay, Deborah Kelsh sums up the sharpened class contradictions in the US and around the world hidden behind pluralist, post- and neo-Weberian mystifications. Kelsh uses the astutely formulated concept of "cultureclass" to denote the way in which the dominant ideology obscures private property – that is, the private ownership of the vital means of production and the private appropriation of material wealth (aggregated surplus value) produced by workers – on which class exploitation is grounded. "Cultureclass" prevents the people from acquiring the necessary knowledge of the totality of social relations of production – a knowledge of the internal contradictions inherent in a crisis-ridden capitalist society. This knowledge equals class consciousness, enabling a radical praxis of critique to transform society. "Cultureclass" separates culture and plural identities from their roots in "the inequitable binary relation of owning," the foundation of capitalist production and exploitation. Preventing a critical analysis of property relations, "cultureclass" serves as the ideological instrument of finance-capital based on the commodification of knowledge, culture, ideas, etc. for corporate profit and capital accumulation. "Cultureclass" is the neoliberal privileging of minds detached from labor, subordinating the call of every person's "freedom from need" to the "free-market" demands of status-obsessed consumerism.

Kelsh's theorizing of "cultureclass" at the opening of this volume is crucial in clarifying the seductive logic of neoliberalism for many educators, technocrats, and professionals. Neoliberalism as the chief ideology of capitalist globalization and the prevailing ethos of neoconservatism – a phenomenon described succinctly by E. Wayne Ross and Greg Queen in their contribution here – has reconfigured the landscape since the 1848 *Communist Manifesto*. But the basic nature of capitalism, namely, the exploitation of labor-power and the private appropriation of social wealth produced by the propertyless majority, remains intact, even while imperial finance-capital has conserved and modified its earlier stages of merchant and industrial capitalism. In this context, one asks: In what way has the ideological apparatus of modern schooling, and education in general, which produces/reproduces class relations (the social division of labor) changed over time? How can the established structures of schooling be revolutionized so as to promote equality, social justice, and a democratic socialist order? This book aims to provide a critique of the traditional mode of schooling designed to reproduce class inequality and an exploration of how to alter that system in an emancipatory anti-imperialist direction.

In 1960, at the height of US prosperity, Harold Benjamin expressed the mainstream view of education as a basic social institution designed for two purposes: "the conservation of sound traditional values, and the encouragement of innovation and the creation of new concepts sufficient to serve the needs of a growing, changing culture" (375). While conserving the basic institutions, education adapts and modifies them; thus, stability and change co-exist (Kozol 2006). On the whole, schools are primarily meant to preserve the values and knowledge maintaining the status quo. But somehow they aren't doing the job well, so problems occur, as indicated by the questions often discussed then: "Who shall be educated? Who shall teach? Who shall control and support the schools? What shall be taught? How shall the teaching be done?" (Benjamin 1960: 375). In 1940, Harvard University President James Conant called on schools to promote "social equality" by diversifying programs to produce not only scholars but also artists, craftsmen, those with "intuitive judgment on practical affairs" (1940). After World War II, the support and buttressing of US global ascendancy became the national goal. While many believe that the Soviet Union's launching of Sputnik rockets in 1957 triggered a progressive reorientation in educational thinking, it was actually the profound sociopolitical upheavals of the 1960s that imbued Benjamin's questions with new urgency. In 1969, those questions were articulated in a libertarian, populist discourse by Neil Postman and Charles Weingartner in *Teaching as a Subversive Activity*. But, while exhorting us to pursue crap detection, their idea of the educated person – a flexible, tolerant, innovative "liberal personality who can face uncertainty and ambiguity" – has morphed into the postmodern indeterminate cyborg: the performative, hybrid, crap deconstructor! Their retooling of education as a survival strategy for the nuclear-space age, a regulation of the body-mind syndromes to cope with the rapidly changing environment of the Cold War, is now a respectable Establishment propaedeutic, part of what Teresa L. Ebert and Mas'ud Zavarzadeh, in Chapter 2, would label a species of instrumentalist "hypohumanities" (see also Ebert and Zavarzadeh 2008).

There is no mystery about the function and purpose of education in the United States from its inception. It was always meant to serve the preservation and reinforcement of capitalism since the nineteenth century. Howard Zinn (1980) recounts how the public school system was designed to inculcate in the literate labor force "obedience to authority" coincident with the rise of the corporate state. Citing standard teacher training texts meant to transform "the child from a little savage into a creature of law and order, fit for the life of civilized society," Zinn reminds us how loyalty oaths, teacher certification, textbook screening, and the requirement of citizenship were introduced to control schooling – a "gigantic organization of know-ledge and education for orthodoxy and obedience" that nevertheless provoked dissent and protest (257–8). This historically defined efficacy of education (in its economic structure and ideological content) as an institution for reproducing class inequality and polarization of power has been acutely examined by Samuel Bowles and Herbert Gintis in their instructive work, *Democracy and Capitalism* (1986).

Notwithstanding its vigorous critique of education as a tool of social integration, legitimation and reproduction, a thesis much more rigorously argued by Pierre Bourdieu in his wide-ranging sociocultural inquiries, Bowles and Gintis were unable to fully argue for a radical transformation of education in a socialist direction. Their failure inheres in their unquestioning positivist and empiricist research procedure, heedless of the dialectical-materialist analytic deployed by Marxist thinkers such as Antonio Gramsci, Georg Lukács, and Paulo Freire, among others. As Madan Sarup (1978) observes, Bowles and Gintis' structuralist-functionalist method is undialectical: not only does it ignore questions about knowledge (purveyed by the curriculum, teacher training, etc.), but it is also blind to the "heterogeneity" of the schooling process manifest in the ways in which learners interpret or make mean-ing of what is going on, how they challenge and creatively react to their learning environment. Citing Dewey's parallel speculation on habit as both a creative and active engagement with the world, Bourdieu (1992) warns against reviving the post-Cartesian dualism of subject and object, spiritual consciousness and material action, and other irreconcilable antitheses. Most US pragmatists (such as Richard Rorty and Stanley Fish), however, have fallen into a chauvinist nominalism once denounced by William James and Charles Sanders Peirce. Although not practicing pragmatists or nominalists, Bowles and Gintis use a deterministic model that may reflect the backwardness of the US political milieu. The use of such a model is a symptom of intellectual marginalization. It does not take into account what Gramsci calls "hegemony," that is, the ideological mode of class domination through popular con-sensus in civil society, and therefore fails to propose a strategy and vision of socialist, national-popular counter-hegemony.

It is precisely this inadequacy of Bowles and Gintis' project that a new postmod-ernist generation of scholars would try to correct. One of the more provocative inquiries intended to supplement, if not revise, the Marxist critique of capitalist schooling is Stanley Aronowitz and Henry A. Giroux's *Education Under Siege* (1985). After reviewing a rich archive of Marxist theorizing, Aronowitz and Giroux reject what they consider its disabling flaw – its economism, scientism, historical reduc-tionism, determinism, etc. – that discounts the primacy of culture which involves the categories of gender, race, popular culture, and other concrete determinants shaping consciousness and individual agency.

Aronowitz and Giroux reject Marx, Engels, and the Western Marxists (Lukács, Gramsci, Frankfurt Critical Theory), as well as the innovative paradigm of habitus/ habitat of Pierre Bourdieu, Althusser's reproductive model, and so on. They invoke the example of Michel Foucault, Ernesto Laclau, Chantal Mouffe and other proponents of the new eclectic "social movements" as the correct path in fashioning a critical pedagogy, a radical theory/practice of schooling, together with the organic intellectuals who would emphasize agency, resistance, and an oppositional public sphere. For Aronowitz and Giroux, critical literacy involves reinventing the connections between knowledge and power sufficient to foster individual/collective empowerment, democratic pluralism, and self-management. While both call for dialectical linkages between structure and agency, stressing the need for creative resistance and transformative struggles, they privilege the moment of subjectivity/ tactical moves over the concurrent moment of theoretical totalizing. They bypass the complex mediations between seemingly disjunctive moments. In their anxiety to rectify the mechanistic deviations of classical Marxism, they reduce praxis into "activistism" (exemplified by the radical style of Saul Alinsky) and the goal of social justice/equality into the empowerment of differences and singularities. In this they anticipate the anarchist compromise of Antonio Negri and Michael Hardt's *Empire* (2000). Consequently, a mass-based liberatory socialist politics, not to speak of an anti-imperialist politics of world revolution mobilizing oppressed "third world" peoples and colonized nations in solidarity with the industrial proletariat of the global North, completely disappears in such revisionist discourses.

We can explain Aronowitz and Giroux's abandonment of the socialist cause by way of the vicissitudes of the US left/progressive movement with the triumph of the neoconservative reaction immediately after the end of the Vietnam War. In general, specific historic realities limit the capacity and horizon of American leftist thought, allowing space for crippling left/right opportunisms. Among others, the lack of a viable labor-union tradition and the entrenched tenacity of a white-supremacist ethos in the US public sphere may explain the distortions of historical-materialist principles and the relapse into various kinds of pragmatist/empiricist solutions. That is why dissenting academics continue to reaffirm their project of decentering authority and the curriculum, preparing their students to be border crossers, critical public intellectuals, "agents of civic courage" in a radical democracy (for example, Giroux 1996: 181–4). But there is no mention of the working class as a significant force for overthrowing capitalism, much less initiating a socialist revolution. It is instructive to contrast this trend with the popular literacy "mission" of the Bolivarian revolution in Venezuela, a pedagogical experiment of historic significance for all anti-capitalist militants (Harnecker 2005; Gott 2005).

This perverse return of former left-wing scholars to an elitist, "holier-than-thou" position is thus confirmed by the erasure of the centrality of alienated labor, the distinctive character of capitalist production relations, in critical pedagogy and social analysis. Culture detached from crucial production relations, from the commodified totality of systemic variables, predominates. A review of Georg Lukács' (1978) inquiry into "the ontology of social being," in particular labor as a model of social practice, might be useful in neutralizing any wrong-headed prejudice against historical materialism. As both Henri Lefebvre (in *Dialectical Materialism*, 1968) and Alfred Sohn-Rethel (in *Intellectual and Manual Labor*, 1978) have shown, the foregrounding of labor (its alienation/commodification in capitalist society, and the attendant class conflicts) in historical materialist inquiry is a methodological postulate that is able to resolve the split of theory and practice, agency and thought, intrinsic in the everyday life of bourgeois society. On the other hand, as Paulo Freire suggests, the dialectical understanding of culture exemplified by Gramsci and Amilcar Cabral cannot be fully appreciated detached from its "role in the liberation of the oppressed" (1996: 116).

Practice and theory are ultimately indissociable. In accomplishing the task of synthesizing a historical-materialist approach with socialist pedagogy, Grant Banfield's essay on "Marxism, Critical Realism and Class" will prove extremely helpful. Banfield demonstrates how Roy Bhaskar's clarification of the dialectical method can help negotiate the perilous antinomies and conundrums in the philosophy of education ever since Plato's *Meno* asked whether virtue can be taught, and what ties knowledge (as justified true belief) with teaching/learning (Senchuk 1995). Dewey's holistic, organic view of education as the growth of experience was once invoked as a maxim of progressive teaching/learning theory. But today, as the texts by Ravi Kumar, Enver Motala, Salim Vally, Mike Cole, Alpesh Maisuria and Robert Faivre show, the learning/teaching experience cannot pretend to be innocent of state policies administering the learning methods, curriculum, environment, and other factors, in the service of corporate profits under the aegis of global capitalist hegemony. Both learning and teaching, as constituents of a "rational life ... in which the critical quest for reasons is a dominant and integrating motive" (Scheffler 1965: 107) cannot be divorced from the political economy of a specific historical stage of class-conflicted society. A revolutionary pedagogy cannot be constituted purely in the realm of ideas; it evolves, in dialectical fashion, as the theoretical rendering of the complex multifaceted praxis/ movement of the working masses, specifically the class-conscious proletariat, as the authentic agent of epochal historical change.

It is fashionable for radicals and progressives today to appeal to Freire, Che Guevara, or Gramsci adapted for *ad hoc* intersectionality politics. But the twin temptation of rationalism and empiricism, either all mind or all circumstance, persists in waylaying any consistent anti-capitalist program. Even the resort to Gramsci evinces the pressure of punctual contingencies in leading many followers to stress either the phase of coercion or the moment of consent in the unfolding dynamic process of hegemony. A cursory look into Gramsci's remarks on the "educational principle" (in *Prison Notebooks*) will show how labor/creative praxis is a necessary axiom in any dialectical comprehension of society and its possible transformation. Gramsci writes: "The discovery that the relations between the social and natural orders are mediated by work, by man's theoretical and practical activity, creates the first elements of an intuition of the world free from all magic and superstition. It provides a basis for the subsequent development of an historical, dialectical conception of the world" (1978: 52). This is also what Bertell Ollman (2003) foregrounds in the Marxist "philosophy of internal relations": subjectivity/agency, the mediation of creative thought/ praxis, cannot be separated from the need to engage in the process of theorizing the process of totality, something which Aronowitz, Giroux, Laclau and Mouffe, and their followers anathematize as class reductionism, technocratic determinism, or worse, Stalinist totalitarianism. Let us keep in mind Marx's reminder: "The weapon of criticism certainly cannot replace the criticism of weapons" (1970: 137).

The closing decades of the last century witnessed the further intensification of the crisis of liberal education signaled by the debate on "political correctness," multiculturalism, canon formation, representation of the nation, and civic identity. One college president rehearsed the conserving and adapting function of schools/ teachers, oblivious to ongoing US aggression in Iraq and previous interventions in Central America, Asia, and elsewhere (Oakley 1992). Because of the disarray in the oppositional public sphere in Europe and North America in the wake of the impe-rialist wars in Iraq and Afghanistan, many progressives have abandoned "overarching narratives, societal critiques and clarion calls for change – of the capitalist system or the social structure," as registered by a *New York Times* survey of the academic scene. Marxist theorist Eric Olin Wright of the University of Wisconsin is quoted in this report: "There has been some shift away from grand frameworks to more focused empirical questions" (Cohen 2008). We cannot recount here the dangers and pitfalls of empiricist scholasticism which have been fully examined by Martin Shaw (1975), Istvan Meszaros (1995), and Samir Amin (1998), among others.

In addition to a return to empiricism and other eclectic nostrums to solve the crisis, we find among critics of the Homeland Security State a revival of reformist illusions amid the trauma of defeat. The controversy over Bush's neoliberal regimen of "No Child Left Behind" (see *The Nation*, May 21, 2007 issue) has revealed how technocratic policies to firm up the class system are premised on the "underlying race- and class-based interpretation of intelligence" (Meier 2007: 21). But there is so far no sustained call for a mass anti-capitalist insurgency among educators.

We find instead more sophisticated testimonies of conciliatory adaptation. One example is the response of Gerald Graff (2008), president of the Modern Language Association, to the government drive to reinforce the reactionary agenda of stand-ardization. While professing a concern for "the free-market ideology underlying the [Margaret Spelling report on the future of higher education]" and its "narrowly vocational vision" (n. p.), Graff argues for a formalist and fundamentalist idea of critical thinking straight out of the old rhetorical textbooks that have served well the tracking and repressively segregating function of education in finance in a profit/ commodity-centered system. Graff's espousal of "intelligent standardization" as "criti-cal to our mission of democratic education" (n. p.) does not even allude or gesture to any ideal of equality, what Dewey conceived of as "the production of free human beings associated with one another on terms of equality" (quoted by Chomsky 1994). These are a few symptoms of the patent bankruptcy of current orthodoxies on how to renew the emancipatory, not to say the virtue-inducing, vocation of a classic liberal education. Hence the need for this unique timely volume of essays that translates into a wide-ranging reflexive praxis the thrust of Marx's injunction (stated in "Theses on Feuerbach") that it is "humans who, as products of specific conditions and upbringing, change circumstances and that it is essential to educate the educator himself" (quoted in Matthews 1980). The collective message of the writers here is the revolutionary one of transforming educational institutions and the ever-changing narrative of the schooling experience into sites/modes of citizens practicing freedom cooperatively – the freedom to imagine and bring about an alternative world free from class exploitation and imperialist domination; the freedom to struggle together for a socialist, genuinely democratic and egalitarian society in which "the free development of each is the condition for the free development of all" (Marx and Engels 1971: 112).

Bibliography

Alinsky, S. (1971) *Rules for Radicals*, New York: Vintage Books.

Amin, S. (1998) *Spectres of Capitalism*, New York: Monthly Review Press.

Aronowitz, S. and Giroux, H. A. (1985) *Education under Siege*, South Hadley, MA: Bergin Garvey.

Benjamin, H. (1960) "The problems of education," in L. Bryson (ed.) *An Outline of Man's Knowledge of the Modern World*, New York: Nelson Doubleday, Inc.

Bourdieu, P. and Wacquant, L. J. D. (1992) *An Invitation to Reflexive Sociology*, Chicago, IL: University of Chicago Press.

Bowles, S. and Gintis, H. (1986) *Democracy and Capitalism*, New York: Basic Books.

Chomsky, N. (1994) "Democracy and education." Mellon Lecture, Loyola University Chicago, 19 October.

Cohen, P. (2008) "The '60s begin to fade as liberal professors retire," *The New York Times* (3 July). Online. Available at http://www.newyorktimes.com (accessed July 3, 2008).

Conant, J. B. (1940) "Education for a classless society," *The Atlantic Monthly* (November): 48. Online. Available at http://www.theatlantic.com/doc/194005/classless-education (accessed July 7, 2008).

Ebert, T. and Zavarzadeh, M. (2008) *Class in Culture*, Boulder, CO: Paradigm Publishers.

Freire, P. (1996) *Letters to Cristina: reflections on my life and work*, New York: Routledge.

Giroux, H. (1996) *Fugitive Cultures: race, violence, and youth*, New York: Routledge.

Gott, R. (2005) *Hugo Chavez and the Bolivarian Revolution*, New York: Verso.

Graff, G. and Birkenstein, C. (2008) "A Progressive case for educational standardization: how not to respond to the Spellings report," *Academe Online* (May/June). Online. Available at http://www.aaup.org/AAUP/pubsres/academe/2008/MJ/Feal/graf/htm (accessed July 12, 2008).

Gramsci, A. (1978) "From 'In Search of the Educational Principle'," in T. M. Norton and B. Ollman (eds) *Studies in Socialist Pedagogy*, New York and London: Monthly Review Press.

Harnecker, M. (2005) *Understanding the Venezuelan Revolution: Hugo Chavez talks to Marta Harnecker*, New York: Monthly Review Press.

Kozol, J. (2006) "Education," *The Atlantic Monthly*, 267(3): 51–79.

Lefebvre, H. (1968) *Dialectical Materialism*, London: Jonathan Cape.

Lukács, G. (1978) *Labour: the ontology of social being*, London: Merlin Press.

Marx, K. (1970) *Critique of Hegel's Philosophy of Right*, New York: Cambridge University Press.

Marx, K. and Engels, F. (1971) "Manifesto of the Communist Party," in D. J. Struik (ed.) *Birth of the Communist Manifesto*, New York: International Publishers.

Matthews, M. R. (1980) *The Marxist Theory of Schooling*, Atlantic Highlands, NJ: Humanities Press.

Meier, D. (2007) "Evaluating 'No Child Left Behind'," *The Nation* (21 May): 20–1.

Meszaros, I. (1995) *Beyond Capital*, New York: Monthly Review Press.

Negri, A. and Hardt, M. (2000) *Empire*, Cambridge, MA: Harvard University Press.

Oakley, F. (1992) "Against Nostalgia: reflections on our present discontents in American higher education," in D. Gless and B. H. Smith (eds) *The Politics of Liberal Education*, Durham and London: Duke University Press.

Ollmann, B. (2003) *Dance of the Dialectic*, Urbana and Chicago: University of Illinois Press.

Phillips, K. (2008) "Lies, damn lies, and government inflation statistics," *Huffington Post*. Online. Available at http://www.huffingtonpost.com/kevin-phillips/lies-damn-lies-and-govern_b_113277.html (accessed July 18, 2008).

Postman, N. and Weingartner, C. (1969) *Teaching as a Subversive Activity*, New York: A Delta Book.

Sarup, M. (1978) *Marxism and Education*, London: Routledge and Kegan Paul.

Scheffler, I. (1965) *Conditions of Knowledge: an introduction to epistemology and education*. Chicago: University of Chicago Press.

Senchuk, D. M. (1995) "Philosophy of Education," in R. Audi (ed.) *The Cambridge Dictionary of Philosophy*, New York: Cambridge University Press.

Shaw, M. (1975) *Marxism and Social Science*, London: Pluto Press.

Sohn-Rethel, A. (1978) *Intellectual and Manual Labour*, Atlantic Highlands, NJ: Humanities Press.

Zinn, H. (1980) *A People's History of the United States*, New York: Harper and Row.

Introduction

Sheila Macrine, Dave Hill and Deborah Kelsh

Class is among the most fundamental of concepts in the classical (orthodox) Marxist tradition because it has the power to explain why capitalism must be transformed into socialism: because under capitalism, "living labour is but a means to increase accumulated labour," the wealth of the capitalist class, instead of accumulated labor being "a means to widen, to enrich, to promote the existence of the labourer" (Marx and Engels 1985: 97). Class is central to analyzing capitalism and explaining that, in order to make socially produced wealth available for "the free development of each" (105), the property relations of capitalism must be abolished. In short, the Marxist concept of class has the power to analyze and explain the existing and inequitable structure(s) of ownership and power in society and thus produce reliable knowledges capable of guiding practices that aim to restructure society as equitable, as able to promote the free development of all humans. Yet as Julian Markels (2005) has recently remarked, "the concept of class as a particular labor process is not only avoided by many recent Marxists but is now unfamiliar to many non-Marxists" (n. p.).

This book is an intervention into the erasure of the Marxist concept of class from the scene of knowledge production in education. It demonstrates the usefulness of the Marxist concept of class by using it to explain the determinate connection between the bas(e)ic and inequitable relations of production and the cultural inequities in capitalism, and to implicate dominant knowledges and pedagogies in the (re)production of those inequities by showing that they manufacture the subjectivities capitalism requires to maintain itself. To be clear: this book takes as its object of analysis the dominant knowledges and pedagogies that, by shrouding and confounding the Marxist concept of class, serve the interests of the capitalist class. It is an explanation of *why* revolutionary knowledges of class must – from the position of the bourgeoisie – be occluded in mainstream educational theory: in order to legitimate the property relations constituting capitalism, which are the cause of exploitation, domination, and oppression.

Class in capitalism, as Marx theorizes it through his critique of capital, is the binary relation of ownership to "private property" that constitutes what Marx calls the "relations of production" (1989: 21). The bourgeoisie, who own the means of production, live off the surplus value, the profit, extracted from the proletariat, those who do not own the means of production and must sell their labor power for a wage in order to live. The relation is inequitable, because the social wealth that is produced by the non-owning class is the property of the owning class. The choices members of either class make in the course of their daily lives – what they eat, where they live, whether and where they seek an education – are shaped by these bas(e)ic and inequitable production (property) relations. Class, in other words, determines social, political, and intellectual inequity. It does so through dialectical, contradictory materialist relations between base and superstructure in which "'[d]etermination,'" as Aijaz Ahmad (2000) has reminded, "does not mean ... the kind of entrapment of which structuralists and Foucauldians speak; it refers, rather, to the givenness of the circumstance within which individuals *make* their choices, their lives, their histories" (6).

In the place of the Marxist concept of class, dominant knowledges have installed what Deborah Kelsh, in Chapter 1, calls "cultureclass," which understands class to be an effect of culture and not the causal relations of production that determine culture. Cultureclass displaces, at the level of knowledge, the constitutive but also historically determined and therefore changeable "outside" of capital without which capitalism cannot exist: the exploitation of labor power. In doing so, cultureclass cuts the dialectical relation between production and culture in which humankind, "by ... acting on the external world and changing it, ... at the same time changes [its] own nature" (Marx 1967a: 173). Cultureclass denies that "there exists a materialistic connection of men with one another, which is determined by their needs and their mode of production" (Marx and Engels 1989: 50), and in doing so it works to naturalize capitalism as the only and final mode of production possible, simultaneously blocking knowledge of capitalism as a mode of production that can be transformed into socialism.

As chapters by Kelsh, Teresa L. Ebert and Mas'ud Zavarzadeh (Chapter 2), and Robert Faivre (Chapter 8) in particular emphasize, changes in culture are effects of class struggle over productivity, the rate of extraction of surplus value from workers. At the level of knowledge, the displacement of the Marxist theory of class, as Ebert and Zavarzadeh explain, is one outcome of capital's long attack on labor that began in the mid-1940s. Its displacement has contributed to the reshaping of the humanities into what they call "hypohumanities," the instrumentalization of the humanities into a pedagogy that contributes to training humans so that their labor can be deployed for profit. The conversion of the humanities into hypohumanities displaces "the knowledges that teach citizen-students a critique-al grasping of everyday practices in their historical and social relations," blocking the understanding of subjectivity in terms of position in the relations of production (relation to property).

In the displacement of class with cultureclass, contemporary research and theory on class in education exemplifies in its own knowledge practices the instrumentalization of knowledges that by occluding property relations contributes to the reduction of humans to "instruments of labour, more or less expensive to use" (Marx and Engels 1985: 88), and thus benefits capitalism.

A priority of this book, then, is to intervene in the dominant knowledges by providing access to the Marxist concept of class from a partisan position that is interested in "combating the real existing world" (Marx and Engels 1989: 41).

Combating the real existing world includes, but goes beyond, "exposing economic (factory and occupational) conditions" in what Lenin (1969) called "exposure literature," leaflets in which workers tell "the whole truth about their miserable existence, about their unbearably hard toil, and their lack of rights" (55). Such literature is evident today in the many texts in education that investigate and narrate inequities in education, from classroom practices to working conditions to hiring practices in academe, but that stop short of connecting those inequities to the inequities of property relations. While exposure literature can serve as "a beginning and component part of Social-Democratic activity" (56), it tends toward "trade-union work" in which all that is achieved is that "the sellers of labour-power learn ... to sell their 'commodity' on better terms" (56). But what is necessary is not "better terms for the sale of labour-power, but ... abolition of the social system that compels the propertyless to sell themselves to the rich" (57).

Combating the real existing world means laying bare the connections of the everyday – including and especially the dominant knowledges – to the "material surroundings" (Marx and Engels 1989: 41), the historical and material conditions that determine them. It means tracing these connections through the mediated layers of the social so that the root cause of inequity – the property relations of capitalism – cannot hide behind the alibis of the dominant knowledges, such as the various versions of cultureclass, that mask rather than explain the cause of the deepening impoverishment of the proletariat and greater profit for the bourgeoisie.

The writers of these chapters, then, combat the real existing world by *using* the Marxist concept of class not simply to expose the fundamental brutality of human exploitation, but also and above all to contest the claims of the dominant knowledges and explain what they evade: the causal connections between the capitalist mode of production and contemporary inequities in culture, including issues involving language, representation, and education.

Ravi Kumar (Chapter 3) details the ways in which the state in India, by substituting for knowledges of class the discourses of multiple cultural identities related to caste, ethnicity, tribe, and so forth, represents itself as working for "development" of the educational system that will benefit the "people" in all their variety. But in fact, as Kumar shows, the state works in the interests of the rule of capital, to the disadvantage of the proletariat as a whole, and in particular, girl children. In such a context, he argues, what is necessary is an understanding of the state as an agent that mediates in favor of capital, an understanding grounded in the Marxist theory of class. It is just such an understanding, he argues, that is necessary to unify and educate all workers so that they do not accept the discourses of the multiple cultural identities and engage in intraclass struggles that benefit capital.

In Chapter 4, Enver Motala and Salim Vally extend the question of the state and education to post-apartheid South Africa, specifically in relation to the connections between class and "race." They explain why social analyses of education in post-apartheid South Africa that do not attend to the question of class not only result in ineffective reforms, but also deny the importance of class struggle for social transformation. While contesting social analyses that prioritize "race" to the exclusion of class, they also argue for the significant and necessary contributions the concept of "race" makes to developing a useful, because many-sided, understanding of capitalist practices of accumulation on an international scale. They urge that educational analyses expand their analytic power by conceptualizing state-education relations in terms of the deep imbrications of both "race" and class.

Mike Cole and Alpesh Maisuria's Chapter 5 contests the valorization of "race" over class in discourses that prioritize "white supremacy," arguing that it limits the development of an understanding of racism in relation to capitalist accumulation. In opposition to understanding racism in terms of "white supremacy," they argue that the Marxist concept of racialization has the capacity to explain both the increase in Islamophobia in Britain, and also the existence of a contemporary form of non-color-coded racialization, what the authors, following Cole's (see Chapter 5, 2004b) theorization of it, call xeno-racialization. Both the increase in Islamophobia and the existence of xeno-racialization need to be understood in the context of changes in the capitalist mode of production. The Marxist concepts of racialization and xeno-racialization and their connections to class form the basis for their suggestions for an alternative vision of education.

Grant Banfield, in Chapter 6, "Marxism, critical realism and class: implications for a socialist pedagogy," draws on critical realism, a philosophy of science, to show that while class is an essential and deep-real feature of capitalist societies, this does not make Marxism determinist, teleological, and reductivist. By theorizing the Marxist base-superstructure theory of the social in terms of critical realism's general meta-theory of the stratification of nature, Banfield argues that capitalist class relations, rooted in material bases consisting of both human and non-human mechanisms, are non-reductive, but that this does not legitimate an "ontologically flat fascination" with the local and particular that disengages from the question of structure and rejects class. On the contrary, theories of the social that do not engage class as an essential and deep-real feature of capitalist societies are insufficient to contribute to radical critique and socialist pedagogy.

In Chapter 7, "Globalization, class, and the social studies curriculum," E. Wayne Ross and Greg Queen put forth a high school social studies curriculum centered on the concept of globalization. Addressing globalization in relation to school curricula and national standards for the social studies, they argue that globalization is perhaps the most important concept in the social studies. They then illustrate through description of a year's units of study how and why the concept of globalization can be used to teach the social studies curriculum, and how and why issues of class and capitalism are central to the endeavor. Greg Queen discusses his experience teaching these units, including responses from students, parents, and administrators, and his own counter responses.

Robert Faivre in Chapter 8, "Class: the base of all reading," addresses recent "crises" in reading, contesting dominant views that they are cultural matters that can be resolved without attention to class. Critiquing contemporary theories of reading – including those advanced in recent US National Endowment for the Arts reports, works by Jim Burke, and John Berger's classic *Ways of Seeing* – Faivre holds that the "crises" in reading are effects of shifts in production, and that what is necessary is the development of conceptual reading capable of developing class consciousness.

The chapter writers demonstrate in both their arguments and in their practices of knowledge production that what is necessary in order to enable the free development of each are analyses and critiques grounded in the Marxist theory of class. By explaining the relation between production practices and culture, by explaining why contemporary knowledges and pedagogies are produced and used to secure, maintain, and update inequitable structures and the subjectivities they require, such analyses and critiques can point to knowledges and pedagogies capable of restructuring society so that the needs of the many take priority over profit for the few.

Bibliography

Ahmad, A. (2000) *In Theory: classes, nations, literatures*, London: Verso.

Lenin, V. I. (1969) *What Is To Be Done?* New York: International Publishers.

Markels, J. (2005) "How to stop paying lip-service to class – and why it won't happen," *The Red Critique* 10. Online. Available at http://www.redcritique.org/WinterSpring2005/howtostoppayinglipservicetoclass.htm (accessed September 8, 2008).

Marx, K. (1989) "Preface," in K. Marx *A Contribution to the Critique of Political Economy*, trans. S. W. Ryazanskaya, ed. Maurice Dobb, New York: International Publishers.

—— (1967a) *Capital: Volume 1*, trans. S. Moore and E. Aveling, ed. F. Engels, New York: International Publishers.

Marx, K. and Engels, F. (1985) *The Communist Manifesto*, New York: Penguin Books.

—— (1989) *The German Ideology*, New York: International Publishers.

1   Cultureclass[1]

Deborah Kelsh

Abstract

This chapter critiques "cultureclass" – the many understandings of class that, despite their local differences, are all informed by poststructuralist and post-Marxist theories that occlude the inequitable property relations that are at the core of the Marxist theory of class. By occluding property relations, dominant understandings of class in social and educational theory convert class into an effect of culture, displacing class as the relation that determines culture and that is the cause of cultural and political inequities. In effect, if not by design, cultureclass protects the interests of the capitalist class: by removing from the scene of knowledge the objective basis for the unity of the proletariat – the fact that the proletariat does not own property and its members must sell their labor power to live – it blocks the development of class consciousness, knowledge of the property relations that at the point of production (re)produce capitalism and all its inequities, that is necessary for the transformation of capitalism into socialism. Cultureclass is rejuvenated particularly at moments of market crises, when it becomes most evident that the property relations of capitalism must be abolished. The chapter critiques cultureclass for limiting theory and research in education, particularly theory and research involving the achievement gap. It argues that contemporary theory and research in education works within the parameters of a society built on human exploitation instead of contributing to knowledge to end the class society that requires that exploitation.

Introduction

Today, the unmet needs of the many tower alongside the vast accumulated wealth of the few. As the United Nations Development Programme (UNDP) 2007 Annual Report noted, "the gap between rich and poor citizens, within both developed and developing nations, is ... growing" (n. p.). Capitalist relations of production, on an ever-increasing scale, separate those who work from the wealth they produce, which is appropriated as their own private property by a tiny minority who do not work but instead live off the work of others. For there to be a society in which "the full and free development of every individual forms the ruling principle" (Marx 1967a: 592), the mode of production must be transformed into one in which material wealth is produced "to satisfy the needs of development on the part of the labourer," rather than one "in which the labourer exists to satisfy the needs of self-expansion of existing values," which is the aim of production under capitalism (621).

To enable the production of reliable knowledges that can guide practices capable of transforming existing property relations, what is necessary is the Marxist theory of class as Marx theorizes it through his critique of capital, as the historically (re)produced binary relation of ownership to "private property" constituting the capitalist relations of production, a relation that determines economic and cultural inequality.

But dominant discourses in education, as elsewhere, take up class and manufacture what I am calling "cultureclass." Cultureclass eclipses "private property" as the cause of the increasingly deep division of "society as a whole ... into two great hostile camps, into two great classes directly facing each other: Bourgeoisie and Proletariat" (Marx and Engels 1985: 80). This division is a historically produced one and as such can be changed by the collective action of the producing class: "the theory of the Communists may be summed up in a single sentence: Abolition of private property" (96). By removing private property from view at the level of knowledge, cultureclass deflects the proletariat from its world historical task of putting an end to class society and exploitation by ending private ownership of the means of production and making that ownership collective. In effect, cultureclass provides a service to the bourgeoisie – protection of private property – at a time of heightened, objective antagonism between the two classes worldwide.

In education, cultureclass has the effect of limiting, by turning attention inward into culture and ignoring the property relations that shape culture, the production of theory- and research-based knowledge. It leads to a curtailed pedagogy that produces educators and students whose subjectivity suits the requirements of business, and leaves need unmet. Thus, while there is an enormous outcry in "left" scholarship against the privatization of education, the "left" use of cultureclass abets that privatization.

Cultureclass is invoked across a range of discourses and registers. My purpose is not to provide a survey of its many (re)iterations. Rather, it is twofold: (1) to articulate the theoretical underpinnings of cultureclass across several contemporary instances of its manifestation, particularly those surfacing in the wake of recent recessions (1980–3; 1990–1; 2001) and in the context of the current (2008) US and world market recessions; and (2) to critique it for justifying capitalism by mystifying the fundamental, dialectical relations of capitalism, those between capital and labor. This chapter, in other words, is a historical materialist critique of the politics of dominant knowledges of class in education and it aims to contribute to the development of knowledge of the political economy of education, ultimately to the abolition of class society that relies on human exploitation. As such, it seeks not to mend the contradictions of capitalism by teaching how to reinterpret them, through the lens of indeterminacy, as pregnant with possible "different futures" (Giroux 2006: 37) that are in fact not different because they all leave in place exploitation. Rather, as does any such critique, it seeks to "push forward the contradictions ... towards crisis and to push forward the most radically progressive tendencies for resolution of these contradictions at and beyond this point of crisis" (Nowlan 1996: 369).

Along with class, however, historical materialist critique – particularly when directed at or occurring among those who regard themselves as "left" – has been dismissed, depicted as a "violence." As one writer has said regarding "intense internal battles" on the left, "[w]hen the left organizes a firing squad, it lines up in a circle" (Apple 2006b: 686). This "joke" ignores what Aronowitz points to when he notes that "[t]he skirmishes within the ranks of the opposition are often dress rehearsals for larger struggles" (2003: 45). That is, the practice of historical materialist critique is a pedagogy of "*radical praxis*" (Nowlan 363), and in two senses. First, it is the praxis (not any "dress rehearsal") by which those who see the necessity of transforming capitalism develop the really useful knowledge and skills – really useful because forged in actual class struggle, from which the "left" is never isolated – to combat (the agents of) capital and develop reliable knowledges capable of guiding revolutionary movement. Second, it is a form of public pedagogy that demonstrates that it is indeed possible and necessary to raise questions and make principled and explanatory critiques regarding the usefulness and legitimacy, for a society deeply divided by class, of dominant knowledges that protect the interests of the capitalist class by obscuring a rigorous and historical materialist understanding of class. That is, the radical praxis of critique refuses to allow critiques of dominant knowledges to be pre-empted by the erasure from the theoretical imaginary of the objective basis – capitalist relations of production – for such critiques. Such critique, Marx argues, "represents a class" (1967a: 16), and because ideas are determined by material practice (Marx and Engels 1989: 58), "[t]he existence of revolutionary ideas in a particular period presupposes the existence of a revolutionary class" (65). In this context, dismissive representations of historical materialist critique in the form of a "joke" unleash violence on revolutionaries from behind a smiling face.

Crises and the manufacture of cultureclass

Crises such as the current world market crisis are effects of the dialectical unfolding of capitalism's internal contradiction between the forces and relations of production, a contradiction that constitutes the material basis for capitalism's tendency towards self-negation: capitalism's own laws of motion develop the forces of production to the extent that they threaten the very basis of capitalist (re)production, the property relations through which what is produced by workers is not available to them because it is the private property of the capitalist (Marx and Engels 1985: 86).

Compelled always to raise the rate of profit, individual capitals must incessantly struggle on two fronts: "against labour and against other capitals" (Shaikh 1992: 176). Against labor, the struggle "manifests itself in the mechanisation of production, in which workers are replaced by machines in order to raise the productivity of labour" (Shaikh 1992: 176). However, "this increased productivity of labour can only be realised in the struggle against other capitals if it is expressed as a lower unit cost of production" (176), which means that individual capitals must always attempt to beat out other capitals by repeatedly "revolutionizing the instruments of production" (Marx and Engels 1985: 83), replacing more workers with more machines in order to lower the unit cost of production. In the long run, this reduces the proportion of variable capital – surplus value that has to be paid out in wages – to the proportion of fixed capital – surplus value reinvested in the new means of production (which quickly become obsolete and must be replaced). But because the new means increasingly reduce the proportion of living labor power required in production, and because living labor power – "the aggregate of those mental and physical capabilities existing in a human being" (Marx 1967a: 167) that Marx (195) opposed to "dead labor," "past, materialised" labor congealed in commodities – is the source of profit under capitalism (Marx 1967a: Chapter 7), the rate of profit has a tendency to fall (Shaikh 1992). The unfolding of the internal contradiction between the forces and relations of capitalism, in other words, is a dialectical movement through which capital in its attempts to increase itself actually undermines its material basis.

Because workers' wages are outstripped in relation to the higher proportion of commodities produced, commodities cannot be sold, surplus value cannot be realized as profit, and thus instead of being able to expand itself, capital is confronted with the crisis situation of having to take a loss: "Crisis results from the impossibility to sell" (Marx 2000, part II: 509). As Marx explains in terms directly applicable to the contemporary world market crisis, "[t]he fixed charges – interest, rent – which were based on the anticipation of a *constant* rate of profit and exploitation of labour, remain the same and in part *cannot be paid*. Hence *crisis*. Crisis of labour and crisis of capital" (516). As individual capitals compete, the internal contradiction of capitalism is multiplied, manifesting itself differentially across a range of sites. Thus today, while hunger haunts the streets of Haiti and food riots roll across sub-Saharan Africa (Lacey 2008), "bulging inventories" of sports utility vehicles sit unsold on lots in the US (Vlasic and Bunkley 2008). Crisis of labor, crisis of capital.

Crises demonstrate both the material basis for the necessity of abolishing class society and the actually existing material conditions of possibility of doing so. But capitalism engages crises as opportunities for "forcible solutions of the existing contradictions" (Marx 1967c: 249). Through "enforced destruction of a mass of productive forces; ... conquest of new markets, and ... more thorough exploitation of the old ones" (Marx and Engels 1985: 86), the individual capitals use crises to attempt to expand the existing value of its capital. At the level of production, such "forcible solutions" manifest themselves in shifts in the means of extracting surplus value (for example, "outsourcing" and "just-in-time production") that are increasingly disruptive to the lives of workers.

In such circumstances, and in order to maintain their relevance and legitimacy, the dominant knowledges – those that serve the interests of the capitalist class by deflecting attention from the capitalist class private property that is the motive force to extract profit from workers at a high rate and a low cost – must engage the question of class. But in order also to maintain themselves as dominant, they must do so in a manner that obscures class in the very act of engaging it – in a manner, in other words, that, rather than enabling class consciousness by producing knowledge of the totality of social relations of production (property relations), manufactures "revised" understandings of class capable of easing workers into updated subjectivities better suited to the updated needs of capital. It is in this context that recent and current engagements with class that dehistoricize, hybridize, invert, and dismiss class as Marx theorized it need to be understood as manufacturing knowledges of class that in effect, if not by design, serve the interests of the capitalist class.

The current world market crisis has pushed to the forefront of inquiry the question of class. The stark manifestation of the binary division of labor on a global scale has put the dominant knowledges in crisis around the question of class, for in the view of many, class is "murky." For example, Nealon and Giroux (2003) claim that class as a concept is "rather murky": what it "maps" "remains an open question" (180). More recently, Lareau (2008a) has asserted that "considerable murkiness swirls around the empirical study of social class" (4). In education, Lubienski (2003) notes "we have moved away from relatively straightforward definitions of class groups (the 'haves' versus the 'have nots' in Marxist terminology) toward murkier, more contested definitions that make it difficult to define and discuss class groups" (32). Similarly, Van Galen (2007) expresses concern that "Marxist analyses and functionalist justifications no longer seem to work, but scholars have been less clear about how to conceive of class within newer theoretical perspectives" (2).

As these comments suggest, the academy is in crisis around the issue of class because, on the one hand, existing understandings of class are said to be too "murky" to have explanatory value. But on the other, the Marxist theory of class, which with sharp clarity posits class as a relation of owning to property (capital) and explains that those who own property increase their wealth by exploiting those who have no property, is rejected out of hand, having been dismissed for the last several decades for its "economic reductivism" (Ahmad 1989; Au 2006; Scatamburlo-D'Annibale and McLaren 2005).

Yet it was during these decades – the same decades during which social wealth was massively shifted from workers to capitalists (Harvey 2005) – that class was in actuality manufactured as "murky," evacuated of its explanatory power, frequently in the wake of recessions as the dominant knowledges sought renewed relevance and legitimacy. Class, to put it differently, was converted into cultureclass through a turn to (neo-)Weberian understandings of class (Kelsh and Hill 2006), as well as to poststructuralist and post-Marxist frameworks that, as Hennessy (2000) has noted, installed a cultural reductivism from which "any consideration of capitalism's relationships of exploitation, accumulation, or domination in social life" was excluded (60). In all of these, class is deracinated from the binary relations of production and displaced into culture as a plurality of identities that are an effect not of the determining relations of production, but of culture. Because it cuts the causal relation between production and culture, cultureclass severs the explanation of cultural inequality from the inequitable binary relation of owning that is the base of capitalist production. In the context of the turn to cultureclass, "economic reductivism" becomes a dismissive code for the Marxist theory of class whose priority is in addressing the social as a totality whose levels are unified because determined by historico-material property relations and their dialectical movement.

"*Post*" *knowledges: erasing and culturalizing class*

Throughout the mid-1970s and 80s, the concept of class was largely displaced (Boltanski and Chiapello 2007: 300; Crompton 1993: ix) as poststructuralism became dominant. Poststructuralism posits that the social operates on the laws of motion of sign systems wherein "the central signified, the original or transcendental signified, is never absolutely present outside a system of differences. The absence of the transcendental signified extends the domain and the interplay of signification *ad infinitum*" (Derrida 1978: para. 5). In the absence of any "central signified," "*differance*" is said to animate social movement(s). As Ebert and Zavarzadeh explain (this volume), by substituting *differance* — "difference *within*" — for "difference *between*," poststructuralism erases any knowable and "objectively existing" "outside" to the social that in the materialist view shapes it (Lenin 1970: 122). It thereby erases from the theoretical imaginary the concept of class as the binary relation of owning to property, the exploitative relation that constitutes the "outside" of capitalism and shapes its "inside," culture.

To take a most influential example, Laclau and Mouffe (1985), in the wake of the 1980–3 recession, echo Derrida's assertion of the absence of any transcendental signified and argue that "[t]here is no *unique* privileged position from which a uniform continuity of effects will follow, concluding with the transformation of society as a whole" (169); "[d]iscursive *discontinuity* becomes primary and constitutive" (191). Having abandoned the base/superstructure opposition and converted the social into a scene of discursive "play," they erase class as an objective entity and argue instead that there is only a "plurality of identities" (167) operating on the logic of "floating signifiers" (113) "without limitation by any exterior" (110), whose partial unity can result only from the practice of articulation (169). In doing so, Laclau and Mouffe, in effect, if not by design, manufactured and disseminated the "left" version of the ruling knowledge of neoliberalism, championed by both US President Reagan and UK Prime Minister Thatcher, wherein the free market, premised on the freedom of individuals, is said to "permit ... wide diversity" "without any centralized authority," as Milton Friedman (1982), the foremost theorist of contemporary (neo)liberalism, put it (15).

Insofar as post knowledges "deny our ability to know" anything outside of discourse (Callinicos 1990: 76), they reject the possibility of any knowledge being reliable enough to guide emancipatory practices. Moreover, they operate on a "ludic" logic that

> rearticulate[s] politics as almost exclusively a cultural politics of representation: as a language-effect, a mode of rhetoric aimed at changing cultural representations and concerned with simply voicing the silenced desires and experiences of ... marginalized people ... In so doing, it has largely abandoned and discredited politics as emancipation ... – that is, politics as a collective practice through which existing social institutions and the exploitative divisions of labor can be transformed so that economic resources and cultural power can be equally distributed without regard to gender, nationality, race, class, sexuality, or physical abilities.
>
> (Ebert 1996: 795)

Because it privileges the semiotic for its ambiguity and reduces political struggle to a series of momentary disruptions with local and fleeting effects, the "post" frame-work, as a number of Marxist critiques have argued (see, for example, Hill, *et al.* 2002; Zavarzadeh, *et al.* 1995; Callinicos 1990; Harvey 1990), is an idealist and rather hollow mode of reading representing the interests of the bourgeoisie in blocking the development of revolutionary consciousness and social transformation.

Tellingly, however, in the wake of the economic recession in the US in 1990–1, when the post theories that so thoroughly erased class as a relation of owning to property began to show signs of explanatory fatigue even to their practitioners, poststructuralism returned to class – but only to "rethink" it in ways that continue to erase property relations and legitimate capitalism.

Dimock and Gilmore (1994), for example, in introducing their anthology *Rethinking Class*, are explicit in their use of ludic logic: they aim to "disturb ... objectivized re-alities" (3). Rethinking class by claiming that their "attempts at class analysis are ... neither predicated on nor reducible to some notion of a privileged historical subject" (2), they make class murky: "questions of cause and effect, of figure and ground, ... become matters of interpretation, matters of uncertain conjecture" (3).

Dimock and Gilmore further occlude the binary theory of class by eliding it with "how to" questions: "how can we continue to use the word with any sense of political efficacy, ... with any sense of analytic authority" when class struggle and the working class are no longer "vital" forces or agents? (1). These questions mask what are in fact the crucial questions: those of *why* class is a necessary concept, and *why* poststructural-ists return to it at the historical moment that they do. By rethinking class, Dimock and Gilmore engage in the ideological work at hand: that of appropriating and updat-ing the concept of class in order to relegitimate the dominant ideology in the wake of the 1990–1 US recession, which put the legitimacy of both poststructuralism and the ruling ideas it serves in question (which is *why* poststructuralists return to class at the moment they do). The ideological services of the two to the bourgeois knowledge industry might be seen in their claim in which, to the relief of the bourgeoisie, they declare that class might "turn out to be as much an effect as it is a cause ... If this weakens the explanatory power accorded class in orthodox Marxism, what is gained is a broader spectrum of permissible questions" (3). Ultimately, Dimock in her own essay (1994) reduces class to a spectral projection, "a projective or reflexive category, emanating from and imaged after the bodily subject" (72).

Engaging in crisis management for the bourgeoisie, Dimock and Gilmore deploy the tactic, as Morton (1990) has theorized it, of "set[ting] the limits of the horizon surveyed ... to occlude the 'troublesome,' while claiming to open up issues to the full spectrum of 'reasonable' views" (57) – the "permissible." The "troublesome" they occlude is the Marxist theory of class as an objective and therefore knowable and transformable position in relation to private property. In contradiction to their denial of a privileged historical subject, Dimock and Gilmore's return to class ultimately serves as an occasion to reinscribe through their performance the "free" individual of liberal pluralism, updated through poststructuralism as one who is not self-identical but divided by "desire to build on [the] limitations" of Marxist class theory (2). Formally rejected by their text, the privileged historical subject of capitalism is nevertheless presupposed, manufactured and legitimated by it.

Culturalizing class by way of Weber

In the absence of class in the dominant discourses, Connell, *et al.* in 1982 used a Weberian-based stratification understanding of class, simply "for want of anything better" (33). In actuality one of the more common ways of dematerializing and culturalizing class is through a return to Weberian class theory.

In the realm of common sense, Weber's understanding of class is understood to be simply a later development of Marx's. Scott and Leonhardt (2005), contributors to *The New York Times'* spring 2005 series of articles on class that are collected in the book *Class Matters*, note that "Marx divided nineteenth-century societies into just two classes; Max Weber added a few more" (8).

The notion that Weberian and Marxist understandings of class are fundamentally commensurate is not only a common sense one, but also pervades dominant "left" scholarship, where the explicit assumption for decades has been that the two theories of class are basically the same because both connect class to property (see, for example, Wright 2008: 26; Johnston 2007: 34; Wright 2002: 839; Giddens 1971: 164). In actuality, what Marx and Weber each mean by "property" is radically different, giving rise to deeply opposed understandings of class, and consequently to opposing theories of knowledge, pedagogy, and subjectivity. The suggestion that they are fundamentally the same legitimates substitution of Weber for Marx while masking that the substitution depoliticizes class by dehistoricizing property, particularizing it into a broad array of "possessions" cut off from the dialectical relations of production that (re)produce capitalist property relations.

The importance of the concept of property to the Marxist concept of class cannot be overstated. Marx and Engels (1985) note that the way in which the Communists, who "represent the interests" of the working-class (95), "support every revolutionary movement against the existing social and political order of things" is by "bring[ing] to the front," "in all these movements" and "as the leading question in each," "the property question, no matter what its degree of development at the time" (120). This is because "property" is central to the concept of capital itself, and through this centrality, to production of knowledges and subjectivities.

By property, Marx does not mean just anything one could be said personally to possess. Rather, the property that is at the core of capitalism is "bourgeois private property," and it is "bourgeois private" because it is used by its owners in definite, historically produced social relations of production. These are the relations of exploitation constituting the capitalist mode of production whose "end and aim" is "to extract the greatest possible amount of surplus value" – profit – from workers (Marx 1967a: 331). Surplus value is value produced in the production of commodities (Marx 1967a: 193) through exploitation of labor power, which is itself a special commodity because it possesses "the specific use-value ... of being- *a source not only of value, but of more value than it has itself*" (Marx 1967a: 193; italics in original). In other words, "surplus value" is "surplus" because it is value that is determined, by capitalist class practices in their totality, to be above and beyond the value that the owner must pay in wages (variable capital) to the laborers to reproduce their labor power, so that they can show up the next day able to work (Marx 1967a: 193–8; 313). The owners of the means of production own this surplus value, which increases their existing property but does not create any such property for the workers who actually produce it. In brief, such property, used to increase itself through the exploitation of non-owners, is "capital," which is "not a thing, but rather a definite social production relation, belonging to a definite historical formation of society, which is manifested in a thing and lends this thing a specific social character" (Marx 1967c: 814). It is because capital is a social production relation whose condition of possibility is bourgeois private property that Marx refers to the relations of production as "property relations" (1989: 21). For Marx, property is capital, and it is the binary relation of owning to that property that divides all persons into the two classes constituting the capitalist mode of production. The bourgeoisie are those who own property; "[t]he proletarian is without property" (Marx and Engels 1985: 92). The capital-labor relation reproduces itself through the relations of exploitation to the extent that bourgeois private property in actuality consists of "the unpaid labour of others." In other words, "property," under capitalism, "turns out to be the right, on the part of the capitalist, to appropriate the unpaid labour of others or its produce, and to be the impossibility, on the part of the labourer, of appropriating his own product" (Marx 1967a: 584).

In contrast, for Weber, class is not the basis of an explanatory theory of the social. It is, rather, a descriptive term. Weber (1978) does note that "'property' and 'lack of property' are ... the basic categories of all class situations" (927), a point that Wright (2008) uses to ground his argument that both Marx and Weber are "really talking about very similar empirical phenomena" (26). Weber's argument, however, is not that a relation of ownership to property *constitutes* classes, but rather that owning or not owning are *categories* into which can be inserted "class situations," and in his theory it is class situation, which he glosses as "market situation," that determines class. It is in this way that his theory eclipses private property and draws class into culture, culturalizing it.

Weber particularizes property into possessions, anything "usable for returns," from "stores" to "cattle" to "products of one's own labor" (1978: 928). In doing so, he dehistoricizes property as Marx theorized it, as the accumulation of capital that is the result of the "expropriation, ... written in the annals of mankind in letters of blood and fire ... of the agricultural producer, of the peasant, from the soil" (Marx 1967a: 715–16). Weber does the same with labor power by particularizing it into an infinite variety of services and skills: "Those who have no property but who offer services are differentiated just as much according to their kinds of services as according to the way in which they make use of these services" (1978: 928).

Because both property and labor power are dehistoricized through particularization, multiple "class situations" are possible: negatively and positively privileged property classes, middle classes defined by skill level, professionals, the self-employed, and so forth (Weber 1978: 303–4). By grouping together "those class situations within which individual and generational mobility is easy and typical" (302), Weber classifies the many "class situations" into four "social classes": "a) the working class as a whole ... b) the petty bourgeoisie, c) the propertyless intelligentsia and specialists ..., d) the classes privileged through property and education" (305). These social classes are unified not on the basis of a relation of owning to the means of production, but instead on the basis of "hav[ing] in common a specific causal component of their life chances" where that "causal component" is the constellation of particularized property, skill, or combination of both possessed by the individuals "under the conditions of the commodity or labor markets" (927). "Always," Weber notes

> this is the generic connotation of the concept of class: that the kind of chance in the *market* is the decisive moment which presents a common condition for the individual's fate. Class situation is, in this sense, ultimately market situation.
>
> (928)

As opposed to Marxist theory, where class is *cause* because it is rooted in the property relations that are the "relations of production" (Marx 1989: 21), Weberian social class is class as *effect*, descriptive of persons as they appear at the level of culture. Weber, that is, inverts the Marxist theory of class: whereas class in Marxist theory is integral to production and determines culture, in Weberian theory class comes into being at the level of culture as an effect of market (class) situation. Weberian class is therefore not an explanatory concept capable of explaining why there are vast differences, for example, in income, wealth, educational attainment, health, and so forth among strata of the population. It is, rather, a tool of classification based on description of property and labor power in the particularized forms they assume on the market, which, as Marx theorized it, is the sphere of circulation of capital in which capital (value produced by labor-power) "now assumes and now strips off in the repetition of its circuit" its "various forms," including money and commodities (1967b: 23). Class in Weber, that is, is an effect at the level of culture of the *circulation* of capital rather than capital's condition of possibility rooted in property (production) relations. Class becomes an array of ambiguous – murky – cultural identities depicting subjects not "as they *really* are; i.e. as they operate, produce materially, and hence as they work under definite material limits, presuppositions and conditions independent of their will," but "as they appear in their own or other people's imagination" (Marx and Engels 1989: 47).

By pluralizing and dehistoricizing property and labor power, Weberian theory occludes the dialectical relation between capital and labor that inheres in the extraction of labor power and the conversion of it into commodities, wages, development of the means of production, and, of course, profit. But it is through this dialectical relation between capital and labor that labor power is converted into cultural and political power, and it is therefore this relation that connects production and culture and explains cultural practices – knowledge production and pedagogy – as having their determinate basis in the material practices of production. In other words, the Marxist theory of class, that explains that the vast majority of the planet's people are objectively unified in historically (re)produced circumstances of non-ownership of the means of production, is central to Marx's labor theory of value. And it is Marx's labor theory of value that makes the Marxist theory of class the explanatory and revolutionary theory of class that is necessary for the development of class consciousness and revolutionary praxis because it is able to explain, without "any mystification and speculation," as Marx and Engels emphasize, "the connection of the social and political structure with production" (1989: 46–7).

The labor theory of value explains that the enormous power of the capitalist class over the lives of all who do not own property that is capital is in actuality the power of the proletariat turned against them for the purpose of raising the rate of profit and producing great wealth for the few. It explains that the power of the capitalist class to command production practices – to "downsize," to "outsource," to cut pay and benefits – resides in its ownership of capital as private property. And, it explains that the power of the capitalist class to legitimate inequitable relations caused by unequal property relations is the labor power of the proletariat turned against that class. "Property," as Marx explains, is "the worker's own objective conditions" that "arise over against him as autonomous forces, the property of someone else, value existing for itself and bringing everything back to itself – in short, capital" (1995: 385). This capital is "value concentrated into a power" (385), and it consists of the very labor power of the workers "embezzled" from them, "because abstracted without return of an equivalent" (Marx 1967a: 611). For example, capital's ability to augment the "value" of capitalism through the promotion and dissemination of ruling ideas – including through No Child Left Behind in the US, the National Curriculum and testing regime in England and Wales, and similar regimes worldwide of controlling and testing officially sanctioned school knowledges – is rooted in the labor power of the proletariat and turned against that class through the "power" of capital held by the businesses that support such ruling ideas, as suggested by Sleeter (2008) and Hoff (2006). The Marxist theory of class is a revolutionary theory because, through the labor theory of value, it explains why it is the historical project of the proletariat, who own only their labor power which they must sell daily to live, to end class contradiction by reappropriating from the capitalist class the property – their own unpaid labor power in the form of capital – that the bourgeoisie live off of but did not produce.

The Weberian framework suppresses inquiry into the gap between the classes as they are constituted in the relations of production central to the capitalist mode of production, making it impossible to question the regime of wage-labor in order to produce knowledge to end it. It is this non-explanatory framework of classes that is typically used to engage questions of class in education and elsewhere, often in terms of socioeconomic status (SES), a concept widely acknowledged to have been "influenced by a Weberian conceptualization that includes a variety of social and economic characteristics capturing class, status, and party positions" (Carpiano, *et al.* 2008: 248).

To take an example of the returns to class that in the wake of the 1980–3 and 1990–1 US recessions rethink class by updating Weber, consider the entry on "class" by O'Hara in Lentricchia and McLaughlin's second edition (1995) of *Critical Terms for Literary Study*, from whose first edition in 1990 class was pointedly excluded. This example is interesting, not so much for what it says, but because it shows cultureclass manufactured and articulated across two historical moments and two disciplines, in each case erasing binary property relations and serving the interests of capital as it attempts to manage crises involving a fall in the rate of profit.

In his essay, O'Hara (1995) treats class as an orphan trope, a term that American literary criticism had "lost contact" with (407), particularly as it went through "revisions

... made in response to better empirical and logical analyses, within the relevant disciplines – the post-Marxist wing of analytic philosophy, radical social theory, and the materialist critique of political economy" (406). And then he adopts Elster's 1985 social sciences analytical Marxist revision of it – articulated in Elster's *Making Sense of Marx*, that was praised by Alan Ryan in the pages of *The Times Literary Supplement* as "ingenious, inventive and imaginative" (1986: n. p.) – so it can be used "strategically, pragmatically, with a certain ironic, even (self-) parodic lightness" (418).

O'Hara claims that

> the best theoretical definition of class that I've discovered appears in Jon Elster's *Making Sense of Marx* (1985): "A class is a group of people who by virtue of what they possess are compelled to engage in the same activities if they want to make the best use of their endowments" (331).
>
> (O'Hara 1995: 415)

Elster updates Weber's understanding of class by folding into Weber's already pluralized notion of property Bourdieu's understandings of social and cultural capital as forms of property, a theorization that draws on and hybridizes Weber's understandings of class and status (Swartz 1997: 41–5) that Weber himself kept distinct (1978: 306–7, 932–3). As O'Hara notes, "endowments" in Elster's view is "a broadly conceived term for ... material and symbolic property or 'capital,'" understood as "'know-how' and/or power-position in society" (416). Once "property" is pluralized to mean any endowment, any group of people who have any possession in common can be said to be a class, or as O'Hara puts it, updating Thompson's (1966) reduction of class to a "happening" (9), "a new class improvising itself into existence" (422). Class becomes "an ever emergent albeit repeatable phenomenon" (416).

Elster himself understands social phenomena such as class to be effects of decisions made by "free" individuals: "the proper explanatory sequence must be to begin with individual motivations and ask how they generate behavioral patterns" (1985: 367). What is common to both Elster and Weber, in other words, is that both begin not with class as that which determines, in the sense of setting limits on, individual action, but with the individual "freely" pursuing interests using whatever it is she regards to be her particular "property." For Weber, these interests are economic (1978: 928), whereas for Elster this is not necessarily so. And this is what appeals to O'Hara: because in Elster's theory "[n]o endowment, however comparatively small in the grand scheme of things, can be beside the point of discussion, negotiation, and care, if only for tactical purposes" (417), "Elster ... encourages us to think of ourselves – intellectuals or otherwise – as the real 'authors' of ... possible visions of radical change" (418).

At the very moment when the effects of the Reagan-Thatcher policy of market deregulation were being felt by workers in the 1980–3 recession, Elster's understanding of class buttressed the neoliberal tenets informing that deregulation, above all, the "freedom of individuals" valorized by Friedman (1982: 12). As Mandel points out in an incisive critique of *Making Sense of Marx*, "[a]t the very time [Elster] was composing his book," "[i]n the midst of recurrent recessions and a 'long depressive wave,' with US industrial production capacity only utilized at an average of 70% ..., capital is busy cutting the wages of its workers in all advanced countries and even more so in most underdeveloped ones" (1989: n. p.). In these circumstances, what Elster offers is not Marx's explanatory theory that can enable class consciousness, but instead a theory that is "ingenious, inventive and imaginative" in the way that under the sign of "Marx" it masks property relations and serves the interests of the capitalist class in containing worker unrest.

O'Hara, for his part, recycles Elster's (neo-)Weberian theory in 1995, reinvigorating the notion of the free individual in the wake of the 1990–1 US recession – and he was not the only one. A reviewer in 1995 remarked that "[i]n the last decade, academic studies of the sociology of Max Weber have continued to pour from the academic press at an alarming rate" (Turner: 116).

The Elster-(Weber/Bourdieu)-O'Hara understandings of class are all ideological in the sense that Marx theorized ideology as an "inverted conception" produced by "the inversion of subject and object that takes place ... in the process of production ... this inverted relationship necessarily produces certain correspondingly inverted conceptions, a transposed consciousness which is further developed by the metamorphosis and modifications of the actual circulation process" (Marx 1967c: 45). Ideology enables description of appearances to occlude explanation of cause. It is an effect of the laws of motion of capital that shields capital, and it is why historical materialist critique is necessary: the work of such critique is to cut through the many inversions produced by capital that hide the property relations that are the root cause of conflict, inequity, and violence. What the Elster-(Weber/Bourdieu)-O'Hara example demonstrates is that the dominant knowledges of class that arise at moments of potential worker unrest are articulations that fabricate from ideological appearance the "ideal expression of the dominant material relationships." Such expression constitutes the ruling ideas whose production is regulated by the capitalist class "which has the means of material production at its disposal" (Marx and Engels 1989: 64), and which serve the interests of that class by blocking the development of class consciousness, all the more when its terms are differentiated into various local "left" and "right" versions and widely disseminated by professional ideologues.

Cultureclass: class management

What unites "post" and (neo-)Weberian versions of class and makes them instances of cultureclass is their erasure of property relations from the theoretical imaginary. Re-engaged in the moments following previous economic recessions, when the actuality of class relations are substantively shifting and disrupting people's lives and therefore cannot be ignored, class is recast in terms of an effect of culture and (re)inserted into dominant discourses as a safe and marketable textware, another difference without any particular priority or relation to actual practices of production. Such "revisions" of class are responses to shifts in production set in motion by capitalist updating of the means of production necessary to remain competitive. They are, that is, responses informed by ideology, responses that augment the ruling ideas of neoliberalism that in turn quicken and attempt to naturalize the shifts in production as being in everyone's interests.

While "[t]he ruling ideas of each age have ever been the ideas of its ruling class" (Marx and Engels 1985: 102) and therefore not in the interests of those from whom surplus value is extracted, in the theoretical climate dominated by a turn towards culture cast in terms of the unknowable and the local, Marxism's materialist understanding that "explain[s] practice from the idea" rather than "the formation of ideas from material practice" (Marx and Engels 1989: 58) is altogether rejected as "economic reductivism," "economic determinism," "economism." In this context, Giroux in 1983, and with no effort to historicize ideas in relation to politico-economic developments informing contestations at the level of culture, rejects "orthodox Marxism" and "radical social theories informed by its basic presuppositions" for having left a "legacy of determinism and pessimism" that he asserts can be traced back to "the failure of orthodox Marxism to bridge the dualism between structure and agency" (122).

However, as Au (2006) has argued, "much of the neo-Marxist critique has erroneously conflated functionalist, economic determinism with Marxism" when in fact, "Marx and Engels themselves have a tradition of struggling against economistic and mechanical interpretations of Marxist theory" (n. p.) and "recognized a non-linear, dynamic, non-mechanistic, *dialectical*, relationship between the economic base and the superstructure" (n. p.; italics in original). Au concludes, then, that "neo-Marxism had no need to reject the original Marxist formulations of the relationship between the economic base and the superstructure for being functionalist, mechanistic, or completely economically determined" (n. p.).

But as revealed by this conclusion, and despite his essay's informative focus on the dialectical relation between production and culture, what Au himself "misses" is that the neo-Marxist conflation of functionalist with historical materialist dialectical Marxism was not one caused by any "error" in reasoning such that there was "no need to reject the original Marxist formulations." This is an idealist formulation that ignores that the conflation was the effect of the power of the bourgeoisie, consisting of surplus value extracted from the proletariat, to widely promote and disseminate through books, journals, and other media put out by its publishing houses – its property – the theoretical focus that would most effectively enable the continued theft of labor power. Quite simply, the bourgeoisie, serving their own interests, made it profitable for a handful of knowledge workers to promulgate the conflation. Given the "publish or perish" imperative of the academy, this move on the part of capital developed a tendency in the academy to go along (with the ruling ideas) in order to get along. In the long run it effectively installed "economism" as a code word, a ruse serving the interests of capital and used to dismiss any return to Marxism that argues that "it is always the direct relationship of the owners of the conditions of production to the direct producers ... which reveals the innermost secret, the hidden basis of the entire social structure, and with it the political form of the relation of sovereignty and dependence, in short, the corresponding specific form of the state" (Marx 1967c: 791).

Giroux, however, alleging a disconnect between structure and agency in Marxism, represents Marxism as hopeless (1983: 59, 85, 122) and argues for "the need to struggle for something other than a change of consciousness, i.e. the transformation of specific social practices in concrete institutions such as schools" (Giroux 1983: 132). Yet when such local change is valorized to the extent that it is cut off from the systemic and determining property relations of global capitalism, as current scholarship is beginning to recognize it has been (Weis and Dimitriadis 2008), it is actually the turn towards the local that is hopeless because it assumes that history has come to an end and that no transformation of the mode of production is possible. Moreover, when local change is valorized over revolutionary systemic transformation of existing property relations, it is a position that, in keeping with neoliberalism, valorizes the agency of individuals over the agency of the proletariat as a class that Marx emphasized:

> It is not a matter of what this or that proletarian or even the proletariat as a whole *pictures* at present as its goal. It is a matter of *what the proletariat is in actuality* and what, in accordance with this *being*, it will historically be compelled to do.
> (1978: 134; italics in original)

What these previous returns to class reveal is that the capitalist class has been quite successful in waging war on labor through its ability, derived from the labor power of the proletariat, to contain the Marxist transformative theory of class and thus the class consciousness of the proletariat.

The now ritualized attack on the Marxist concept of class has over the course of five decades emptied social analyses of the very concept necessary for the development of proletariat class consciousness that enables the "really revolutionary class" (Marx and Engels 1985: 91) in its world historical task of transformation – a task which that class is widely regarded to have abdicated owing to its "failure" to have developed class consciousness. Noblit (2007) reiterates this familiar refrain and uses it to declare class nonexistent: "[t]he failure of working people to behave in ways in which class theory requires, forces us to admit that materiality is insufficient for class to be constructed as objectively real" (317). But as Lustig (2004) has argued, this mistakes "the absence of the cure for the passing of the disease" (46). Class consciousness, that is, is never served up raw. Class consciousness is a knowledge, and like any knowledge, it is not developed solely by the experiential, for experience is never made sense of outside of theory. As Lenin indicates when he argues that "Without revolutionary theory there can be no revolutionary movement" (1969: 25), class consciousness involves theoretical knowledge. At the level of theory, it involves grasping as integrated all aspects of the social totality both as they interact and as they are determined by and impact back on the relations of production. As a theoretical knowledge, class consciousness is enabled by access to concepts, especially that of class as property relations constitutive of the relations of production – the very concept that "left" scholarship has systematically dismissed.

Thus, in the return to class in 2008, at the very moment of a world market crisis when the US and nations worldwide stand on the precipice of a deep recession, when Van Galen notes that "the academy is relatively silent about class" and wonders "[w]hy, even as we've come far in our understanding of race, ethnicity, and gender in schooling, do we seem to be late to class?" (2007: 2, 1), it is not, as Weis cynically contends, that "academics ... participated in the production of our collective ignorance around issues of social class" because "discussion ... of social class" was "tempered, if not altogether ignored, since the 1980s, as scholarship targeted more specifically to issues of race and/or gender, as well as broader issues of representation, has taken hold" (Weis 2004: 167; see also Weis 2008: 1–2). What accompanied the rise of imperialist neoliberal practices and the increase in social inequality that have gone largely uncontested by the academy, contributing to a proletariat that has "learned to accept the logic of the market as a functional equivalent of democracy" (Frank 2000: 57), was not any simple "inattention" to class. It was an attack on it on the part of "left" knowledge workers themselves as they valorized "post" knowledges, justified capitalism, and served the interests of the bourgeoisie by bloc(k)ing class consciousness through the conversion of economic inequality into cultural differences – a move that fragmented the proletariat and "provided the right a useful technology" for evading class wars (Michaels 2006: 109).

What is necessary now, in order to be serious about transforming the existing material conditions in which "accumulation of wealth at one pole is accumulation of misery, agony of toil, slavery, ignorance, brutality, mental degradation, at the opposite pole, i.e. on the side of the class that produces its own product in the form of capital" (Marx 1967a: 645), is a theory of class that can explain, without "any mystification and speculation," as Marx and Engels emphasize, "the connection of the social and political structure with production" (1989: 46–7), and in so doing provide the revolutionary knowledges necessary to transform the existing mode of production.

Cultureclass and the contemporary

Most contemporary texts engaging the concept of class, however, extend the notion that class, once again, needs "rethinking" (see, for example, Johnston 2007: 31; Noblit 2007: 315; Aronowitz 2003: 2).

While the call for "rethinking" signals that the dominant knowledges are presumably distancing themselves from the "murky" understandings of class manufactured through post and (neo-)Weberian frameworks, it also signals an ongoing dismissal of the Marxist theory of class. In fact, Van Galen calls for rethinking class "within newer theoretical perspectives" (2007: 2), specifically those of the "'new economy' of knowledge and service work" (2). Thus the call for rethinking class works to open the field to "new" understandings – which, once again, turn out to make class murky.

The "newer" theoretical frameworks within which class is being updated are taken up in light of "several decades" during which "neoliberal and neoconservative politicians have reshaped educational policy around the ideology that schools need to incorporate markets, competition, and choice in order to prepare students for the global economy" (Hursh 2005: 13). These frameworks, then, involve globalization and the issues it raises in relation to education and class, among them the "class-linked forms of pressure on schools, families, and youth" (Weis 2008: 3), as well as the question of the "roles ... our educational institutions play in reproducing or interrupting class dynamics" (Apple 2007: viii).

With these concerns, education has turned primarily to the frameworks of globalization that Held and McGrew (2007) call "critical globalism." These "[i]ssu[e] principally from poststructural and post-Marxist scholarship" (171) – precisely the scholarship out of which emerged the dismissal of the Marxist theory of class. So although compelled now by the starkly evident binary division of labor on an international scale to address class, education returns to class, but from within an understanding of the contradictions of capitalism that continues to be informed by post and (neo-)Weberian frameworks that prioritize culture over production.

Once again, "post" knowledges

Theories of critical globalism have at their core the idea that "a new globalized social formation is ... in the making" (Held and McGrew 2007: 171) – what others (for example, Drucker 1994) have called a post-capitalist formation.

Theories of post-capitalism are repeated with regularity on both right and left. However, from right to left they always foreground the increasing centrality of knowledge to the labor process and the production of (surplus) value. For example, conservative columnist David Brooks, student of the late William F. Buckley, argues for a "cognitive age paradigm emphasiz[ing] psychology, culture and pedagogy" as "the real source of prosperity" (2008). Thomas L. Friedman, *The New York Times* columnist and one of the capitalist class's most effective ideologues for "globalization" and neoliberal economic policies, argues that "solutions" "create value" (2006: 180). Lash and Urry (1996), finding reasons for optimism in the "end" of what they call "organized capitalism," argue that in "the mode of information" that replaces "mode of production" (319) it is information flows (326) that drive production. On the left, Hardt and Negri argue that what is central to a society in which "information and communication have come to play a foundational role in production processes" (2000: 289) is "immaterial labor" – "labor that creates immaterial products, such as knowledge, information, communication, a relationship, or an emotional response" (2004: 108) and that is involved with the production of "not only commodities but also subjectivities" (2000: 32).

The increasing centrality of knowledge to production is used to argue for the need to change how class is understood. Aronowitz, for example, suggesting that "the fundamental relations within capitalist society" have changed, argues that "immaterial labor" – the knowledge work of "a new class of salaried managers and trained scientific and technical intellectuals" – has changed the "class map" (2003: 2, 3). Dolby and Dimitriadis (2004) assert that "as 'productive labor' fades as the real basis of the economic structure," "the structural conditions of capital have shifted dramatically" (8). McCarthy (2004) agrees that there is a "deepening reorganization of capital," emphasizing the post-capitalist notion that "symbolic mobilization is now an ascendant practice" such that "[s]tyle and taste are now driving the economic" (160).

Weis (2004), concurring with these views, rewrites shifts in capitalism as "a radical break with past practice" (8). It is this assumption of a "radical break" from capitalism that marks theories of post capitalism as part of the ensemble of knowledges constituting "post-ality," which by

> sever[ing] the past of capitalism from what is regard[ed] to be its radically different and "new" present (which unlike its past is now free from exploitation)

... attempts to solve – in the theoretical imaginary – the historical and material contradictions of capitalism caused by the social division of labor.

(Zavarzadeh 1995: 1)

The assumption they all share – despite differences in register, which are themselves highly effective in installing post capitalism across a range of sites as the new common sense – is the assumption articulated by "management guru" ("Farewell" 2005: n. p.) Peter Drucker: the fundamental contradiction between capital and labor is being superseded as "[k]nowledge ... becom[es] the sole factor of production, sidelining both capital and labor" (1994: 20). Since (the thinking goes) labor increasingly involves knowledge, and because knowledge itself is seen as *both* product *and* means of production – knowledge workers are said to "own the 'means of production,' that is, their knowledge" (Drucker 1994: 64) – the shift to knowledge work is seen as eroding the antagonism and indeed the relation between capital and labor. While "[t]he traditional 'factors of production' – land ..., labor, and capital – have not disappeared, ... they have become secondary" and "can be obtained ... easily, provided there is knowledge" (42). Thus what eventually becomes the "knowledge society" is seen as "capitalism *sans* the capitalists" (78) and indeed without classes (96).

Hardt and Negri's version of this (to take an example from the "left") holds that immaterial labor – labor that remains "material" but that produces an "immaterial" product such as an idea or relation (2004: 109) – changes the character of cooperation, making it "internal to labor and thus external to capital" (147), such that "the cooperative powers of labor power (particularly immaterial labor power) afford labor the possibility of valorizing itself" (2000: 294). In turn, this means that "[p]rivate property" still exists, but as an "obsolescence" (410–11). While in the post-capitalist view the relation of owning to the means of production is no longer seen as the bas(e)ic relation that compels exploitation and determines developments in culture, exploitation nevertheless does not disappear: it "expand[s] everywhere, ... tending to occupy the entire social terrain" (209). What disappears, however, is the "outside" of capitalism, the production relations that determine culture. They become subsumed within culture. As Hardt and Negri (2000) put it, "social relations completely invest the relations of production, making impossible any externality between social production and economic production" (209).

In brief, post-capitalist theories – whether articulated from "right" or "left" – highlight the increasing centrality of knowledge to production and read its apparent and apparently increasing autonomy from property relations as a harbinger of a (d)evolution of capitalism in which production is subsumed within culture. Revolution, in this framework, becomes not only unnecessary, but impossible, since with the "outside" (production relations) erased, "everything," once again, "can be said to have become 'cultural'" (Jameson 1991: 48).

What these theories ignore is threefold. First, "immaterial labor" – knowledge work – is not an autonomous source of surplus value; it is made possible by material labor (Ebert and Zavarzadeh 2008: 54; Sayers 2007). Second, and relatedly, knowledge work becomes integral to the conversion of surplus value into what Marx (2000, Part III), following Richard Jones, calls "auxiliary capital." Marx glosses auxiliary capital as "the part of constant capital which is not made up of raw materials" (436). Auxiliary capital involves what Marx calls "science" (443) which, broadly, means application of knowledge that results in discoveries: "discovery of new use-values or of a new use for well-known use-values, and new inventions of machinery" (440). In this connection, Marx mentions the telegraph (440). The part of the telegraph that is "not made up of raw material," and therefore constitutes auxiliary capital, consists of the codes – a discovery made possible by science – used to transmit communications. Auxiliary capital, then, consists of the discoveries made by knowledge work – DNA codes, for example. But in order for this knowledge work to be productive of surplus value, it must always be incorporated into means of production that require material labor. Codes used in the telegraph are useless without the machinery of the telegraph, machinery that must be produced by material labor. As Marx puts it, "[c]apitalist production leads to separation of *science from labour* and at the same time to the use of science in material production" (443). The increase in capital's use of knowledge work may make it *appear* that knowledge work alone can create value, but in actuality the increase represents the more complete integration of knowledge workers into the creation of means useful for the extraction and realization of surplus value. Third, the increasing centrality of knowledge work to production does not change the production relations – exploitation of the non-owners by the owners – that are fundamental to capitalism. This holds true whether knowledge work is productive or unproductive labor (producing absolute or relative surplus value or subtending the extraction and realization of surplus value). As Marx argued, the wage laborer, "even one of the better paid, ... works part of his time for nothing" (1967b: 132).

Positing immaterial labor as having an increasing autonomy from property relations serves as a warrant for declaring the Marxist theory of class bankrupt and revising class as an effect of culture that can be categorized in (neo-)Weberian and post frameworks according to differences in knowledge, skills, and power. What the turn to such frameworks does is reinvigorate a poststructuralist politics that detaches "power" from the exploitation of wage labor and privileges resistance to capitalism, over emancipating humans from class society. In effect, post-capitalist theories serve to mask the binary and inequitable property relations of capitalism, even as the practices they enable become more blatantly barbaric.

In the moment of a world market crisis in which the productive forces threaten private property and create what Aronowitz refers to as objective and subjective conditions "ripe" for the development of an alternative left (2006: 68–9), the class consciousness of the proletariat might be enabled through uncompromising historical materialist critique of the property relations through which capitalism has produced the misery of the many. Yet with Marxist theory delegitimized for decades (extensively so in the US), contemporary theorists, including Aronowitz, once again turn away from the Marxist theory of class and open space to reintroduce (neo-)Weberian and post frameworks of class.

"Post" knowledges: replacing the property line with the power line

Informed by post-Marxist and poststructuralist theories of the social, dominant contemporary knowledges of class displace the property line as the fundamental basis of class with what Weiner (2004), borrowing Kelley's locution and engaging Aronowitz's theory of class in his recent *How Class Works*, calls "the power line." Aronowitz (2003) "proposes to define the class divide according to the line of power" (10). His basic move – in light both of historical developments in capitalism that increasingly involve "immaterial labor" in production (3–4) and the rise of "many social movements [that] have lost their punch and have been absorbed into the liberal establishment" (155) – is to "shift ... the concept of class from a cleavage based exclusively on relations of ownership of capital ... to relations of power in all of its domains" (58–9).

This is a Foucauldian understanding of power. Consistent with the ludic logic of poststructuralism, Foucault (1990) argues that "there is no binary and all-encompassing opposition between rulers and ruled" (94) that "explains" power relations (95). Because there is no binary opposition, there is no fundamental cause of inequity, no systemic inequitable relation from which humans need to emancipate themselves. Indeed, in Foucault's view, "[p]ower is everywhere ... because it comes from everywhere" (93), and is "always local and unstable" (93). Thus the existing power relations in their totality cannot be transformed. What takes the place of revolutionary class struggle is "a plurality of resistances, each of them a special case" (96). By pluralizing and dehistoricizing power, Foucault's "post" theory of power removes from view the conditions of possibility for revolution to emancipate humans from exploitation by humans for profit for the few.

While he critiques the limits of postmodern theories, such as Foucault's and Laclau and Mouffe's, for enabling only "incremental reform" (159), Aronowitz (2003) nevertheless explicitly turns to Foucault's theory of power (53) to argue that power comes not only from the binary relation of ownership to the means of production, but also from the relations within the "class fractions ... divided" into social movements on the basis of "bio-identities" that have been united in their "insist[ence] on their absolute separation from class politics" (2003: 141–2). Thus, while Aronowitz asserts that his "understanding of power differs from the tendency of postmodern social theory" (53), it in fact returns to the very "post" framework he claims to reject. Power in its "subjective" form that involves "the effects of the interventions of specific groups and individuals" (2006: 68) is pluralized and detached from labor power: "While ownership of productive property remains one of its key elements, power relations in the state and everyday practices are outcomes of struggles that are, in turn, indeterminate from the perspective of the relations of production" (61).

In this view, power is not determined by the social relations of production; power is not the materiality of labor-power turned against the proletariat from which it was appropriated by the bourgeoisie. Rather, as it is in Weber (1978), power is pluralized and dehistoricized into types of "authority" that are considered to be "legitimate" (212–15). Yet as Sahay (1998) has argued, to abstract power from the relations of production "is ultimately a (class) *political* strategy to dehierarchize power as a 'reversible' construct in which the lines of opposition between the 'powerful' and the 'powerless' are blurred." This strategy effectively "neutraliz[es]" power as a concept enabling the "powerless ... to wage a concerted struggle against the powerful." Unable to "explain *why* power is deployed in the first place," the strategy reveals itself as a "reverse strategy" that, by dehistoricizing power, makes power "a transcendental' category: the effect of a transhistorical 'will to power' which eternally subsists in the social" (para. 10).

Once the power line replaces the property line, classes are not unified on any objective basis, nor do they have any causal relation to one another. Indeed, as Aronowitz notes, "class formation is contingent" (2003: 39): "class occurs when insurgent social formation(s) make demands that cleave society and engender new social and cultural relations" (11).

What Aronowitz does is theorize social movements consisting of "women, blacks, and the physically disabled" each as "a modality of class politics," that is, as "class fractions" (142) – but not as class fractions with an objective unity rooted in property relations. Rather, they are fractions of a *possible* class whose verifiable existence is to be adjudicated, not in relation to members' objective unity as subjects of exploitation, that is, with reference to *cause* (the base), but in terms of whether they "make historical difference" (38), that is, with reference to *outcome* at the level of the cultural and political (the superstructure). Aronowitz's detour through post theory, in short, returns to a Weberian framework in which classes, as Weber argued, are "phenomena of the distribution of power within a community" (1978: 927) where power is detached from labor power – power, Weber notes, may "exist ... on other grounds" than the economic – and possession of power is adjudicated with reference to outcome: "we understand by 'power' the chance of a man or a number of men to realize their own will in a social action even against the resistance of others who are participating in the action" (926).

Aronowitz replaces transformation of the mode of production, which he dismisses as a necessary aim (2003: 39), with "change." Agreeing that Marxist "notions of transformation" must be rejected, McCarthy (2004) argues in favor of "thinking about change within the terms of modulation" where the focus is on "working with and against constraint, in the struggle for happiness" (162). The "struggle for happiness" displaces the struggle to end exploitation by abolishing class society. Indeed, such arguments work to manufacture subjects who accept exploitation as a "happy" circumstance, as the work of Giddens (2003) suggests. Returning to arguments for a "third way" between capitalism and socialism, Giddens does not argue for transformation but instead in favor of what he calls "*controlled inequality* ... we should accept some inequalities in order to prevent worse ones developing" (20). However, as Lenin argued, in part against the "evolutionary socialism," advocated by Weber's colleague Eduard Bernstein and which stands as the precursor to all modern and (post)modern versions of the third way, "there is no middle course (for humanity has not created a 'third' ideology, and, moreover, in a society torn by class antagonisms there can never be a non-class or above-class ideology)" (1969: 41). There is no third way because there is no "happy" capitalism – because capitalism is the exploitation of humans by humans.

Once again, the turn to Weber

Quite explicit versions of (neo-)Weberian understandings of class are used in research concerned to close the achievement gap between students from lower and higher income families. The achievement gap was identified in the Coleman Study (1966) that found that "variation in school resources had very little – almost nothing – to do with what we now term the test score gap between black and white children," and that "family backgrounds of black and white students, their widely different social and economic conditions, accounted for most of the difference" (Rothstein 2004: 13). This finding has for "four decades" been "consistently confirmed" (14). Moreover, the gap shows no signs of abating in the next decade because "the same broad ... social conditions that supported educational inequality in the twentieth century are still operating" (Gamoran 2008: 170).

(Neo-)Weberian social class is used in such research because the dehistoricized particularizations of property and labor constituting Weber's "class situations" present, as Weber put it, "opportunities for income" on the market (1978: 927), and income has proven useful in predicting "intergenerational economic status transmission" (Bowles and Gintis 2002: 3). Thus, researchers read backwards from (neo-)Weberian social class into "class situations" and treat the factors that constitute them and present "opportunities for income" as factors that cause and can therefore explain the achievement gap, ignoring that the "ultimate" cause is the fundamentally inequitable relation of owning to property (Engels 1968: 704–6). With the expansion of "possessions" to include "endowments" of any sort, as in the Elster-O'Hara updating of the Weberian understanding of class, these causal factors include not only the classic Weberian factors such as wealth, income, education credentials, and skills, but also what Bourdieu theorized as cultural and social capital – "possessions" in which the "material types of capital ... present themselves in ... immaterial form" (Bourdieu 1986: 46).

Apple (2007), for example, following McNall, Levine, and Fantasia who retain the Marxist understanding of classes as relational but then merge this feature into a Weberian framework (1991: 1–4), puts forth just such an updated, (neo-)Weberian understanding of class when he states that "what class means is more than simply one's place in an economic structure" (2007: viii), that is, the connection between "income and advantage" cannot be "totally explained by economic resources" (2007: ix). He goes on to suggest that "[c]ultural and social resources are crucial as well. Particular dispositions, propensities, and appreciations – and an 'ease' in displaying them – as well as who you know, play important roles here." These resources, he notes, are those theorized by Bourdieu in "his taxonomy of various kinds of capital: economic, cultural, and social" (2007: ix; see also Bourdieu 2006a: 61–3). In short, class, Apple argues, quoting McNall, Levine, and Fantasia, "has both objective and subjective components" (viii), and therefore it "functions as a structure and as a process, as both economic and cultural" (ix).

The objective/subjective framework makes class "murky." It blurs the determinate relation between base and superstructure, reducing it to a nondeterminate interaction in which the classes constituting the "base" have already been replaced by Weberian classes constituted in the superstructure as the outcome of market exchanges (class situation). Li (2008), for example, explicating the objective/subjective framework that Apple (2007; 2006a) advocates, notes that class is both objective, "defined in terms of material standards of living usually indexed by income or wealth" (class as effect of Weberian "class situation") and subjective, "a sociological process through which people live their lives" and "survive, and cope." Li goes on to explain that "[s]ocial class is therefore not simply a static construct but a developing one that can be changed through one's socialization process" (151). The objective/subjective framework posits class as a Weber-Bourdieu hybrid, as an effect of cultural practices – of how individuals and groups negotiate the existing class situation of their lives using whatever "capital" they have at hand. It erases the base, the inequitable property relations of capital, in effect erasing the conceptual space to conceptualize the existence of the proletariat as a class objectively unified by non-ownership of "property." This erasure at the level of knowledge has consequences at the level of the political: any basis for an objective interest on the part of the "nonpropertied" in transforming the relations of production is entirely occluded, dispersed into an infinite number of possible "market situations" that become the focus of attention.

For example, Rothstein, while supporting reforms involving improvement of instruction, argues that "the influence of social class characteristics is probably so powerful that schools cannot overcome it, no matter how well trained are their teachers and no matter how well designed are their instructional programs and climates" (2004: 5). He therefore advocates "public policies that narrow the social and economic gaps between lower- and middle-class children" (9) – policies, for example, that fund extended early childhood and extended-day and -year school programs, as well as healthcare services that, together, Rothstein believes can "narrow" the achievement gap (131).

But what the reforms aim to do is "eliminate[e] *the impact* of social class on children in American society" (Rothstein 2004: 149; emphasis added), not transform the property relations that produce the achievement gap. Rothstein's proposal, in other words, is an example of what Marx and Engels (1985) call "conservative socialism," which argues that "only a change in the material conditions of existence, in economical relations, could be of any advantage" to the proletariat. But, by "changes in material conditions," this form of socialism does not mean "abolition of the bourgeois relations of production," but "administrative reforms" (114). It "is desirous of redressing social grievances, in order to secure the continued existence of bourgeois society" (113).

That Rothstein's proposal is in effect an effort to maintain bourgeois society is clear in the fact that, while it leaves in place inequality of property relations, it advocates committing funds to reforms to enable equality of opportunity – equalizing "life chances" in Weber's terms. Equality of opportunity is precisely what Friedman (1982) argues is at the very core of (neo)liberalism (as opposed to egalitarianism which argues for "material equality or equality of outcome" that "defend[s] taking from some to give to others ... on grounds of 'justice'" (195), what today is called the "liberal" "left" view). Equality of opportunity, as Friedman points out, is actually "equality of rights." In particular, equality of opportunity means an "equal right to freedom" (195), which is the fundamental value of (neo)liberalism because it is necessary to the workings of the free market insofar as it enables competition on the market: no one is to be restricted by law from producing, exchanging, or selling whatever she wants (8–15). Michaels (2006), in his argument against turning economic into cultural difference, unpacks the connection between equality of opportunity and the maintenance of bourgeois society: "[t]he whole point of the commitment to equal opportunity is to make sure not only that people have a right to their property but also that they have a fair chance to earn that property" (133).

The argument for equality of opportunity, in other words, turns out to be an argument for "the importance of hard work and ability" (Michaels 2006: 133) – what Weber (1992) regarded as the values, summed up in the phrase "the spirit of capitalism" (17–19), that are "the fundamental basis of" capitalism because together they make "the making of money ... the ultimate purpose of ... life" (19). Rothstein's conservative socialism, in short, works to reinvigorate the exercise of the equal right to freedom that is in actuality the right to compete on the market that works in the interests of the maintenance of free market capitalism, not its abolition. As Marx and Engels point out, "[t]he essential condition for the existence, and for the sway of the bourgeois class, is the formation and augmentation of capital; the condition for capital is wage labour. Wage labour rests exclusively on the competition between the labourers" (1985: 93). In brief, equality of opportunity/right to freedom is a value that is an expression of the capitalist interest in increasing the value of capital, and demonstrates that the bas(e)ic property relations of capitalism shape the superstructure.

Taking what appears to be a different tack, a "noneconomic solution" (Ream and Palardy 2008: 258), the main focus of a large and growing body of current work in education largely focuses on developing understanding of how various strata of the proletariat (what this research, following Weber, refers to in terms of upper, middle, and working classes and the poor) do or do not use cultural and social capital to "maintain and change class position" (Van Galen and Noblit 2007: 53) – that is, maintain or change factors contributing to class situation in order to enable social mobility among these strata of the proletariat. They, too, however, are proposals for equality of opportunity that, by focusing specifically on cultural practices, reinvigorate the values that are expressions of the capitalist interest in increasing the value of capital.

To take several representative instances, Lareau uses a hybrid understanding of class that draws on both (neo-)Weberian models concerned with credentials and "power line" versions concerned with authority (2003: 261) together with a *partial, empirical application of Bourdieu's broader theoretical model*" (276), to show "how class works in the rituals of daily life" (2008b: 117). In particular, she is interested in how middle-class parents, both black and white, ensure children's success by "routinely scann[ing] the horizon for opportunities to activate their cultural capital and social capital on behalf of their children." These are not only interventions on their children's behalf, but also act as a form of pedagogy: "By teaching their daughters and sons how to get organizations to meet their individualized needs, white and black middle-class mothers pass along skills that have the potential to be extremely valuable to their children in adulthood" (118).

Relatedly, Devine (2008) argues for the necessity of examining schools as a site "where class inequalities are reproduced" and understanding how that happens in order to provide opportunities for upward social mobility at a time when it seems to be stalling or perhaps in decline (100). Kroeger (2007) looks at the practices of the middle class in a diverse urban setting to determine "tensions and possibilities" in their practices – whether middle-class parents in fact work only for their own or also for others' children (204) – and suggests "school leaders and teachers [need] either to question more carefully and to stop the beneficial but recapitulative activity of the middle class, or to marshal their forces more powerfully to benefit schools in new and different ways" (229). Payne (2003) argues that "[s]chools are virtually the only places where students can learn the choices and rules of the middle class" (80). Using a (neo-)Weberian framework delineating three classes (poor, middle, and wealthy) described in terms of "resources" ranging from financial to spiritual (16), she argues that "[t]he ability to leave poverty is more dependent upon other resources than it is upon financial resources" (17). Primarily, she argues that the discourse practices and hidden rules of the middle class need to be explicitly taught in order to enable students in poverty to "move from one class to the next" (18).

Despite their local differences and contestations over them (Payne's work, widely disseminated in *The New York Times Magazine*, has been criticized by many in the academy for its deficit approach to the question of poverty; see, for example, Bomer, *et al.* 2008; Gorski 2006), what unites all of the "noneconomic solutions" that address the achievement gap is their belief that identifying how individuals and strata of the proletariat use cultural and social "capital" to their advantage and the disadvantage of others will contribute to a body of knowledge of what is necessary to be changed in education in order to enable future workers' equality of opportunity on the market.

In the aggregate, contemporary scholarship concerning the use of social and cultural capital by various strata of the proletariat urges that members of the so-called middle class, including educators, stop engaging in exclusive practices that benefit their own children to the detriment of others, but also widely disseminate their skills in developing and using social capital ("who you know and how you use them") and cultural capital ("how to act in dominant culture"). This is an argument for updating the "values" of the lower strata of the proletariat to meet the needs of capitalism as it engages in the "forcible solutions" necessary for it to survive its most profound crisis since 1929–33. As such, it is a revisionist argument.

Revisionism, as Luxemburg (1970) explains, does "not expect to see the contradictions of capitalism mature"; it believes there is no alternative to capitalism. Consequently it aims "to lessen, to attenuate, the capitalist contradictions" – in short, to "adjust" "the antagonism between capital and labor" by "bettering ... the situation of the workers ... and conserv[ing] ... the middle classes" (60).

To teach cultural and social capital, abstracted from conceptual education in the property relations that underpin the ascendance of the values cultural and social capital represent, is to attempt to attenuate the capitalist contradictions: it inculcates future workers into the values required for workers to compete to be used by capitalism in its aim of adding more value to the existing value of various capitals. It is a proposal that encourages the so-called middle class to disseminate its knowledges of how to work within the system rather than change it.

Yet teaching social and cultural capital reduces education to training in the skills (the how) useful to capital and displaces education as critique-al engagement with the question of the relation between the value of such skills and capital's relentless drive, rooted in its property relations, to enhance the value of itself (the why). Knowledge workers who advocate such training in social and cultural capital do the work of ideologically managing the proletariat, rather than educating persons in such a way as to enable them to organize to put an end to the property relations that convert humans into "instruments of labour, more or less expensive to use" (Marx and Engels 1985: 88).

To be clear, it is necessary to support reforms that might have a chance of improving the local circumstances of many. As Marx and Engels argue, it is necessary to "fight for the attainment of the immediate aims ... of the working class" (1985: 119). This is so because the attainment of immediate aims such as legislation to "protect ... the working-class both in mind and body" has the effect of "maturing the material conditions, and the combination on a social scale of the processes of production," and, by "matur[ing] the contradictions and antagonisms of the capitalist form of production, ... thereby provides, along with the elements for the formation of a new society, the forces for exploding the old one" (Marx 1967a: 503).

Support for the attainment of immediate aims, however, does not logically exclude critique of the limited extent of the aims. As Marx and Engels (1985) argue, it is necessary to "take up a critical position" (119) in relation to reform movements, and to do so in order to educate the proletariat regarding "the hostile antagonism between bourgeoisie and proletariat." In this way, critique seeks to position workers not simply to accept reforms as all that can ever be done, and in accepting them contribute to maintaining capitalism, but rather to "use, as so many weapons against the bourgeoisie, the social and political conditions that the bourgeoisie must necessarily introduce along with its supremacy" (120). To say this differently: critique of reforms seeks to educate workers in understanding why the attainment of immediate aims will not reconcile the objective antagonism between the two classes whose effects dominate the lives of workers and limit individual development, and why only the abolition of class society can put an end to the inequities workers experience in their everyday lives.

It is in this context that cultureclass, which suppresses inquiry into property relations in the context of a world crisis that foregrounds the very limits of existing property relations, must be understood as capitalist class interested management of workers at the level of culture through wide dissemination of knowledges capable of updating worker subjectivities adapted to the updated production relations required by capitalism to extract more profit.

Conclusion

Cultureclass, in all its various forms, is a response to sharpened contradictions of capitalism, but one that emerges from within a framework that, long anchored in the privileging of the arena of culture to the exclusion of production relations, continues to repudiate Marx's binary theory of class. It severs, at the level of knowledge, the connection between culture and the production practices in which all persons participate in order to (re)produce themselves. While the culturalization of class occurs through a variety of means – erasure, hybridization, or inversion of the historical materialist logic of causality that establishes that "[t]he social structure and the State are continually evolving out of the life-process of definite individuals ... as they operate, produce materially, and hence as they work under definite material limits, presuppositions and conditions independent of their will" (Marx and Engels 1989: 46–7) – what unites all of them is that they are idealist knowledges.

Insofar as cultureclass attempts to "explain practice from the idea" rather than "the formation of ideas from material practice" (58), its multiple versions all follow what Lenin argued is a "subjectivist line" that "cuts human reason off from nature," and "makes nature a *part* of reason, instead of regarding reason as a part of nature" (Lenin 1970: 142). Politically, cultureclass is reformist, diverting inquiry into inequality inward, into cultural relations and away from the constitutive but also historically determined and therefore changeable "outside" of capitalism without which capitalism cannot exist: the extraction, by and for owners of private property, of surplus value (profit) from the non-owners. For that constitutive outside, and at the level of knowledge, cultureclass substitutes practices of individuals that take place within culture, the "inside" of capitalism. In doing so, cultureclass works to naturalize capitalism as the only and final mode of production possible as it simultaneously (re)presents the social as a series of relatively autonomous arenas and blocks knowledge of capitalism as a mode of production that can be transformed into socialism.

Conley, in the concluding chapter of his co-edited book with Lareau (2008) in which he argues for "folk versions" of class, reflects as follows on that book's myriad versions of what I am calling cultureclass:

> *the very paradox of class is that the moment we are measuring some aspect of it adequately – say, income – and specifying a causal pathway of some sort, then we have taken our finger off what class really is.* If it is income buying us advantage, then it is not social class exactly, but rather financial resources. If it is explicit skills or credentials that land us the killer job, then it isn't social class per se that gets us there ... It is the silent force between the cracks of wealth, income, occupation, and education that constitutes the mortar of the class system.
>
> (2008: 371, italics in original)

In essence, Conley recognizes that contemporary reductions of class to cultureclass are inadequate for the socially necessary intellectual labor that inquires into the cause(s) of inequality in order to explain and change it. But, rather than turning to the Marxist theory of class that demystifies "the silent force ... of the class system" and shows it to be the embezzled labor power of the proletariat turned against them by the mediations of the capitalist class, Conley, in fine post-al fashion, spectralizes class:

> That unspoken – unspeakable even – thing that hangs in the air ... that is the essence of social class ... Think of social class as a ghost that haunts this volume,

tapping you, dear reader, on the shoulder occasionally as you are about to turn the page. But each time you spin your head around to catch a glimpse, it has disappeared from view.

(371–2)

But class is not dead. Class is not a specter. Its materiality is evident even and especially in the conversion of the brutality of capitalist relations into a nineteenth-century folk tale of spirit hauntings. To be sure, the hour is growing late. But the intellectual task at hand is not to entertain. It is to lay bare the dialectical workings of class and provide a materialist explanation of why class society continues, and why it must be transformed. The task is to show that class is, indeed, here, there, ... everywhere.

Note

1 For red critique.

Bibliography

Ahmad, A. (2000) *In Theory: classes, nations, literatures*, London: Verso.

Apple, M. W. (2007) "Foreword," in J. A. Van Galen and G. W. Noblit (eds) *Late to Class*, Albany: State University of New York Press.

—— (2006a) *Educating the "Right" Way: markets, standards, god, and inequality*, 2nd edn, New York: Routledge.

—— (2006b) "Rhetoric and reality in critical educational studies in the United States," *British Journal of Sociology of Education*, 27(5): 679–87.

Aronowitz, A. (2006) *Left Turn: forging a new political future*, Boulder: Paradigm Publishers.

—— (2003) *How Class Works: power and social movement*, New Haven and London: Yale University Press.

Au, W. (2006) "Against economic determinism: revisiting the roots of neo-Marxism in critical educational theory," *Journal for Critical Education Policy Studies*, 4 (2). Online. Available at http://www.jceps.com/index.php?pageID=article&articleID=66 (accessed July 18, 2007).

Boltanski, L. and Chiapello, E. (2007) *The New Spirit of Capitalism*, trans. G. Elliott (2004), London: Verso.

Bomer, R., Dworin, J. E., May, L. and Semingson, P. (2008) "Miseducating teachers about the poor: a critical analysis of Ruby Payne's claims about poverty," *Teachers College Record*, 110 (12). Online. Available at http://www.tcrecord.org ID number: 14591 (accessed March 3, 2008).

Bourdieu, P. (1986) "The forms of capital," trans. R. Nice, in J. E Richardson (ed.) *Handbook of Theory of Research for the Sociology of Education*, Westport, CT: Greenword Press.

Bowles and Gintis (2002) "The inheritance of inequality," *Journal of Economic Perspectives*, 16(3): 3–30.

Brooks, D. (2008) "The Cognitive Age," *The New York Times*, 2 May. Online. Available at http://www.nytimes.com (accessed May 2, 2008).

Callinicos, A. (1990) *Against Postmodernism: a Marxist critique*, New York: St. Martin's Press.

Carpiano, R. M., Link, B. G. and Phelan, J. C. (2008) "Social inequality and health," in

A. Conley and D. Conley (eds) *Social Class: how does it work?* New York: Russell Sage Foundation.

Coleman, J. S. (1966) "Equality of educational opportunity (Coleman) study (EEOS)," [computer file]. ICPSR06389-v3. Washington, DC: U. S. Department of Health, Education, and Welfare, Office of Education/National Center for Education Statistics [producer], 1999. Ann Arbor, MI: Inter-university Consortium for Political and Social Research [distributor], 2007-04-27. doi: 10.3886/ICPSR06389.

Conley, D. (2008) "Reading class between the lines (of this volume): a reflection on why we should stick to folk concepts of social class," in A. Lareau and D. Conley (eds) *Social Class: how does it work?*, New York: Russell Sage Foundation.

Connell, R. W., Ashenden, D., Kessler, S. and Dowsett, G. W. (1982). *Making the Difference: schools, families and social division*, St. Leonards: Allen & Unwin.

Correspondents (eds) (2005) *Class Matters*, New York: Times Books, Henry Hold and Company.

Crompton, R. (1993) *Class and Stratification: an introduction to current debates*, Cambridge, UK: Polity Press.

Derrida, J. (1978) "Structure, sign, and play in the discourse of the human sciences," in J. Derrida, *Writing and Difference*; trans. A. Bass. Chicago: The University of Chicago Press. Online. Available at http://www.hydra.umn.edu/derrida/sign-play.html (accessed October 30, 2006).

Devine, F. (2008) "Class reproduction and social networks in the USA," in L. Weis (ed.) *The Way Class Works: readings on school, family, and the economy*, New York: Routledge.

Dimock, W. C. (1994) "Class, gender, and a history of metonymy," in W. C. Dimock and M. T. Gilmore (eds) *Rethinking Class: literary studies and social formations*, New York: Columbia University Press.

Dimock, W. C. and Gilmore, M. T. (1994) "Introduction," in W. C. Dimock and M. T. Gilmore (eds) *Rethinking Class: literary studies and social formations*, New York: Columbia University Press.

Dolby, N. and Dimitriadis, G. (2004) "Learning to labor in New Times: an introduction," in N. Dolby and G. Dimitriadis (eds) with P. Willis, *Learning to Labor in New Times*.

Drucker, P. F. (1994) *Post-capitalist Society*, New York: HarperBusiness.

Ebert, T. L. (1996) "For a red pedagogy: feminism, desire, and need," *College English*, 58(7): 795–819.

Ebert, T. L. and Zavarzadeh, M. (2008) *Class in Culture*, Boulder: Paradigm Publishers.

Elster, J. (1985) *Making Sense of Marx*, Cambridge: Cambridge University Press.

Engels, F. (1968) Engels to H. Borgius in Breslau, in *Karl Marx and Frederick Engels: their selected works*, New York: International Publishers.

"Farewell, Peter Drucker: a tribute to an intellectual giant." (2005) Online. Available at http://knowledge.wharton.upenn.edu/article.cfm?articleid=1326 (accessed November 3, 2008).

Foucault, M. (1990) *The History of Sexuality, Vol. I: an introduction*, trans R. Hurley, New York: Vintage Books.

Frank, T. (2000) *One Market Under God*, New York: Anchor Books.

Friedman, M. (1982) *Capitalism and Freedom*, Chicago: The University of Chicago Press.

Friedman, T. (2006) *The World is Flat*, New York: Farrar, Strauss and Giroux.

Gamoran, A. (2008) "Persisting social class inequality in US education," in L. Weis (ed.) *The Way Class Works: readings on school, family, and the economy*, New York: Routledge.

Giddens, A. (2003) *The Progressive Manifesto*, Cambridge, UK: Polity.

—— (1971) *Capitalism and Modern Social Theory*, Cambridge, UK: Cambridge University Press.

Giroux, H. A. (2006) *America on the Edge: Henry Giroux on politics, culture, and education*, New York: Palgrave Macmillan.

—— (1983) *Theory and Resistance in Education: a pedagogy for the opposition*, New York: Bergin and Garvey.

Gorski, P. (2006) "The classist underpinnings of Ruby Payne's framework," *Teachers College Record* (February 9). Online. Available at http://www.tcrecord.org ID Number 12322 (accessed July 24, 2006).

Hardt, M. and Negri, A. (2004) *Multitude*, New York: The Penguin Press.

—— (2000) *Empire*, Cambridge, MA: Harvard University Press.

Harvey, D. (2005) *A Brief History of Neoliberalism*, Oxford: Oxford University Press.

—— (1990) *The Condition of Postmodernity*, Cambridge, MA: Blackwell.

Held, D. and McGrew, A. (2007) *Globalization/Anti-globalization: beyond the great divide*, 2nd edn, Cambridge, UK: Polity Press.

Hennessy, R. (2000) *Profit and Pleasure: sexual identities in late capitalism*, New York: Routledge.

Hill, D., McLaren, P., Cole, M. and Rikowski, G. (2002) *Marxism Against Postmodernism in Educational Theory*, Lanham, MD: Lexington Books

Hoff, D. J. (2006) "Big business going to bat for NCLB," *Education Week*, 26(8): 1, 24. Online. Available at http://www.edweek.org/ew/articles/2006/ (accessed October 18, 2006).

Hursh, D. (2005) "Neoliberalism, markets and accountability: transforming education and undermining democracy in the United States and England," *Policy Futures in Education*, 3(1): 3–15.

Jameson, F. (1991) "The Cultural Logic of Late Capitalism," in F. Jameson *Postmodernism, or the Cultural Logic of Late Capitalism*, Durham: Duke University Press.

Johnston, B. J. (2007) "Class/culture/action: representation, identity, and agency in educational analysis," in J. A. Van Galen and G. W. Noblit (eds) *Late to Class: social class and schooling in the new economy*, Albany: State University of New York Press.

Kelsh, D. and Hill, D. (2006) "The culturalization of class and the occluding of class consciousness: the knowledge industry in/of education," *Journal for Critical Education Policy Studies*, 4 (1). Online. Available at http://www.jceps.com/index.php?pageID=article&articleID=59 (accessed December 21, 2006).

Kroeger, J. (2007) "Social heteroglossia: the contentious practice of potential place of middle-class parents in home-school relations," in J. A. Van Galen and G. W. Noblit (eds) *Late to Class: social class and schooling in the new economy*, Albany: State University of New York Press.

Lacey, M. (2008) "Across Globe, Empty Bellies Bring Rising Anger," *The New York Times* (April 18). Online. Available at http://www.nytimes.com (accessed April 18, 2008).

Laclau, E. and Mouffe, C. (1985) *Hegemony & Socialist Strategy: towards a radical democratic politics*, London: Verso.

Lareau, A. (2008a) "Introduction: taking stock of class," in A. Lareau and D. Conley (eds) *Social Class: how does it work?* New York: Russell Sage Foundation.

—— (2008b) "Watching, waiting, and deciding when to intervene: race, class, and the transmission of advantage," in L. Weis (ed.) *The Way Class Works: readings on school, family, and the economy*, New York: Routledge.

—— (2003) *Unequal Childhoods: class, race, and family life*, Berkeley: University of California Press.

Lareau, A. and Conley, D. (eds) (2008) *Social Class: how does it work?* New York: Russell Sage Foundation.

Lash, S. and Urry, J. (1996) *Economies of Signs and Space*, London: SAGE Publications.

Lenin, V. I. (1970) *Materialism and empirio-criticism*, Moscow: Progress Publishers.

—— (1969) *What Is To Be Done?* New York: International Publishers.

Lentricchia F. and McLaughlin T. (eds) (1995) *Critical Terms for Literary Study*, 2nd edn, Chicago: The University of Chicago Press.

Li, G. (2008) "Parenting practices and schooling: the way class works for new immigrant groups," in L. Weis (ed.) *The Way Class Works: readings on school, family, and the economy*, New York: Routledge.

Lubienski, S. T. (2003) "Celebrating diversity and denying disparities: a critical assessment," *Educational Researcher*, 32(8): 30–8.

Lustig, J. (2004) "The tangled knot of race and class in America," in M. Zweig (ed.) *What's Class Got to Do With It?* Ithaca: Cornell University Press.

Luxemburg, R. (1970) "Reform or revolution," in M. Waters (ed.) *Rosa Luxemburg Speaks*, New York: Pathfinder.

McCarthy, C. (2004) "Thinking about the cultural studies of education in a time of recession: *Learning to Labor* and the work of aesthetics in modern life," in N. Dolby and G. Dimitriadis (eds) with P. Willis *Learning to Labor in New Times*, New York: RoutledgeFalmer.

McNall, S. G., Levine, R. F. and Fantasia, R. (1991) *Bringing Class Back In*, Boulder: Westview Press, 1991.

Mandel, E. (1989) "How to make no sense of Marx," *Marxist Internet Archives*. Online. Available at http://www.marxists.org/archive/mandel/1989/xx/nosense.htm (accessed September 12, 2008); originally published in R. Ware and K. Nielsen (eds) *Analyzing Marxism. New essays on Analytical Marxism, Canadian Journal of Philosophy*, Supplementary Volume 15, 1989, The University of Calgary Press: 105–32.

Marx, K. (2000) *Theories of Surplus Value: Books I, II, and III*, Amherst, NY: Prometheus Books.

—— (1995) "Results of the immediate process of production," in D. McLellan (ed.) *Karl Marx, Capital: a new abridgement*, Oxford: Oxford University Press.

—— (1989) "Preface," in K. Marx *A Contribution to the Critique of Political Economy*, trans. S. W. Ryazanskaya, ed. Maurice Dobb, New York: International Publishers.

—— (1978) "Alienation and social classes (from *The Holy Family*)," in R. C. Tucker (ed.) *The Marx-Engels Reader*, 2nd edn, New York: W. W. Norton & Company, Inc.

—— (1967a) *Capital: Volume I*, trans. S. Moore and E. Aveling, ed. F. Engels, New York: International Publishers.

—— (1967b) *Capital: Volume II*, ed. F. Engels, New York: International Publishers.

—— (1967c) *Capital: Volume III*, ed. F. Engels, New York: International Publishers.

Marx, K. and Engels, F. (1985) *The Communist Manifesto*, New York: Penguin Books.

—— (1989) *The German Ideology*, New York: International Publishers.

Michaels, W. B. (2006) *The Trouble with Diversity: how we learned to love identity and ignore inequality*, New York: Metropolitan Books, Henry Holt and Company.

Morton, D. (1990) "Texts of limits, the limits of texts, and the containment of politics in contemporary critical theory," *diacritics*, 20(1): 57–75.

Nealon, J. and Giroux, S. S. (2003) *The Theory Toolbox: critical concepts for the humanities, arts, & social sciences*, New York: Rowman & Littlefield Publishers, Inc.

Noblit, G. W. (2007) "Class-declasse," in J. A. Van Galen and G. W. Noblit (eds) *Late to Class: social class and schooling in the new economy*, Albany: State University of New York Press.

Nowlan, R. A. (1996) "Critique as radical praxis," in D. Morton (ed.) *The Material Queer: a lesbigay cultural studies reader*, Boulder: Westview Press.

O'Hara, D. T. (1995) "Class," in F. Lentricchia and T. McLaughlin (eds) *Critical Terms for Literary Study*, 2nd edn, Chicago: The University of Chicago Press.

Payne, R. K. (2003) *A Framework for Understanding Poverty*, Highland, TX: aha! Process, Inc.

Ream, R. K. and Palardy, G. J. (2008) "Reexamining social class differences in the availability and the educational utility of parental social capital," *American Educational Research Journal*, 45(2): 238–73.

Rifkin, J. (1996) *The End of Work*, New York: G. P. Putnam's Sons.

Rothstein, R. (2004) *Class and Schools: using social, educational, and economic reform to close the black-white achievement gap*, New York: Economic Policy Institute and Teachers College Columbia University Press.

Ryan, A. (1986) "The Marx problem book," *The Times Literary Supplement* (April 25). Online. Available at http://www.geocities.com/hmelberg/elster/ryan86.htm?200812 (accessed September 12, 2008).

Sahay, A. (1998) "Transforming race matters: towards a critique-al cultural studies," *Cultural Logic*, 1 (2).

Sayers, S. (2007) "The concept of labor: Marx and his critics," *Science & Society*, 71(4): 431–54.

Scatamburlo-D'Annibale, V. and McLaren, P. (2005) "Class dismissed? Historical materialism and the politics of 'difference'," in Z. Leonardo (ed.) *Critical Pedagogy and Race*, Malden, MA: Blackwell Publishing.

Scott, J. and Leonhardt, D. (2005) "Shadowy lines that still divide," in Correspondents (eds) *Class Matters*, New York: Times Books, Henry Holt and Company.

Shaikh, A. (1992) "The falling rate of profit as the cause of long waves: theory and empirical evidence," in A. Kleinknecht, E. Mandel, and I. Wallerstein (eds) *New Findings in Long Wave Research*, London: Macmillan Press.

Sleeter, C. (2008) "Teaching for democracy in an age of corporatocracy," *Teachers College Record*, 110(1): 139–59.

Swartz, D. (1997) *Culture & Power: the sociology of Pierre Bourdieu*, Chicago: The University of Chicago Press.

Thompson, E. P. (1966) *The Making of the English Working Class*, New York: Vintage Books.

Turner, B. S. (1995). Book review. *Politics, Death, and the Devil: self and power in Max Weber and Thomas Mann*. By Harvey Goldman. *The Journal of Modern History*, 67(1): 116–18.

United Nations Development Programme (2007) "Inclusive Globalization," in United Nations Development Programme Annual Report, *Making Globalization Work for All*. Online. Available at http://www.undp.org/publications/annualreport2007/IAR07-ENG.pdf (accessed November 3, 2008).

Van Galen, J. A. (2007) "Introduction," in J. A. Van Galen and G. W. Noblit (eds) *Late to Class: social class and schooling in the new economy*, Albany: State University of New York Press.

Van Galen, J. A. and Noblit, G. (eds) (2007) *Late to Class: social class and schooling in the new economy*, Albany: State University of New York Press.

Vlasic, B. and Bunkley, N. (2008) "Toyota Scales Back Production of Big Vehicles," *The New York Times* (July 11). Online. Available at http://www.nytimes.com (accessed July 11, 2008).

Weber, M. (1992) *The Protestant Ethic and the Spirit of Capitalism*, trans. T. Parsons, London: Routledge.

—— (1978) *Economy and Society: an outline of interpretive sociology*, Vols 1 and 2, G. Roth and C. Wittich (eds) trans. E. Fischoff, H. Gerth, A. M. Henderson, F. Kolegar, C. W. Mills, T. Parsons, Berkeley: University of California Press.

Weiner, E. J. (2004) "The work of power and the power of work: teaching for class consciousness in the neoliberal age," *Policy Futures in Education*, 2 (3–4): 539–4.

Weis, L. (2008) "Introduction," in L. Weis (ed.) *The Way Class Works: readings on school, family, and the economy*, New York: Routledge.

—— (ed.) (2008) *The Way Class Works: readings on school, family, and the economy*, New York: Routledge.

—— (2004) *Class Reunion: the remaking of the American white working class*, New York: Routledge.

Weis, L. and Dimitriadis, G. (2008) "Dueling banjos: shifting economic and cultural contexts in the lives of youth," *Teachers College Record*, 110(10): 2290–316.

Wright, E. O. (2008) "The continuing importance of class analysis," in L. Weis (ed.) *The Way Class Works: readings on school, family, and the economy*, New York: Routledge.

—— (2002) "The shadow of exploitation in Weber's class analysis," *American Sociological Review*, 67: 832–53.

Zavarzadeh, M. (1995) "Post-Ality: the (dis)simulations of cybercapitalism," in M. Zavarzadeh, T. L. Ebert, and D. Morton (eds) *Post-Ality: Marxism and postmodernism*, Washington: Maisonneuve Press.

Zavarzadeh, M., Ebert, T. L. and Morton, D. (eds) (1995) *Post-Ality: Marxism and postmodernism*, Washington: Maisonneuve Press.

2 Hypohumanities[1]

Teresa L. Ebert and Mas'ud Zavarzadeh

In bourgeois society the school has three principal tasks to fulfill. First, it inspires the coming generation of workers with devotion and respect for the capitalist regime. Secondly, it creates from the young of the ruling classes "cultured" controllers of the working population. Thirdly, it assists capitalist production in the application of sciences to technique, thus increasing capitalist profits.

Nikolai Bukharin and Evgeny Preobrazhensky,
The ABC of Communism

Do you suffer from class consciousness? Come to Oxford and be cured.

Raymond Williams,
Politics and Letters

Abstract

This chapter argues that the humanities have been transformed into "hypohumanities," largely through the transformation of the interpretive logic of the humanities. Hypohumanities are the instrumentalization of the humanities by contemporary post-humanities. Post-humanities erase the class and labor relations that shape education by foregrounding digital skills in teaching and obscuring the place of human labor in education. At the same time, they forge a new (post)identity politics that dissolves "species being" into natural relations. Consequently they turn education into simply training the future work-force in the useful signs-skills and transhuman affects that are needed by network capital. This transformation is one outcome of the class struggle and triumph of capital over labor in the years following World War II. It is part of the tendency to culturalize class. Hypohumanities displace the production of critique-al consciousness in student-citizens – a consciousness that can connect cultural practices to the social relations of production and use cultural critique for social change – with production of subjects who accept existing relations. While the dominant interpretive logic of this transformed version of the humanities is seen to be anti-instrumental, it actually constitutes a new instrumentalism that validates the most recent changes in labor relations under capital and teaches people how to occupy the waste-land of time left for them by global capitalism, in which non-employment and imposed leisure play an important economic role. Hypohumanities teach thoughtful unthoughtfulness, thought as an ongoing play-full-ness, as a resistance to closure, to concluding and to acting on that conclusion. It hides the secret of class – that labor power produces surplus value, which is the source of value – when what is necessary is to put that secret in the open and thereby contribute not to what *is*, but to what can *become*.

Introduction

Contemporary humanities have been changing and changing radically. But the most radical changes are not in the theoretical themes by which the humanities have put in question such traditional concepts as language, truth, objectivity and the subject. Although these thematics have attracted a great deal of attention, the most significant changes are the ones that have quietly transformed humanities into what we call "hypohumanities." These include structural changes (such as those in the curriculum), the re-coding of knowledge (what counts as the humanities), and above all transform-ing the interpretive logic of the humanities, which is our primary interest here.

Hypohumanities are the *instrumentalization* of the humanities by contemporary "post-theory" ("post" as in poststructuralism, postcolonialism, post-Marxism and what used to be called postmodernism) which turns the humanities into a discursive training ground to teach useful signs-skills to the future workforce of capital. This instrumentalization of the humanities is a class issue. It displaces the knowledges that teach citizen-students a critique-al grasping of everyday practices in their historical and social relations, emptying them of substance, and substituting a "body without organs," politics without politics, and materiality without materialism, while putting genealogy in the place of history. Hypohumanities are a pedagogy for tutoring a new workforce of global capitalism in the excessive pleasures of consumption and hyper-interpretation that masquerade as "freedom." They substitute the digressive pleasures of the flaneur – a textual loitering – for critical consciousness and the historical understanding necessary for social change. Under the banner of the innov-ative, they actually teach an "enlightened false consciousness" of ironic enjoyment in acquiescence to the rule of capital over labor. Hypohumanities are being taught (without irony) to student-citizens in advanced capitalist societies as progressive cultural sciences that can make the complexities of culture intelligible. We argue that the intelligibility that hypohumanities offer normalizes the world for transnational capitalism and needs to be countered by a historical materialist critique.

The changes that are being legitimated as hypohumanities are, of course, histori-cal: they are effects of the volatility and transformations in the class struggle and the triumph of capital over labor in recent years. The newly hegemonic hypohumanities are, as Marx and Engels wrote in *The German Ideology*, "nothing more than the ideal expression of the dominant material relationships ... grasped as ideas" (1976: 59). The purpose of this essay is to unpack the connections between the theoretical subtle-ties and textual practices of hypohumanities and the material relations of capital and labor.

Beginning with the surplus enjoyment of difference, we argue that the rewriting of the humanities as hypohumanities is largely accomplished by translating "class" into *differance* (Derrida 1982: 1–27). *Differance*, as the difference of difference from itself, turns difference *within*, thereby making impossible class as difference *between* "Freeman and slave, patrician and plebeian, lord and serf, guild-master and journeyman, in a word oppressor and oppressed ... Bourgeoisie and Proletariat" (Marx and Engels 1977: 41).

Class and the instrumentalism of *differance*

Differance for Derrida (1982) is the condition of signification; it is the "non-full, non-simple, structured and differentiating origin of differences" (11). In its conventional sense, difference (with an e) is a cultural device for stabilizing identities by placing one identity in opposition to another: masculine is masculine because of the difference *between* it and the feminine; it is an opposition to the other. The difference *between*, in other words, stabilizes identities (masculine/feminine) by representing each identity as self-same and free from difference; each identity resituates the difference within itself in its "outside," which allows it to oppose itself as a coherent totality to the other, who is also represented as a full identity without self-difference. Derrida's argument is that "the outside is the inside" (1976: 44), and therefore *differance* (with an a) puts difference (with an e) in play and opens up its difference from itself. In doing so *differance* destabilizes difference between as the ground of stable identities (such as the masculine) by transferring the difference *between* identities to a difference *within* them. The masculine in this narrative is not masculine because it is self-present but because it suppresses differences within itself. To be recognized as masculine, it represents the features of the feminine within itself as absent. The masculine is as marked by features of the feminine as the feminine is marked by the masculine: they are two versions of *differance*. Their "stable" identity (difference-less-ness) as two distinct genders that act as cultural opposites is an arbitrary convention, a metaphysics of presence. They are effects of the representations produced by texts of culture and the playfulness of the sign and not instances of plenitude.

Derrida's "*differance*" produces "a system that no longer tolerates the opposition of activity and passivity, nor that of cause and effect, or of indetermination and determination" (1982: 16). It puts an end to opposition and rewrites opposites as a "movement of difference ... between two differences" (5). One of the outcomes of Derrida's reading of *differance* is the way it shapes the interpretive logic of the hypohumanities: it puts "in ruins" the concept of class – as a structure of antagonism and opposition over social surplus labor – by demolishing the difference *between* "worker" and "owner." Neither is anything in itself; neither is a complete and self-sufficient identity with a fixed meaning in opposition to another fixed meaning. Instead, meaning/identity is the effect of relations within differences. *Differance* is, therefore, "a structure and a movement" that makes "difference" no longer "conceivable on the basis of opposition" (Derrida 1981b: 27). The "proletariat" in the narrative of *differance* is not the opposition of a presence to an absence, an "inside" to an "outside" such as the "bourgeois" (Marx and Engels 1977: 41). Rather, a worker's identity is the effect of suppressing the differences within himself that he shares with his putative opposite – the owner. The two are not in relations of *opposition* but of *supplementarity*, "two significations whose cohabitation is as strange as it is necessary" (Derrida 1976: 144). They are versions of *differance*. Class struggle, which is based on the opposition of classes, is seen as a fiction in this narrative – a fiction of the metaphysics of plenitude obtained by binary oppositions. Thus, it should be abandoned. In this view one should deploy *differance* to break the homogeneity of capital and produce a heterogeneous economic system that allows for "class diversity" (Gibson-Graham 2006: 52) instead of aiming to overthrow capitalism and its class structures because "the revolutionary task of replacing capitalism now seems outmoded and unrealistic" (263).

Derrida's notion of *differance* deconstructs Marx and Engels' (1977) oppositional analytics of labor in which "society as a whole is more and more splitting up into two great hostile camps, into two great classes directly facing each other: Bourgeois and Proletariat" (41). Classes, in this narrative, are not effects of an outside such as the "domination of the capitalist over the worker" (Marx 1976a: 899), but the outcome of *differance* (the difference of differences) which is inaudible and exists only in textuality/writing. Classes, in other words, are representations and not instances of self-presence, which is another way of saying classes are "metaphors for particular language games" (Jenks 1993: 74).

Differance, however, to use Derrida's own expression, has not "fallen from the sky" (1982: 11), but is the outcome of class struggles. Like all concepts it too is "the theoretical expression, the abstraction of the social relations of production" (Marx 1976b: 80). Or to again recall Marx and Engels in *The German Ideology*, "the ruling ideas are nothing more than the ideal expression of the dominant material relations, the dominant material relations grasped as ideas" (1976: 59). *Differance* is the concept by which the dominant social relations eliminate (class) collectivity from the scene of the social and, in the name of the "war on totality" (Lyotard 1984: 82), valorize singularity and individuality – which are the grounding values of the "free" market – and consequently represent the way things are as the way they ought to be. In the regime of *differance*, change is never changing because what is changed is a version of *differance* that moves back and forth, from change to what it is changed from. Hypohumanities, through their interpretive logic of *differance*, naturalize existing social relations; they are the ideology of the ruling order represented as cutting-edge knowledge.

This, of course, is why the humanities matter to capital, and why there are ongoing contestations (such as the writing of this essay) over its interpretive logic as well as its borders of exclusion and inclusion. The humanities teach the future workforce its cultural logic, reading strategies, and signs-skills by which it codes and decodes cultural representations, all of which are necessary for an efficient workplace. Class critique brings to the humanities an understanding of social relations that puts in crisis both the humanities – as the institutional pedagogies of capital – and capital's own legitimacy. It does so, in part, by explaining culture, not as an autonomous sphere of the imaginary but as the historical manifestation of the social relations of production; not as an arena of untraceable desires, changeless values and immanent aesthetics but as a struggle zone in which people become aware of social conflicts over the appropriation of the surplus of social labor – which determines the conditions of their lives under capital – and "fight it out" (Marx 1989: 21).

The marginalization of class in the humanities has not happened in a social vacuum nor has it been the effect of purely philosophical debates. The cultural is always the effect of the material. It is the effect of specific historical and material conditions and the level of class struggles, namely the triumph of capital over labor after World War II. Owing to the economies of war, the rate of profits for capital had increased substantially from its near collapse during the Great Depression. In its invigorated state, capitalism was determined to regain not only its lost management power in the workplace, which it had conceded to workers, but also, and equally important, its political power and ethical legitimacy in culture (Fones-Wolf 1994). In his *American Labor in Midpassage*, Bret Cochran calls postwar capital's class war against labor and its aggressive assault on class consciousness the "businessman's intellectual re-conquest of America" (1959: 2). The attack on labor has gradually increased since the mid-1940s and gained strength during the "long boom," especially in the 1980s – the height of the hegemony of capital and its conservative governments (Reagan, Thatcher, Kohl, Pinochet, Deng Xiaoping) and the triumph of the counter-revolution in the Soviet Union. From the late 1940s to early 1970s, capitalism reduced class militancy through a temporary truce with workers (because of the shortage of labor) by increasing wages, healthcare and other welfare benefits. However, after the end of the long boom and the collapse in 1971–2 of the Bretton Woods agreements of 1944, globalization gained new momentum, and capital found new access to more cheap labor of workers of the world. Consequently capital began not only to take away workers' benefits but also to keep their wages stagnant while increasing their productivity – the rate of surplus labor (Ebert and Zavarzadeh 2008).

The long boom has played an important role in the representation of the relation of capital to labor. It is during the long boom and the transformation from so-called Fordism to Post-Fordism that the cultural myth of the "embourgeoisement" of workers becomes popular, the movement of "cultural studies" is started, and the trend is set for left intellectuals to culturalize class (Williams 1977); marginalize classical Marxism (Hall 1996); embrace Post-Fordism; and argue that the social is no longer determined by objective "production" relations but has become an assemblage of heterogeneous meanings derived from consumption (Baudrillard 1970). This leads many to announce the demise of the working class (Gorz 1982) and declare "the death of class" (as Pakulski and Waters do in their book by the same title [1996]). This is the time in which narratives about a "new" capitalism – in which class has no central place – begin to take shape. It is therefore important to pause here and say a few words about it.

The long boom is represented as the "golden years" of capitalism, as a period of cross-class harmony and the "end of ideology" not only in official and mainstream analyses but also in left-liberal narratives (Hobsbawm 1994) and, perhaps most significantly, in "socialist" accounts. In his *The Future of Socialism*, for example, Anthony Crosland argues that the long boom is proof that "Capitalism has been reformed almost out of all recognition" (1956: 517). In the "new" capitalism, it is said, the relation of capital and labor has changed from conflict to a new form of cooperation. Cyclical crises, such as the Depression of the 1930s, are assumed to have vanished for good, and the working class itself is said to have rapidly become part of the "middle class" (Drucker 1994). The "most striking feature" of the long boom "was a quite breath-taking growth in production" (as Armstrong, Glyn, and Harrison [1991] write in *Capitalism Since 1945*: 117). In short, the long boom is seen as "capitalism's great leap forward" (Beaud 2001: 213–61).

The long boom is also seen as the forerunner of a new economic order that is variously called by such names as post-industrial (Bell [1976] *The Coming of Post-Industrial Society*) or "post-Fordist" (Aglietta [2001] *A Theory of Capitalist Regulations: The U.S. Experience*): an order in which the nature of labor itself (seemingly) changes. The old (manual) labor capitalism is believed to have been displaced by a new "knowledge capitalism" that reshapes all variants of capitalism – including Anglo-American, social market capitalism (Sweden), state capitalism (France), and the Japanese model – into a "global knowledge-based economy" and modes of a new "knowledge capitalism" (Burton-Jones 1999: 20–2). One feature of knowledge capitalism, according to these theories, is that not only have workers become well-off but their very mode of work has changed. The "old" style "proletariat" is being replaced with a "new" style "cybertariat" (Huws and Leys 2003). As a consequence of these changes, "production" is said to have been displaced by "consumption" – lifestyle not class, in other words, shapes the everyday.

But the long boom was a period of fleeting prosperity followed by years of stagnating wages, loss of healthcare insurance and other benefits, and massive layoffs. In resistance to both the reformism fostered by the long boom and the obscured class consciousness of the workers, Walter Reuther argued that the goal of workers should not be "to patch up the world so men can starve less often ... but remake the world so that working people will get the benefit of their labor" (Dubofsky and Dulles 2004: 349).

The long boom did not bring about the end of class; it increased class fissures. Like all boom periods in the history of capitalism, the prosperity of the long boom was achieved by increasing surplus labor (exploitation) of workers. In the case of the long boom, surplus labor was increased by adding the exploitation of the workers of the global South to that of the workers of the North and by transferring wealth from the South to the North by, for example, institutionalizing "loans" to third world countries and other financial devices.

The exploitation of workers in the global South was "legalized" through the "new" anti-labor arrangements that were first imposed on the world through the Bretton Woods agreements in 1944. The Bretton Woods agreements set the basic frame for the postwar global financial regime and instituted the International Monetary Fund, the International Bank for Reconstruction and Development (the World Bank), and the General Agreement on Tariffs and Trade (the World Trade Organization). The collapse of the Bretton Woods agreements in 1971–2, the end of the gold standard, and the US's abandonment of the fixed rate of exchange in 1973, all set the stage for contemporary globalization and its neoliberal economics that have normalized the war on the workers of the world in the name of global competitiveness.

Hypohumanities are the cultural codification of globalization (which they valorize as a new cosmopolitanism) and neoliberal philosophical assumptions and values, which were initially stated in the Mont Pelerin Society's "Statement of Aims" in 1947.

Among other things, the manifesto declared, "The central values of civilization are in danger," because of the "decline of belief in private property and the competitive market" (n. p.).

Another significant event in this process of cultural codification was Derrida's first influential lecture in the US, "Structure, Sign, and Play in the Discourse of the Human Sciences" (1978), which was delivered at the Johns Hopkins University conference on "The Language of Criticism and the Sciences of Man" in 1966 and became available in humanities classrooms through a popular paperback edition of the conference lectures in 1970 (Macksey and Donato 1970).

One of the consequences of the triumph of capital and its increasing cultural hegemony has been the tendency of the left in the global North to continue, in the name of a resistance to capitalism, to maintain class, but only as a signifier that is always in play (and thus has no decidable meanings [Derrida 1981a: 174–285]). At the same time, much of the left deplores and rejects the use of class as a materialist concept that explains the extraction of surplus labor at the point of production that brings about the conditions that determine life under capitalism. The rejection of class as a materialist analytic usually takes the form of an argument by the left that concludes that such a materialist (not to be confused with materiality) view of class is "ossified and simple," if not simplistic. Class, accordingly, only becomes "useful if thought about in the double sense of both markers of status-based resource privilege and as a system marking differential usage, distribution and expropriation of resources" (Hutnyk 2004: 190). "Production" – the main materialist determinate of class relations – is completely erased from such a left-libertarian and neo-Weberian culturalist view, which claims "class does not make as much sense if rigidly restricted to a bipolar opposition" theory as Marx and Engels argued for in *The Manifesto of the Communist Party* (Hutnyk 2004: 191). Materialist theory, which maintains that class is the effect of the relations of property, is not only seen as simplistic and reductive but is also thought to be used only by the naïve, the dogmatic, and Stalinists. (By the way, the cure for Stalinism, according to Derrida, is to read more Heidegger [Derrida 1993: 208].) Hutnyk's "it does not make much sense" is based on the popular claim articulated by the mass media and in think-tanks of the North (and rooted in the "long boom" debates) that capitalism has changed, and, in the "new" cybereconomy of a globalized culture, class has become a "class process" (Gibson-Graham 2001: 6–10); it is not a structure of social antagonism nor is it determined by "property ownership" (Gibson-Graham 2006: 179). These views of class are, in the last analysis, an extension of the capitalist theory that social conflicts are not caused by labor relations, or as Ernesto Laclau puts it, "class antagonism is not inherent to capitalist relations of production" (2000: 202). Culturalist theories of class are ultimately all grounded in the mythography that labor has become "immaterial" (Hardt and Negri 2004) – a fantasy that is ontologized by Giorgio Agamben who regards labor to be a "solidarity that in no way contains an essence" (1993: 19). The left in the North is more worried about essentialism than capitalism. Its vision of the future is, therefore, "a vision of economic heterogeneity rather than of an alternative (noncapitalist) homogeneity" (Gibson-Graham 2006: 179).

Going against these accommodationist left tendencies, we argue that class is a relation of owning. However, it is not any owning but owning what produces more owning – it is owning labor (living and past) because labor is "a commodity that has the peculiar property that its use is the source of new value" (Marx 1976a: 270). Under capitalism one is what one owns. People of the world are therefore divided into only two classes: those who own the labor of others and make profits from it, and the others who own only their own labor and sell it for wages, which they pay back to the owners of labor to buy the food, medicine, houses, cars ... they need to go back to work for the owners of labor.

The instrumentalization of the humanities is part of the tendency to culturalize class. Under the influence of post-theory, hypohumanities represent any attempt to produce a critique-al consciousness in student-citizens – a consciousness that is able to relate cultural practices to the social relations of production and deploy culture critique for social change – as an in-difference to difference and thus as logocentric residues of a metaphysics of presence and a will to power (which is a code, among other things, for a cultural critique that deviates from liberalism and, therefore, is said to be a species of Stalinist public pedagogy). By cleansing the humanities of class, hypohumanities rewrite "education" as "training" and reduce critique-al citizenship to a pragmatics of finding and holding jobs as long as they are needed by capital – humans are bearers of useful skills for capital, and hypohumanities are the depository of these skills.

Our statement that post-theory is the agent for instrumentalization of the humanities and the reduction of "education" to "training" might strike some readers as odd or even eccentric because post-theory is often regarded in the mainstream academy and cultural circles as anti-instrumentalist and a strong ally of the humanities, an advocate of critique, and a supporter of the freedom of meaning and the transformative power of language. So, we need to make clear at the outset what we mean by instrumentalism and why we regard post-theory to be a means of instrumentalization of the humanities. After outlining our critique of instrumentalism, we will focus on some of the ways in which post-theory has turned education into training. As we develop our views, we argue for bringing back "theory" and class critique to the humanities. We have already started our analysis of post-theory and will do more as we go on. Here, however, we need to make clear our understanding of theory, since far from abandoning theory in the humanities, we argue for deploying it in humanities knowledges and pedagogies.

By "theory" we do not mean its popular sense, which is the inquiry into the "production and ... reception of meaning" (de Man 1986: 7), specifically, the application of linguistics "to literary texts" (8) and whose object is "literariness" (9), namely, theory as textuality in play. According to this view (Derrida 1988), "theory" is an account of the tropic self-displacement of the text as "it deconstructs it-self" (Derrida 1991: 274), and, as a "verbal event" (de Man 1986: 17), it becomes an allegory of (its own) (un) readability (de Man 1979). We argue that texts do not theorize themselves, nor do they read or deconstruct themselves, or become allegories of self-referentiality. They are always read from a specific historical class position. Meaning is a social relation. It is not the excess of signification of the signifier, the materiality of the letter, or the self-difference of the trace. By theory, therefore, we mean knowledge of social totality, which is knowledge of "the relations of productions in their totality" as they "constitute .. the social relations, society, and moreover, a society at a definite stage of historic development" (Marx 1976c: 29). It is in this sense that we argue theory is an integral part of understanding in the humanities. To put it differently, theory is, as Marx writes, a "material force" (Marx 1974: 182), and in this sense, as Lenin (1961) argues, "Without revolutionary theory there can be no revolutionary movement" (369). This idea, to continue quoting Lenin, "cannot be insisted upon too strongly at a time when fashionable preaching of opportunism goes hand in hand with an infatuation for the narrowest form of practical activity" (369). Without theory as knowledge of social totality – which, among other things, brings class critique back to the humanities – the humanities become lessons in (business) communications for the workers and pedagogies of the pleasures of the text for managers. We will return to this question in our discussion of theory and ideology.

The debate over instrumentalism in recent theory has been a formalist discussion over tendencies toward pragmatism (in philosophy), which treats truth (reason) not as a self-reflexive critique that evaluates concepts and examines how accurately they represent the real, but in terms of its operational usefulness. William James's canonic statements – that "the truth is the name of whatever proves itself to be the good in the way of belief, and good, too, for definite, assignable reasons" (1974: 59), or that "'the true' ... is only the expedient in the way of our thinking ... Expedient in almost any fashion" (1974: 145) – are echoed in the writings of such contemporary pragmatic philosophers as Richard Rorty (*Objectivity, Relativity, and Truth* 1991). Post-theory, which is formally critical of instrumentalism (Mouffe 1996), is itself an instrumentalism of *différance*, an instrumental textualism that regards truth to be what is good in the way of representation, or to use James's other term, as what is expedient in the way of rhetoric. To be more clear, in post-theory truth is not understood as an effect of language's relation to its outside but as its textual self-referentiality, its usefulness in the self-reflexive questioning of the text's own desires for absolute and fixed meanings. The range of its reference is always limited to the local textualities of "language games" (Thebaud and Lyotard 1988). Post-theory truth, to put it differently, is an instrumental performativity: a construction by language for specific (pragmatic) uses in a (con)text that makes its own claims to any transcendental (non-pragmatic) truth undecidable through the play of its tropes and the aleatoriness of its citationality (Butler 1999).

This aleatory textuality – language without reference – is represented in hypohumanities as a resistance to fixed meanings and, therefore, as an anti-instrumentality that frees cultural meanings (e.g. "black," "gay," "woman," ...) from their hegemonic framings. We argue that this seeming anti-instrumentality is the new instrumentalism of contemporary capital in which age, sexuality, race, and gender are gradually losing their importance because in advanced capitalism people "are all instruments of labour, more or less expensive" (Marx and Engels 1977: 52–3). Contemporary capitalism does not need homophobia to survive (big corporations give insurance and other benefits to the domestic partners of their employees), but it cannot survive without cheap labor which it must obtain regardless of the source and subject of labor.

Our understanding of instrumentalism, therefore, is not merely epistemological but historical. We argue that instrumentalism is the deployment of human labor for profit and thus the repression of human freedom: "the realm of freedom really begins only where labour determined by necessity and external expediency ends ... true freedom, the development of human powers as an end in itself, begins beyond it ..." (Marx 1981: 958–9). Instrumentalism is a class issue; it equates truth with what produces results within the existing social relations of production and, in doing so, legitimates what *is* as what *ought to be* by normalizing "the silent compulsion of economic relations" that sets "the seal on the domination of capitalist over the worker" (Marx 1976a: 899). Hypohumanities is the pedagogy of training humans so that their labor is useful for capital's international division of labor. It constructs a cognitive climate (in the classroom) for the domination of capital over labor by lifting "the spiritual world" out of "its social context" where "culture is held up as a realm of authentic values and self-contained ends in opposition to the world of social utility and means" (Marcuse 1968: 94–6). Culture as an autonomous zone of the social is the instrument by which hypohumanities disconnects the material relation of culture from its labor relations and, by doing so, erases critique from the humanities, turning them into lessons in skills and pleasures – instruments that are necessary for work and leisure under capital.

It might be helpful here to provide an example of post-theory as an anti-instrumental instrumentalism that shapes hypohumanities. The theory of culture that is implied in our discussion of the humanities – namely culture as the superstructural articulation of the social relations of production where class conflicts are articulated and fought out – is an example of what is thought to be an "instrumentalist" theory of culture (Sterne 2005: 80–4). It is displaced by the anti-instrumentalist notion of culture which designates culture as a "meaningless, nondirected activity" (99). Anti-instrumental culture in these narratives is understood as a discursive strolling, a digressive digression, a way of talking free from the burden of saying anything. It is culture without being cultural, lacking referents of use. The unburdening of culture from the cultural is intensified in the linguistic turn (within the "cultural turn") by theorizing culture as a form of "writing," which is the other name of the textuality of the negative – spacing, difference, and the supplementation. In anti-instrumental theories, culture is a loiterly act: a "moving without going anywhere," a delightful "dilatory" and "digressive" activity, a writerly ecstasy or "loiterature," which is another name for culture as "peripatetic desire" (Chambers 1999). Culture is not, in other words, an explanatory concept but a figure that intervenes in itself and rids itself of commitment, of cultural politics. Its politics becomes a politics in "the last instance" which, like Althusser's moment of determination, will never arrive (Sterne 2005: 82).

"Meaningless, nondirected activity," however, far from being anti-instrumental, is the new instrumentality of contemporary capitalism in which non-employment and imposed leisure play an important economic role. Anti-instrumental culture is instrumentality in a new idiom, a script by which people are taught how to occupy the waste-land of time left for them by global capitalism. Culture as meaningless strolling is an aesthetic instrumentality for the "producerly" subject trained in the hypohumanities (Fiske 1989: 115–17). The producerly subject is the subject of the pleasures of consumption in which consumption is represented as a form of production because the subject makes meanings and constructs identity through consumption. Producerly consumption is the latest revision of Benjamin's late-modernist revision of Baudelaire's modern flaneur – which is itself based on an ecstatic rewriting of "purposiveness without purpose" instituted in Western philosophy by Kant at the rise of capitalism (1951: 17–31, 68–73). Anti-instrumental culture is the discursive machine of hypohumanities for producing the subject of capitalism.

Under capitalism there is no escape from instrumentalism because it commodifies human labor and perpetuates the realm of necessity. All bourgeois "rebellions" against instrumentalism (from Horkheimer and Adorno's left anti-instrumentalism to contemporary late-aesthetic non-instrumentalism) are strategies for inventing more agile and effective forms of instrumentalism. Our critique of instrumentalism, therefore, is not limited to a reiteration of the familiar anti-pragmatism, anti-positivism, anti-rationalism in cultural theory. Instead, we critique these criticisms themselves because, in the name of anti-instrumentalism, as we have just demonstrated, they actually reproduce instrumentalism in newer and more efficient forms to culturally validate the most recent changes in labor relations under capital.

Hypohumanities as the signs-craft of the new cybertariat

Through teaching "writing" and "reading," hypohumanities instruct the subject in the labor force how to grasp the world as a textual construct and interpret it as a heterogeneous assemblage of localities that have to be read in their own terms as spaces of meanings (Trifonas 2000: 13–52). They reject the world-historical everyday as a metaphysical projection and consider class to be errant tropes in language games. In hypohumanities "writing" and "reading" are taught as technical skills by which the student interprets the world-as-text in terms of a self-displacing rhetoric that disperses all fixed meanings into the indeterminate play of signs. Reading and writing in hypohumanities are techniques of immanent description and resignification that are set apart from "critique" – which produces "explanations" and is the basic practice in critique-al humanities.

Explanation is a causal analysis that establishes a relation of determination between, for example, the war and capitalism, or the poverty of the poor and the prosperity of the rich. It understands one to be the effect of the other. Reading and writing in hypohumanities are interpretations without ascribing cause-and-effect (Ronell 1989). In the name of honoring the text's "own terms" and its textual singularity, such a-causality protects the text from its "outside" (e.g. the labor relations that actually shape a text's figurations). Within a hypohumanities theory of language, reading is a recognition of the self-referentiality of texts and their negative epistemology, namely, their opacity which makes them "unreadable," to use Paul de Man's term – their assertions "radically exclude each other." Therefore, the text becomes its own referent without any reference to its outside (1979: 72, 77, 245).

Hypohumanities, in short, put in question the logic of cause-and-effect and turn the self-displacing tropics of the text into a self-fashioning "logic." The logic of cause-and-effect connects the "inside" to the "outside" (for example, linking labor relations to T. S. Eliot's "The Waste Land" or to Derrida's *Hospitality*) and therefore marks textual "immanence" as a social relation. It is grounded in the materialism of the world and is the outcome of the dialectics of nature and human labor. In contrast, cause-and-effect explanations are represented in the hypohumanities as fictions (as non-rationality) that are invented to contain the excess meanings of the sign.

The hypohumanities pedagogy of reading and writing is grounded in Nietzsche's argument that events are too complex to be explained; they exceed reason (explanation). Therefore, explanations always have a remainder that does not fit into any system of representation. Reading is an account of this excess, this unexplainable overflow. Far from being a rational explanation, Nietzsche argues, cause-and-effect is a fiction because, according to Nietzsche, we first feel the effect – pain for example – and then find the cause – such as a broken rib. In other words, we reverse the chronology to make order out of what is essentially arbitrary (1969: 263–7, 300–1, 367–8).

If the relation between cause and effect, as Nietzsche implies, is pure fiction, then any attempt at a rational explanation of the relations among capital and labor, imperialism, hunger, war, and the market would also be arbitrary – an expression of the will to power that depicts itself as a quest for truth.

Through his criticism of cause-and-effect, Nietzsche (1969) produces a new anti-instrumental instrumental logic for advanced capitalism, one that is grounded in the neo-positivism of the aleatory: things are the way they are, and any explanation of the reason for their being the way they are – for example, by class analysis – is simply an amusing plotting that relates unrelated "events." We can enjoy the pleasure of the text's complex rhetorical emplotting but should have no illusion about its truth. Hypohumanities teach reading as a lesson in Nietzschean non-causality and the non-representability of the excess meanings of experience (265–6). It depicts it as freeing the plural meanings of the signs of culture without making any determinate of another. In the world that emerges from hypohumanities reading, nothing can be changed because nothing causes anything, and all actions for bringing about change are practices in constructing different fictions of the future. Change is aleatory as is history, which is void of "regulative mechanism" (Foucault 1997: 154). Reading in hypohumanities is an interpretation of the world as effects of "haphazard conflicts" (Foucault 1997: 154) and the performativity of errant tropes.

Hypohumanities are, we argue, part of an ongoing class offensive by capital to rewrite critique-al humanities as hypohumanities so as to represent the world as a discourse in the sense that "History and society are an infinite text" (Laclau 1980: 87) and to obscure the materialism of the world, which is the effect of class relations or more specifically the laws of capitalist accumulation (Marx 1976a: 771).

It is, of course, true that mainstream humanities also taught writing and reading as technical skills because humanities have always been truncated to the "communications" skills needed by big business. There is, therefore, a pedagogical continuity between the two – a continuity, by the way, that is caused by the continuing domination of the same class relations. Both the dominant humanities and the hypohumanities replacing them are responses to capitalism's need for a new work force – a "cybertariat" (Huws and Leys 2003) proficient in communications skills but indifferent to critique. However, there is a radical difference in the way the two pedagogies of skills actually work and, more importantly, in the way they philosophically justify their pedagogies and, through teaching writing and reading, teach the cultural values that capital needs in its workforce.

In mainstream humanities, the focus on teaching writing as a technical skill is grounded in the humanistic Quintilian maxim that "eloquence has its fountain-head in the secret springs of wisdom" (1856: n. p.). In other words, the subject already knows, and technical skills are a means for enabling that knowledge to be expressed. Content, to be more precise, is implicitly equated with immanent human knowledge, whose source, at different times, is said to be divine (Descartes 1960, *Meditations Concerning First Philosophy*), experience (Hume 1967, *A Treatise of Human Nature*), or the unconscious (Freud 1950, *The Interpretation of Dreams*).

In hypohumanities, however, the substantial subject is subverted. The subject in hypohumanities is not a stable "natural" subject in command of what he intends to say; rather he is a discontinuity, a *coupure*, in the chain of signifiers (Lacan 2002: 297), who tends to "disappear or slip away beneath the signifying chain by means of which he is constituted within the register of the symbolic as a *je*" (146). This is a subject whose "unconscious is structured in the most radical way like a language" (234). The technical skills of writing, therefore, are not a means for expressing what is already in the subject, since what is already there is what is "discovered in the study of actual languages, languages that are or were actually spoken" (234). Since there is not an already formed subject, writing skills in hypohumanities have a much more important role: in a sense, they construct the subject. Subjectivity is meaning, and since meaning is itself an indeterminate effect of the play of the sign, the subject is depicted as a loop of aleatory signs and traces activated by a tropics of desire.

The construction of the subject as meaning and desire takes place within language. But in hypohumanities narratives, language itself is not constructed as substantial (containing meanings) but as differential – as a producer of contingent meanings through difference: "in language there are only differences. Even more important: a difference generally implies positive terms between which the difference is set up; but in language there are only differences without positive terms" (Saussure 1989: 120).

Writing is taught as a practice of difference – signs without contents (Johnson 1995). Students learn to manipulate signs and seek meaning not in the relations of signs to the social conditions but within the sign-system itself – "there is nothing outside of the text" (Derrida 1976: 158). Everything is representation, but language itself is not representational; it makes what it represents. Robert Scholes naturalizes this pedagogy of writing by declaring: "The human condition is a 'condition of textuality'" (2001: 77). Teaching writing, therefore, becomes part of a more general approach to textuality, namely one that moves beyond a non-linguistic understanding of writing. "The object of discussion" in teaching writing, which is now part of literary theory, "is no longer the meaning and or the value" of writing "but the modalities of production and of reception of meaning and value prior to their establishment" (de Man 1986: 7). This is a formalist pedagogy that teaches writing as signs-skills and obscures the content in an indeterminate play of signs. Such a formalist pedagogy turns content into anti-content – into a site for the destruction of meaning – and represents this as cutting-edge writing pedagogy. However, the content of anti-content, as we will argue, is the class interest of the owners – its self-referentiality is one of the masks of dominant ideology. In part, through this meaningful non-meaning, the very notion of "dominant ideology" is now marginalized in cultural theory.

The question of content is of great significance in understanding hypohumanities and we need to unlayer it. In hypohumanities the content of reading and writing (as difference) is said to be the effect of the play of the signifiers and not the effect of the social relations, historical situation, or class conditions within which it takes place. Since texts are self-referential – allegories of their own (un)readability – the content of a text is the text itself; there is no outside to the text. The meaning (content) of what is written, in other words, is never determinate but always an excess of signification that overflows all systems of representations whether historical, social, or class, and its excess is a mark of its autonomy from all "outside" determinations. The text is not only self-referential but self-determinate. The excess of meaning is a voiding of all explanations: writing is difference and difference *is*. Nor is it available to representational reason. This "*is*-ness" – difference without grounds – is the very condition of the arts – writing, painting, music, film – in hypohumanities.

Obscuring the contents of cultural texts (film, writing, music, painting ...) is characteristic of all class societies. However, at times of heightened class antagonism, valorizations of form acquire a discursive urgency and become a dominant cultural imperative because they effectively eclipse content – which is not only the outcome of social antagonism but also an index of social relations.

In hypohumanities, this privileging of the medium of writing (signs) has such diverse sources as poststructuralist theories of self-referential textualities, the media theories of Marshall McLuhan, and neo-and post-Marxist theories of discourse, to name only a few. McLuhan and Derrida are both deeply affected by the formalism of Mallarme and James Joyce, and these tendencies converge in many recent writings, such as those by Jean Baudrillard. McLuhan argues that "the medium is the message" (1968: 23–35) because media – including writing – achieve their representational purpose not by reference (contents) but through the apparatus of representation. The "formative power in the media," according to McLuhan, "are media themselves" (35). The significance for McLuhan of a cultural practice, such as a cubist painting, is not in its immediate referent (content) but in its autonomous "configuration" (28). Its "being" is in itself as a floating sensory: what in theories of the following generation is called by Deleuze and Guattari the "body without organs" – "that which one desires and by which one desires" (1987: 165). The body without organs is a body free from the hierarchy of organs – phallus, mouth, vagina – that is, a body "opposed not to the organs but to that organization of the organs called the organism" (158). Stuart Hall (whose work has had a deep impact on cultural studies in the hypohumanities) generalizes McLuhan's theory when he writes, "The word is now as 'material' as the world" (1990: 128). They both substitute semiotics for class.

The emptier the medium is, namely, the freer it is from the "organization" of ideas ("message"), the more intense and excess-ive will be the play of its sensory performativity. McLuhan's grounding social theory is that it does not matter whether a medium – a machine, for example – turns out "cornflakes or Cadillacs" (1968: 23).

What does matter is that the medium – the regime of (mechanical) machines in this case – restructures human practices "by the technique of fragmentation that is the essence of machine technology" (23). By the same token, the essence of the post-machine "automation technology" is the opposite. "It is integral and decentralist in depth, just as the machine was fragmentary, centralist, and superficial in its patterning of human relationships" (23). "Automation" and "machines," which McLuhan sees as opposites, are actually two historically determined different means of exploiting labor under capitalism. Their differences are not that one "fragments" and the other "integrates," but that one is more exploitative than the other – one extracts more surplus labor and is therefore more profitable than the other.

Conservative aesthetes, however, are not the only ones to deride content. Contemporary left critics are even more anxious to distance themselves from content out of fear that they may be accused of a lack of subtlety and of falling back into discussions of what Fredric Jameson scornfully lists as issues from "those days" (by which he means the militant 1930s), namely, the "relation between literature and the labor movement" (1974: ix). Discussing such issues, for him, is vulgar: they are more "for use in night school" than the "graduate seminar." Such issues of content are merely the object, he maintains, "of intellectual and historical curiosity" (ix).

For Jameson (1974), a Marxist criticism that is appropriate to "the conditions of the world today" (ix) bypasses class because class issues and class conflicts have disappeared from "the daily experience" of social life today (xvii) and, furthermore, the "class model has never been worked out satisfactorily ... for American social reality" (401). In other words, if class is not visible, it can be ignored. As far as he is concerned, it is not the task of ideology critique to make the invisible visible. No longer is the role of a Marxist critic, for Jameson, to demonstrate that class is constitutive of the social under capitalism and mark its presence in all social practices. His response to the current situation is that since class is mystified by theories of post-industralization (xvii), a "new" Marxist criticism should turn away from class and focus on hermeneutics (401–16). He quietly surrenders to the "post-al" notion of the end of class and the end of ideology. Jameson, thus, hollows out the cultural from its content by stating that the "new" Marxist criticism should be anti-positivistic (a code word for the valorization of form) and therefore hermeneutic. Its hermeneutic models, he maintains, should be drawn from the work of writers such as Goethe and Wilhelm von Humboldt, who have explored the "inner form" by founding their critical views on Plotinus (401). The model for revolutionary left criticism today, according to Jameson, is the mystical idealism of Plotinus, as translated by nineteenth-century Romantic writers, and not the materialism of Marx, Engels, Lenin, Trotsky or Plekhanov (ix). Jameson further develops his Neoplatonist marxism in *The Political Unconscious* (1981: 17–102) and deploys it to advance his version of hypohumanities (*Postmodernism or, the Cultural Logic of Late Capitalism* 1991). His "new" marxism is concerned with the "operation of interpretation itself" (401) – the same thing, as we have seen, that formalist critics call not meaning (content) but the "production ... of meaning" (de Man 1986: 7).

In marginalizing content, Jameson goes much further than many formalist critics. In his *Postmodernism or, The Cultural Logic of Late Capitalism*, Jameson claims that "depthlessness" (1991: 6) is the "supreme formal feature of all postmodernisms" (9). It reduces cultural products to their form-medium which, among other things, means culture is itself fundamentally material (67–96). Therefore, there is no longer any place within culture for a materialist ideology critique that teases out the class relations in daily practices. In other words, there is no "outside" to the materiality of culture itself (no "base" determines it), and thus a materialist ideology critique of contents (the "relation between literature and the labor movement") is critically vulgar.

However, like labor, content is historically the decisive term even though in idealist aesthetics it is overwhelmed by form – either by being theorized as a form in disguise or by being dissolved into form in a state of artistic ambiguity. Materially, content structures form within specific social relations of production; both are, ultimately, articulations of material class relations. Under capitalism, however, content is alienated from form, which is represented as autonomous and is said to be the driving force of the cultural ("The medium is the message"). This alienation is a symptom of the contradictions of labor and capital and the class antagonism that the valorization of form attempts to obscure.

This becomes more clear in the recent history of the relation between socialism and capitalism. Hypohumanities' pedagogy of writing – with signs-as-difference – is part of larger contemporary efforts to hollow out the contents from all cultural texts. It is affiliated with such other contemporary cultural practices as, for example, abstract expressionism. Abstract expressionism is represented as absolute text – a text without metaphysics, like hypohumanities' claim about self-referring textuality. However, what is depicted as a rapture of pure color is, like the ecstasy of absolute signifiers in writing, an articulation of the interests of the class in dominance.

Nelson Rockefeller describes abstract expressionism as "free enterprise painting" (Saunders 2001: 258). It was widely regarded to be an enunciation of capitalist values – "anti-Communist ideology, the ideology of freedom, of free enterprise. *Non figurative and politically silent*, it was the very antithesis to socialist realism" (254, emphasis added). The blankness of abstract expressionism and the self-referential texts of hypohumanities are anti-content content: by masquerading as non-content, they convey the interests of the class in dominance.

However, content (the referent) is historical and determined by the social relations of production. Far from being referentially blank with zero-degree of content, the absolute text is not a self-reflexive and self-referential instance of a representation that doubles back on itself and becomes an allegory of its own unreadable opacity. Rather its (seeming) blankness is a forceful and aggressive voiding of the social. It asserts not just the indeterminacy of textuality and the autonomy of art, but in doing so, it negates the objectivity of the social relations of production, and states, to use Laclau's words, that "society does not 'exist'" (1990: 183).

The "blank" (anti-content) content of abstract expressionism was so strongly pro-capital that, as Francis Stonor Saunders (2001) argues, the CIA used it as part of its cultural arsenal to fight socialism and all forms of socialist arts and writings. An important site for the popular dissemination of postwar abstract expressionism, MoMA (the Museum of Modern Art) was a close collaborator with the CIA in advancing the cause of the indeterminacy of the sign (signifier, color, musical note) on behalf of capitalism and in the fight against socialism. In an *ArtForum* article on "Abstract Expressionism: Weapon of the Cold War," Eva Cocroft discusses the ideology of blankness and writes that the

> links between cultural cold war politics and the success of Abstract Expressionism are by no means coincidental ... They were consciously forged at the time by some of the most influential figures controlling museum policies and advocating enlightened cold war tactics designed to woo European intellectuals ... In terms of cultural propaganda, the functions of both the CIA's cultural apparatus and MoMA's international programs were similar and, in fact, mutually supportive.
>
> (Quoted in Saunders 2001: 263)

Abstract expressionism is exemplary of art without referents and is held up, like anti-referential writing, as an instance of free art and, by extension, of human freedom itself. The CIA's support (on behalf of capitalism) for writing without reference and for art without content goes beyond support for a particular school or textuality or art. It is support for apolitical theories of art and the apolitical intellectuals who disseminate them. Hypohumanities is, above all, about training a workforce that is highly informed about *how* to do things but incurious about *why* they are being done – other than that doing them is part of "my job." This indifference is reinforced by post-theory theories about the "producerly" subject whose identity is constructed not by her work but by her lifestyle: the consumption of objects through which she produces meanings and thus locates herself in a cultural space of desire. The constitution of the subject as producerly is part of the anti-content that hypohumanities teaches through pedagogies of writing and reading.

This is another way of saying that blank content – writing as self-reference without any referent to its outside – is an anti-content content through which the labor force of the future is trained. Unlike mainstream humanities, in which the student is instructed in the values of culture in a rather moralistic idiom, hypohumanities' pedagogies are subtle, indirect, and nuanced. Consequently, when the student-citizen acts on them, it seems to him that he is acting not in response to an outside imperative but to an inside desire.

In its pedagogy, hypohumanities represent the interpretation of texts as having (social) content as an outdated way of reading that is deterministic, rigid and mimetic. Instead, it teaches reading content as constituted by the playfulness of the sign and, therefore, as indeterminate, non-mimetic and undecidable. Content, in this sense, is produced through reading and not by objective social relations. Content can be anything that reading protocols produce. Teaching the protocols of interpretation – *how* to read – therefore, becomes the primary task of hypohumanities' pedagogy. In critique-al humanities, the question of reading is always a question of *why* – questioning the logic of the social that shapes the text and not decoding the text in its own terms.

The hypohumanities logic of "how" – interpretation as difference – teaches that meaning (content) is free from limits because the signifier never settles on any signified. The freedom of the signifier is taken as the allegory of freedom as such – the autonomy and indeterminacy of language and culture. Culture in hypohumanities is simply a linguistic interlacing. The freedom of the sign teaches the student-worker that by producing free meanings he, too, is free. Freedom of language becomes a metaphor for individualism and individual freedom – whose most effective expression is said to be freedom of speech in which the free consciousness of the free individual is activated. The only social system that is seen as allowing the full activation of free individuality is democracy, which is assumed to be impossible without a stable free market. The freedom of the signifier, in other words, is the allegory not of its self-reference but of the free-enterprise system, capitalism. This is the lesson of the anti-content of writing-as-difference. Hypohumanities represent the freedom of meaning as the sublime of human culture and its political regimes. It tutors the student-worker on how to accept her place within this free world and to freely submit to exploitation – even to be happy that she has a "job." It teaches thoughtful unthoughtfulness.

Gerald Graff's *Clueless in Academe: how schooling obscures the life of the mind* (2003) is a manual on teaching thoughtful unthoughtfulness for producing an educated but uncritique-al labor force. He does not simply offer a technical manual for training good subjects for capital; he also offers a "philosophy" for tutoring them in entrepreneurial values. He thinks it is delusional to defiantly fight corporate culture and, for instance, to argue (as we are doing in this essay) for a critique-al humanities. He, therefore, turns the cultivation of the entrepreneurial spirit into an educational policy because "capitalism is probably here to stay" (Buffington and Moneyhun 1997: n. p.). Since, in his assessment, there is no "alternative" to capitalism "right now," the function of education is a pragmatic training of students to work within the system of wage labor. "Big, sweeping, doctrinaire attacks on capitalism" for commodifying education "are a dead end," as far as Graff is concerned, because they will not "help students" get a job. Instead of "marginalizing" themselves by working to overthrow capitalism, Graff advocates that the humanities accept the existing social relations of property and adopt the principle of local reformism and work from within (Buffington and Moneyhun 1997: n. p.).

This argument is repeated, with regional differences in vocabularies, in similar books that legitimate capital from the left: Bill Readings 1996, *The University in Ruins*; Robert Scholes 2001, *The Crafty Reader*; Michael Berube 2006, *What's Liberal About the Liberal Arts?*; bell hooks 2003, *Teaching Community: a pedagogy of hope*; Henry Giroux 2006, *America on the Edge*; Cary Nelson 1997, *The Manifesto of a Tenured Radical*; J. Hillis Miller 1999, *Black Holes*. While using different idioms, they all defend capitalism with populist, pragmatist arguments. The value of these writings for capital lies not merely in their conservative contents but more immediately in their left rhetoric. Their left rhetoric, unlike Roger Kimball's *Retaking the University* (2008), for example, lends cultural credibility and ideological trustworthiness to capital because these texts are written by "well-known" leftist critics of capitalism. (Graff, for instance, says that he is "a sort of sentimental socialist" [(Buffington and Moneyhun 1997: n. p.]).

The pragmatic logic of Graff's "left" populism is repeated almost daily in the media. In his "In Praise of the Maligned Sweatshop," for instance, Nicholas D. Kristof (2006) writes that sweatshops in Africa set up by capitalists of the North are in fact "opportunities" and advises that "anyone who cares about fighting poverty should campaign in favor of sweatshops." His argument is summed up by two sentences, printed in bold and foregrounded in his essay: "What's worse than being exploited? Not being exploited" (A21).

Graff's (2003) pedagogy of reading teaches the same ideological conclusion by normalizing the core cultural values of capitalism that are articulated in "popular culture." He undercuts critique-al humanities by representing them as elite and thus alienating to students; he then teaches them non-alienating lessons in what he calls "argument" through popular culture. Stating that anti-intellectualism – which is actively fostered by capitalism through popular culture – is really a different form of thoughtfulness (211–31), he displaces conceptuality with experience and replaces abstract thinking – the condition of all knowledge – with the concrete sensuality of anecdotes (155–72). His reason for embracing the experiential, which he says he shares with Michael Berube (279), is that: "to the non-egghead, any two eggheads, no matter how far apart, are virtually indistinguishable" (7). The intelligible is opaque; only the sensible – the tissue of experience – makes a difference. Graff's "argument," which he refers to in a mocking-populist tone as "arguespeak" (21), is that the most effective "argument" is not an "argument" in any alienating conceptual sense, rather it is the robust pleasures of the experiential. Underlying almost all of the essays collected in his book is the assumption that lived experience is the real, and the most real of the real is the spontaneity of the student. The clueless becomes clued when he trusts his own spontaneity, rejects the congealed conceptuality of abstract thinking, and returns to the concrete. This is another way of saying that what Graff teaches as "argument" is the circuit of ideology. "'Lived experience' is not a *given*, given by a pure 'reality,' but the spontaneous 'lived experience' of ideology in its peculiar relationship to the real" (Althusser 1971: 223). What passes as the concrete singular is a homogenized sentiment marketed through popular culture.

This raises the issue of the fundamental difference between hypohumanities' pedagogies and the pedagogies of critique-al humanities, which refuse to accept the putative freedom of the sign as anything but the formal feature of a closed system and, therefore, insist that human freedom is not freedom of meanings but freedom from necessity.

The "secret" and its thoughtful unthoughtfulness

Hypohumanities are the convergence of theory and the (corporate) popular imaginary in which the world has been transformed into a new exciting sphere of work and desire. In this popular imaginary, the contemporary is represented as the effect of technologies of the text – the fading of hardware and the materialization of software – and a time of groundbreaking cyber-innovations that have made culture "primary and constitutive, determining its shape and character as well as its inner life" (Hall 1997: 215); they have also made the economy and the economic "inherently cultural phenomena" (Salaman 1997: 236). In this new world, labor itself is said to have been transformed into immaterial labor (Hardt and Negri 2004) and knowledge-capitalism has displaced "things" with "ideas." In the popular imaginary, we now "live in an environment" where "Joe Friday's 'Just the facts ma'am'" is supplanted by the belief that "if you can touch it, it's not real" (Peters 1992: 8), a time of the "triumph over materialism" by technologies of information and the rise of a "quantum economy" (Gilder 1989). The theoretical is not very different because "as objects become more mobile they progressively dematerialize and are reproduced as symbols ('signs')" (Waters 2001: 64).

These changes celebrated by both the popular and the theoretical are believed to have been responsible, at least in part, for turning the world into an interconnected network and accelerating what is often called "globalization," which in these narratives is basically the formation of a worldwide "free market." We call this theory of globalization which evolves around consumption (the market) and the supposed ending of the (national) state, "*Transnationalism*." Transnationalism is represented in the cultural common sense as a brand new world that is decentered and deterritorialized, and as a democratic place whose organizing logic is no longer the coercive regulating force of states. In this emerging world civil society is envisioned as an arena for the unbound desires of autonomous consumers freely expressing themselves through exchanges across transnational markets (Friedman 2005; Giddens 2001; Stiglitz 2007). In the new global community, in other words, "The material and power exchanges in the economic and political arenas are progressively becoming displaced by symbolic ones, that is, by relationships based on values, preferences and tastes rather than by material inequality and constraint" (Waters 2001: 160).

Globalization is understood to rearticulate time and space – the emergence of the borderless immediate – to produce a more fundamental epistemological change in the very order of reality by dematerializing "objects" into "signs." In *The Globalization of Nothing*, for instance, George Ritzer (2004) argues that globalization is the move away from "something" (the local materiality of a dense, layered, and distinctive content) towards "nothing" (the dispersal of substance). The progression of globalization, for Ritzer, is the "loss amidst monumental abundance (of something)."

The nation(-state) was historically necessary for the development of capitalism because it helped to centralize political power, which in turn reorganized economic institutions (banking, taxation, insurance, investment, laws of property, among others) in response to capital. "Independent or loosely connected provinces with separate interests, laws, governments and systems of taxation, became lumped together into one nation, with one government, one code of laws, one national class-interest, one frontier and one customs tariff" (Marx and Engels 1977: 94). The nation-state's historical role is now changing since global capitalism needs globally (not nationally) uniform banking, insurance, investment, and tax laws that favor and protect capital against the interests of workers across all borders.

What was once one of the conditions for the accumulation of profit is now becoming its fetters. But the nation-state, contrary to corporate theories of globalization, is neither dead nor is it coming to an end. Rather its role in support of capital has been modified. Its sovereignty is decreased so that it can no longer effectively block capital in its transnational movements. However, it serves capital's interests locally (by reducing its taxes, giving it police protection, lowering environmental standards, doing away with pension laws, ...). The nation-state, to again quote Marx and Engels, remains "a committee for managing the common affairs of the whole bourgeoisie" (1977: 44). Globalization is the articulation of the logic of history as class struggle and the withering of the state. However, globalization-as-transnationalism is only a stage towards globalization which is an *internationalism* grounded in production. It realigns the people of the world not along nationalities but classes.

All theories of globalization-as-transnationalism are ultimately legitimizations of imperialism which is a structural feature of capitalism (Lenin 1976). By assuming that imperialism is the effect of politics – "wars" among sovereign states – and not constitutive of the system of wage labor, writers such as Antonio Negri and Michael Hardt (2000) argue that since there are no longer sovereign states, imperialism has ended. This is another way of saying that capitalism is structurally free from imperialist aggression aimed at the appropriation of global surplus labor. "Business leaders around the world," writes Michel Hardt, "recognize that imperialism is bad for business because it sets up barriers that hinder global flow" (2002: n. p.). However, imperialism is a structural feature of capitalism as a regime of property relations and not simply politico-military events among states, a business policy (as Hardt argues) or cultural politics (such as, "the link between literature and the achievement of national self-consciousness," as Readings writes in *The University in Ruins* [1996: 77]). These "new" positions supposedly born out of the "new" conditions of capitalism are simply rehearsals of the "old" Kautskian views that capitalism would "enter upon a new phase, a phase marked by the transfer of trust methods to international politics, a sort of super-imperialism," that is, a post-imperialist modality (Kautsky 1914: n. p.). The idea of ultra-imperialism – grounded in the notion that imperialism is not "the highest stage of capitalism" (Lenin 1976) but an effect of intra-state conflicts which, as Kaustsky maintains, are contrary to the interests of capitalism – is now the master theory of the neoliberal left. "Kautsky's ultra-imperialism," writes Doug Henwood (2001: n. p.) with the usual defensive humor that has become the regulating rhetoric of "progressive" neoliberalism, "seems like a not-bad characterization of the world in the early twenty-first century" (n. p.). Hardt and Negri's "empire," according to Henwood, is not only "absolutely right" about the "dispersion of power in the new order," but is much more relevant now than Lenin's theory of imperialism (n. p.). The invasions of Afghanistan and Iraq in the "early twenty-first century" have turned these left theories of the (end of) imperialism into a dark joke. The end of the state, claimed by contemporary critics and bourgeois theorists, is not what Marx and Engels have called the "withering away" of the state. The state "withers away" not because capitalism becomes transnational but because capitalism, itself, comes to an end.

Bill Readings' *The University in Ruins* (1996) is a map of the transnational hypohumanities – which forms the ground of "values" for training the new labor force for global capitalism. Keeping in mind Fukuyama, who declares the triumph of liberal capitalism as the end of history (1992: 64–7, 276–7), Readings maintains that the new university is posthistorical (119–34) and repeats the view that globalization is a condition in which "the nation-state ceases to be the elemental unit of capitalism" (44). In this new, post-nation-state, capitalism, which, in Kenichi Ohmae's words, is run by "Investment, Industry, Information, Individual" (1995: 2–5), not only the market and individual (entrepreneur) are free from the normative force of the state, but also pedagogy itself is de-regulated – as the space of aleatory trajectories of the sign. This is a post-normative and post-conceptual hypohumanities whose lessons are of affect and caring and in which "ideas" are translated as "interests" because its teaching is aimed not at explaining but at entertaining – bringing pleasure not knowledge:

> I have certain principles (more accurately habits or tics of thought); they are not grounded in anything more foundational than my capacity to make them *interesting* to others, which is not the same thing as convincing other people of their "rightness."
>
> (Ohmae 168, emphasis added)

Explaining becomes an imposition of norms and as such acts against the freedom of the subject of interpretation. Persuasion, in this version of hypohumanities, is an honoring of the subject's desires and a recognition of his freedom.

After declaring that the end of the nation-state has put an end to Humboldt's notion of the university as a disseminator of national culture, as well as to the university of reason (the Kantian academy), Readings (1996) announces the birth of the University of Thought (166–79). "Thought," in Readings, is modeled after "politics" in Derrida: it is an empty signifier whose main function is to keep the space of thought open and protect it from becoming the site of thinking (anything in particular) because thinking will impose closure on Thought. Thought is not conscious thinking that may lead to the production of a coherent knowledge and enable people to change their world; it is its opposite. Thought is a "structurally incomplete practice" whose main purpose is to "hold open the temporality of questioning so as to resist being characterized as a transaction that can be concluded" (19). Thought, in other words, is a resistance to closure, to concluding and to acting on that conclusion. In fact, if Thought reaches a conclusion it becomes an "idea," and "ideas" are "answers," which is another way of saying, they are acts of closure. In this pedagogy of non-closural acts of reading for pleasure, humanities are aesthetic judgments, not cognition. Thought, in other words, is an ongoing play-full-ness, which is its own purpose, because, as Readings puts it, Thought "has no intrinsic meaning" (159).

Thought without thinking is an ideological device for thoughtful unthoughtfulness. Hypohumanities of Thought convert Thought into a private meditation on meditation to produce a worrying subject (represented as self-reflexive) – who suspects he is unthoughtful when he thinks (since "I am thoughtful because I am in Thought") – and "persuade" him to believe that the orders he carries out are not decisions made by others ("owners") but are the result of his own serious "thoughtfulness." Hypohumanities, in this narrative, should not fill Thought with "thinking" because such substantializing of Thought will give it a referent in the social relations of production and will, consequently, put a stop to the play of the sign and totalize the "ruins" (of the university in ruins) into a critique-al humanities.

To shield Thought from thinking (i.e. to recognize its essential social construction), Readings (1996: 175) warns against social commitment because he seems to know that any commitment will recognize Thought as a strategy for cleansing the social from critique. The commitment to deploy Thought to build a new society should be abandoned because it leads to "answers" (totalization) and thus closes the questions that help to maintain Thought as open. Thought is its own end. This is essentially an aesthetic model of pedagogy that is itself totalizing if not totalitarian.

The empty openness of Thought is, of course, a normalization of the hollow pluralism of liberal hypohumanities, which in the name of heterogeneity produces a highly homogeneous (aesthetic) consensus as the ground for politics. The student-citizen – under the alibi of broadmindedness and tolerance of the "other" – is persuaded to be pragmatic (Readings 1996: 178) and accept the existing social order. Any change is viewed as a violation of Thought and the imposition of thinking (about "socialism," for example). All such thinking is part of "big politics," which is always a project of change and smacks of "bad utopianism" (178), the cure for which is Thought without thinking.

In Readings' (1996) narrative the university has lost its old coherence and is now "in ruins" – it has "lost its historical *raison d'être*" (19) in the "sense that the institution has outlived itself" (6). Thus the only pragmatic way for the university to continue as a university is to become a place for pedagogy in "ruins" and teach new lessons that abandon "cognition" for "judgment," "objectivity" for "values," and "critique" (along with the critique-al humanities) for "aesthetics" ("interests," Thought). The "ruins," in other words, should not be un-ruined; pedagogy should not seek to "re-unify those ruins" (19) and produce a new "whole" (totality) out of them. "We should not attempt to bring about a rebirth or renaissance of the University," Readings writes, "but think its ruins as sedimentation of historical differences that remind us that Thought cannot be present to itself" (171). The university in ruins then is not a fallen university; on the contrary, it is a freed university. Freed from "reason" and "culture" into Thought (without thinking).

The university in ruins is the university of transnationalism. Its "ruins" are allegories of the singularity of the consumer in her autonomous, unstructured desires and her utter uniqueness and unrepresentable alterity. Thoughtful unthoughtfulness is the identity of the transnational subject of labor. Any thinking (coherence) will destroy that subjectivity and make it unfit for transnational capitalism's labor force. The new subject demanded by transnational capitalism is the nomadic subject-in-ruins: the fragmentary subject of the market who acquires his/her intermittent identity not by cultural belonging but by his/her chances in the ever shifting market and process of consumption – not consuming specific objects but a practice of consumption; not thinking specific ideas but "Thought" without thinking.

Readings teaches that in the post-national hypohumanities of Thought, critique becomes "obsolete since there is no outside to cultural ideology. Culture no longer hides anything; there is nothing behind culture for ideology critique to find …" (1996: 120). His lessons are based on corporate narratives that, in the age of high capital, culture becomes everything and therefore there is no place from which one can critique it. His statement that "there is nothing behind culture" (but more culture) is the logic of transnationalism.

But there *is* "something" behind culture.

The "something" that Thought hides in Thought itself – by prohibiting thinking that might find "something" – is the secret of class. It is the secret that the exchange of "labor power" for "wages" is an unequal exchange. "Labor power" is "a commodity which its possessor, the wage-worker, sells to capital" (Marx 1976c: 202). It is

> life-activity the worker sells to another person in order to secure the necessary means of subsistence. Thus his life-activity is for him only a means to enable him to exist. He works in order to live. He does not even reckon labour as part of his life; it is rather a sacrifice of his life. It is a commodity which he has made over to another.
>
> (Marx 1976c: 202)

And he has made it over in exchange for "wages," which are the "direct consequence of estranged labour" (Marx 1975: 280).

The exchange is not an equal exchange because "labour power" is a commodity unlike any other. It is a commodity which has the unusual property that its use is a source of new value. It is "a commodity whose use-value possesses the peculiar property of being a source of value" (Marx 1976a: 270). The "process of consumption of labour-power is at the same time the production process of commodities and of surplus-value" (279). "Surplus value" is appropriated by the capitalist. This is the secret that culture hides: that labor power produces surplus value, which is the source of value. Culture, through its legal codes, makes the exchange look "equal in the eyes of the law" (271) although it is anything but equal.

Critique (as in critique-al humanities) puts that secret in the open, and puts an end to the endless interpretations in hypohumanities that cultivate a taste for the secret (Derrida and Ferraris 2001) and linger in what *is* and postpone for ever what can *become*.

Note

1 For Peter McLaren.

Bibliography

Agamben, G. (1993) *The Coming Community*, Minneapolis: University of Minnesota Press.

Aglietta, M. (2001) *A Theory of Capitalist Regulation: the U.S. experience*, new edn, London: Verso.

Althusser, L. (1971) *Lenin and Philosophy*, New York: Monthly Review Press.

Armstrong, P., Glyn, A. and Harrison, J. (1991) *Capitalism since 1945*, Oxford: Blackwell.

Baudrillard, J. (1970) *La Societe de consummation*, Paris: Gallimard.

Beaud, M. (2001) *A History of Capitalism 1500–2000*, new edn, New York: Monthly Review Press.

Bell, D. (1976) *The Coming of Post-Industrial Society*, New York: Basic Books.

Berube, M. (2006) *What's Liberal About the Liberal Arts?* New York: W.W. Norton & Co.

Buffington, N. and Moneyhun, C. (1997) "A Conversation with Gerald Graff and Ira Shor," *JAC*, 17, 1:1–21.

Burton-Jones, A. (1999) *Knowledge Capitalism: business, work, and learning in the New Economy*, New York: Oxford University Press.

Butler, J. (1999) *Gender Trouble*, 10th anniversary edn, New York: Routledge.

Chambers, R. (1999) *Loiterature*, Lincoln: University of Nebraska.

Cochran, B. (1959) *American Labor in Midpassage*, New York: Monthly Review Press.

Crosland, A. (1956) *The Future of Socialism*, London: Jonathan Cape.

Deleuze, G. and Guattari, F. (1987) *A Thousand Plateaus: capitalism and schizophrenia*, Minneapolis: University of Minnesota Press.

de Man, P. (1979) *Allegories of Reading: figural language in Rousseau, Nietzsche, Rilke, and Proust*, New Haven: Yale University Press.

—— (1986) *The Resistance to Theory*, Minneapolis: University of Minnesota Press.

Derrida, J. (1976) *Of Grammatology*, Baltimore: The Johns Hopkins University Press.

—— (1978) "Structure, Sign, and Play in the Discourse of the Human Sciences," in *Writing and Difference*, Chicago: University of Chicago Press.

—— (1981a) *Dissemination*, Chicago: University of Chicago Press.

—— (1981b) *Positions*, Chicago: University of Chicago Press.

—— (1982) "Differance," *Margins of Philosophy*, 1–28.

—— (1988) *The Ear of the Other: otobiography, transference, translation*, Lincoln: University of Nebraska Press.

—— (1991) "Letter to a Japanese Friend," in P. Kamuf (ed.) *A Derrida Reader: between the blinds*, New York: Columbia University Press.

—— (1993) "Politics and friendship," in E. A. Kaplan and M. Sprinker (eds) *The Althusserian Legacy*, London: Verso, 1993.

—— and Ferraris, M. (2001) *A Taste for the Secret*, Cambridge: Polity.

Descartes, R. (1960) *Meditations Concerning First Philosophy*, New York: Prentice Hall.

Drucker, P. F. (1994) *Post-Capitalist Society*, New York: HarperCollins.

Dubofsky, M. and Dulles, F. R. (2004) *Labor in America: A History*, 7th edn, Wheeling, IL: Harlan Davidson.

Ebert, T. L. and Zavarzadeh, M. (2008) *Class in Culture*, Boulder: Paradigm Publishers.

Fiske, J. (1989) *Reading the Popular*, New York: Routledge.

Fones-Wolf, E. A. (1994) *Selling Free Enterprise: the business assault on labor and liberalism: 1945–60*, Urbana: University of Illinois Press.

Foucault, M. (1997) "Nietzsche, Genealogy, History," in D. E. Bouchard (ed.) *Language, Counter-Memory, Practice*, Ithaca: Cornell University Press.

Freud, S. (1950) *The Interpretation of Dreams*, trans. A. A. Brill, New York: The Modern Library.

Friedman, T. L. (2005) *The World Is Flat: a brief history of the twenty-first century*, New York: Farrar, Straus and Giroux.

Fukuyama, F. (1992) *The End of History and the Last Man*, New York: Free Press.

Gibson-Graham, J.K. (2001) "Toward a Poststructuralist Political Economy," in J. K. Gibson-Graham, S. Resnick and R. Wolff (eds) *Re/Presenting Class: essays in postmodern Marxism*, Durham: Duke University Press.

—— (2006) *The End of Capitalism (as we knew it): a feminist critique of political economy*, Minneapolis: University of Minnesota Press.

Giddens, A. (ed.) (2001) *The Global Third Way Debate*, Cambridge, UK: Polity Press.

Gilder, G. (1989) *Microcosm: the quantum revolution in economics and technology*, New York: Simon and Schuster.

Giroux, H. (2006) *America on the Edge*, New York: Palgrave Macmillan.

Gorz, A. (1982) *Farewell to the Working Class*, Boston: South End Press.

Graff, G. (2003) *Clueless in Academe: how schooling obscures the life of the mind*, New Haven: Yale University Press.

Hall, S. (1990) "The meaning of New Times," in S. Hall and M. Jacques (eds) *New Times*, London: Verso.

—— (1996) "The Problem of Ideology: Marxism without Guarantees," in D. Morley and K.-H. Chen (eds) *Stuart Hall: critical dialogues in cultural studies*, New York: Routledge.

—— (1997) "The centrality of culture: notes on the cultural revolutions of our time," in K. Thompson (ed.) *Media and Culture Regulation*, London: Sage.

Hardt, M. (2002) "Folly of our Masters of the Universe." *The Guardian* (December 18). Online. Available at http://www.guardian.co.uk/ (accessed December 10, 2006).

—— and Negri, A. (2000) *Empire*, Cambridge: Harvard University Press.

—— and Negri, A. (2004) *Multitude: war and democracy in the age of empire*, New York: Penguin.

Henwood, D. (2001) "Does it Mean Anything to be a Leninist in 2001?" Online. Available at http://www.leftbusinessobserver.com/Lenin.html (accessed February 18, 2007).

Hobsbawm, E. (1994) *Age of Extremes*, London: Abacus.

hooks, b. (2003) *Teaching Community: A Pedagogy of Hope*, New York: Routledge.

Hume, D. (1967) *A Treatise of Human Nature*, Oxford: Oxford University Press.

Hutnyk, J. (2004) *Bad Marxism: capitalism and cultural studies*, London: Pluto.

Huws, U. and Leys, C. (2003) *The Making of a Cybertariat: virtual work in a real world*, New York: Monthly Review Press.

James, W. (1974a) "Pragmatism's Conception of Truth," in *Pragmatism*, New York: New American Library.

—— (1974b) "What Pragmatism Means," in *Pragmatism*, New York: New American Library.

Jameson, F. (1974) *Marxism and Form*, Princeton: Princeton University Press.

—— (1981) *The Political Unconscious: narrative as a socially symbolic act*, Ithaca: Cornell University Press.

—— (1991) *Postmodernism or, the Cultural Logic of Late Capitalism*, Durham: Duke University Press.

Jenks, C. (1993) *Culture*, New York: Routledge.

Johnson, B. (1995) "Writing," in F. Lentricchia and T. McLaughlin (eds) *Critical Terms for Literary Study*, Chicago: University of Chicago Press.

Kant, I. (1951) *Critique of Judgment*, New York: Hafner-Macmillan.

Kautsky, K. (1914) "Imperialism and the war." Online. Available at http://marxists.org/archive/kautsky/1914/09/war.htm (accessed May 7, 2007).

Kimball, R. (2008) *Retaking the University*, New York: Encounter Books.

Kristof, N. D. (2006) "In Praise of the Maligned Sweatshop," *The New York Times* (June 6), A21.

Lacan, J. (2002) *Ecrits: a selection*, trans. Bruce Fink, New York: Norton.

Laclau, E. (1980) "Populist rupture and discourse," *Screen Education*, 34: 87–95.

—— (1990) *New Reflections on the Revolutions of Our Time*, London: Verso.

—— (2000) "Structure, history and the political," in J. Butler, E. Laclau and S. Zizek, *Contingency, Hegemony, Universality*, London: Verso.

Lenin, V. I. (1961) *What Is To Be Done? Collected Works*. Vol. 5. Moscow: Foreign Languages Publishing.

—— (1976) *Imperialism, the Highest Stage of Capitalism. Collected Works*. Vol. 22. Moscow: Progress.

Lyotard, J.-F. (1984) *The Postmodern Condition*, Minneapolis: University of Minnesota Press.

Marcuse, H. (1968) *Negations: essays in cultural theory*, Boston: Beacon Press.

Marx, K. (1974) "Contribution to the critique of Hegel's philosophy of right. Introduction," *Collected Works*. Vol. 3. New York: International Publishers.

— — (1975) *Economic and Philosophic Manuscripts of 1844, Collected Works*. Vol. 3. New York: International Publishers.

— — (1976a) *Capital*. Vol. 1. trans. B. Fowkes, intro. E. Mandel, New York: Penguin.

— — (1976b) *The Poverty of Philosophy, Collected Works*. Vol. 6. New York: International Publishers.

— — (1976c) *Wage-Labour and Capital and Value, Price and Profit*, New York: International Publishers.

— — (1981) *Capital*. Vol. 3. Trans. David Fernbach, intro. E. Mandel, New York: Penguin.

— — (1989) *A Contribution to the Critique of Political Economy*, M. Dobb (ed.) New York: International Publishers.

— — and Engels, F. (1976) *The German Ideology, Collected Works*. Vol. 5. New York: International Publishers.

— — (1977) *Manifesto of the Communist Party*, Moscow: Progress.

Macksey, R. and Donato, E. (1970) *The Languages of Criticism and the Sciences of Man: the structuralist controversy*, Baltimore: Johns Hopkins University Press.

McLuhan, M. (1968) *Understanding Media*, New York: Mentor Books.

Miller, J. H. (1999) *Black Holes*, Stanford, CA: Stanford University Press.

Mont Pelerin Society (1947) "Statement of Aims." Online. Available at http://www.montpelerin.org/mpsGoals.cfm (accessed January 5, 2007).

Mouffe, C. (ed.) (1996) *Deconstruction and Pragmatism*, London: Routledge.

Nelson, C. (1997) *Manifesto of a Tenured Radical*, New York: New York University Press.

Nietzsche, F. (1969) *The Will to Power*, New York: Vintage.

Ohmae, K. (1995) *The End of the Nation State: the rise of regional economies*, New York: The Free Press.

Pakulski, J. and Waters, M. (1996) *The Death of Class*, London: Sage.

Peters, T. (1992) *Liberation Management*, New York: A. A. Knopf.

Quintilian (1856) *Institutio Oratoria*, trans. Rev. John Selby Watson. Book XII, Chapter 2. Online. Available at http://honeyl.public.iastate.edu/quintilian/12/chapter2.html (accessed May 3, 2007).

Readings, B. (1996) *The University in Ruins*, Cambridge: Harvard University Press.

Ritzer, G. (2004) *The Globalization of Nothing*, London: Sage.

Ronell, A. (1989) *The Telephone Book*, Lincoln: University of Nebraska Press.

Rorty, R. (1991) *Objectivity, Relativism, and Truth*, Cambridge: Cambridge University Press.

Salaman, G. (1997) "Culturing Production," in P. Du Gay (ed.) *Production of Culture/Cultures of Production*, London and Thousand Oaks: Sage.

Saunders, F. S. (2001) *The Cultural Cold War: the CIA and the world of arts and letters*, New York: New Press.

Saussure, F. (1989) *Course in General Linguistics*, La Salle, Illinois: Open Court.

Scholes, R. (2001) *The Crafty Reader*, New Haven: Yale University Press.

Sterne, J. (2005) "The burden of culture " in M. Berube (ed.) *The Aesthetics of Cultural Studies*, Oxford: Blackwell.

Stiglitz, J. E. (2007) *Making Globalization Work*, New York: W. W. Norton.

Thebaud, J.-L. and Lyotard, J.-F. (1988) *Just Gaming*, Minneapolis: University of Minnesota Press.

Trifonas, P. P. (2000) *The Ethics of Writing*, New York: Rowman and Littlefield Publishers, Inc.

Waters, M. (2001) *Globalization*, London: Routledge.

Williams, R. (1977) *Marxism and Literature*, Oxford: Oxford University Press.

3   Persistent inequities, obfuscating explanations

Reinforcing the lost centrality of class in Indian education debates

Ravi Kumar

Abstract

This chapter argues that the bourgeoisie in India, using the state to serve its own interests, has produced an education system that is highly tilted against the poor and in favor of those who can afford to buy education. Both left and right debate the system, but neither right nor left raises the question of class in relation to the capitalist class interested use of the state to maintain an education system that contributes to the perpetuation of capitalism. By substituting for knowledges of class the discourses of multiple cultural identities related to caste, ethnicity, tribe, and so forth, the state represents itself as working for "development" of the education system that will benefit all. But in fact, the state divides all, pitting worker against worker, disadvantaging the proletariat as a whole and, in particular, girl children. This chapter argues that what is necessary is an understanding of the state as an agent that mediates interests in favor of capital, an understanding grounded in the Marxist theory of class. It is just such an understanding that is necessary to unify and educate all workers so that they do not accept the discourses of multiple cultural identities and therefore engage in intraclass struggles that benefit capital. A critical pedagogy that locates education within the context of the relation between the state and the bourgeoisie can contribute to the development of the understanding that the struggle for equal educational opportunities is the struggle against capitalism.

Introduction

Our day-to-day engagements reveal numerous instances in which the state, as an institution that represents the interests of "the most powerful, economically dominant class" (Engels 1884: n. p.), marginalizes or quite ingeniously manipulates critical spaces in an effort to draw them back into the conceptual framework promoted and naturalized by the state. The framework promoted and naturalized by the state represents the state as an agency of change working in the interests of all people, where "the people" are understood not in terms of class (position in relation to production), but in terms of (multiple) cultural identity/ies (e.g. those related to caste, ethnicity, tribe, and so forth) largely unconnected to class. The debates on education in India starkly reveal these maneuvers from within this dominant framework.

While inequality in education and the institutionalization of this inequality by the state in India (Kumar and Paul 2006) has been established beyond doubt, mainstream analyses of the gross inequities in Indian education typically evade situating education in relation to the political economy of capitalism.

This paper does not provide an extensive review of how educationists look at the so-called educational crisis in India (see Kumar 2006b), but it seeks to address the larger common thread running through their ideas, of evading the necessity of situating education in the political economy of capitalism, where it becomes clear that the so-called crisis is in actuality not a crisis but can be explained by the historical trajectory of India to follow the dictates of capital and privatize.

A brief overview of contemporary education debates

Education debates in India during the last decade need to be located in the context of debates over (1) the rise of right wing politics; and (2) persistent illiteracy: as per the Census of India statistics (Census of India 2001), only 64.8 percent persons were literate in 2001. The condition of female literacy is dismally low at 53.7 percent. In some of the states female literacy is much lower, such as Haryana (49.3 percent), Rajasthan (37.3 percent), Uttar Pradesh (36.9 percent), and Bihar (29.6 percent).

Without going into the detailed history of debates in Indian education, one may conclude that debates over both the rise of right wing politics and persistent illiteracy sharpened in the post-liberalization era when private capital became pro-active and the state was relegated to being a secondary player in the social sector. However, it is important to understand the apparent demotion of the state in the moment of the rise of private capital in relation to a critical (rather than common sense) understanding of the uses to which the bourgeoisie has put the Indian state at various historical moments: immediately after Independence in 1947, the Indian bourgeoisie was in its initial stages and drew up the Bombay Plan that asked the state to manage the heavy industries, contain foreign finance and leave those industries to the private sector which they could manage (see Mukherjee 2002). By 1980, we find mounting pressure from the Indian bourgeoisie on the state to open up the economy, ease many restrictions, and provide much greater freedom to operate (see Kumar 2006a).

The developments in education also need to be understood critically and in relation to the shifting ways in which the bourgeoisie uses the state in its interests (for a brief overview of India's educational history, see Kumar 2006b). It was the "historic" Kothari Commission (or Education Commission 1964–6), appointed by the central government and still referred to in the Indian education debates, that recommended the Common School System (CSS). According to its 1966 report, "a Common School System of public education should be evolved in place of the present system which divides the management of schools between a large numbers of agencies whose functioning is inadequately conditioned" (Government of India [GOI] 1966: 229). The report, which advocated access to equitable education for all students, said that

> the main problem before the country is to evolve a common school system of public education which will cover all parts of the country and all the stages of

school education and strive to provide equality of access to all children. This system will include all schools conducted by government and local authorities and all recognized and aided private schools. It should be maintained at an adequate level of quality and efficiency so that no parent would ordinarily feel any need to send his child to the institutions outside the system such as independent or unrecognized schools.

(GOI 1966: 231)

It is interesting to note that the concern of the Commission was to connect under state control the different kinds of schools that were under different government bodies or were government aided, suggesting a move toward equity enabled by the state. However, the Commission did not want to comment on the privatization of schooling, which has emerged as the biggest challenge for equal access to equitable education.

The education policy or the government documents after that reiterated the need to have a CSS until the National Policy on Education (NPE) in 1986. Thereafter, the concept of a CSS has occasionally been paid lip service. Now the education system is highly tilted against the poor and in favor of those who can afford to buy it. There are layers of schools within the government schooling system, such as the schools with best facilities, like the chain of Kendriya Vidyalayas and Navodaya Vidyalayas, and the schools with worst facilities, meant for the poor and deprived, like the "other" formal as well as non-formal education centers and schools. In this extremely strenuous and long trajectory we stand at a critical juncture where private capital not only co-opts the voices of dissent but also transforms this dissent into a "within-system" reform-seeker.

The education debate today in India (as elsewhere) is comprised, on the one hand, of weak and sporadic voices against neoliberal assault, while on the other hand, of the overwhelming state apparatuses and intellectual-activists supported by private capital which see education as enhancement of human capital. Recent years have seen the state adopting an apparently "*ad hoc* policy" of meeting targets in the education sector as part of a global strategy of neoliberal capital to bring education under more strict capitalist control. The idea of a public-private partnership appears as the most conspicuous method of inducing fully fledged privatization in education as outlined by many government documents (GOI 2001a: 39, para 2.2.70; GOI 2004). Thus we find an overwhelming emphasis on "alternative methods" of education (which is in fact an attractive nomenclature for poor quality parallel streams of education).

A vast majority of the population faces discrimination and is not in a position to scale up the ladder of educational attainment like the rich sections. Among such sections we have poor dalits (who are among the Scheduled Castes, considered "outcastes," that constitute the lowest rung of caste hierarchy) (Nambissan 1995; 2006) and girl children from rural areas and poor households (Nambissan 2004). We find that the poor, seen as those who cannot afford to purchase education, are being deprived of education more and more as they cannot afford it (National Sample Survey Organisation [NSSO] 2001: 18–19). The National Family and Health Survey (NFHS) clearly shows how many children (and more so in the case of girls) drop out of schools due to economic reasons (International Institute for Population Sciences [IIPS] and ORC-Macro 2000). It has been argued by many that despite the government's declaration that the education is free it is not really so (Tilak 1996; Kumar 2006c).

The "alternative" non-formal education has appeared as a panacea for all educational ills in such a situation. The Government of India, which had begun the much critiqued District Primary Education Programme of multi-grade teaching[1] (Kumar, *et al.* 2001a–b), launched the Sarva Shiksha Abhiyan (SSA) to operationalize the commitment that it has made through the 86th Constitutional Amendment to make education a fundamental right.[2] However, this operationalization has been plagued with problems that will have long-term effects because the teachers are poorly paid and are appointed on contract (GOI 2000), and even the infrastructural facilities are deficient. Instead of regularizing the government schools, new schools for the drop outs were opened up, thereby sustaining the distinction between those who can afford to purchase education and those who cannot. This reveals the direct link between education and the market forces of capitalism.

These historico-material conditions have sharpened the contradictions in the Indian education debate. However, those who critique the education policies and state withdrawal are very few, and a larger brigade of intellectual-activists are seen going along with the system in the name of "viability," "do-ability," or "something is better than nothing." Those who have been arguing for state control and management of the social sector demand complete state control and funding of a common, uniform pattern of education of equitable quality for all, while those who go along with the system have been supporting the parallel systems of education for poor and girl children on the grounds of a resource crunch. Hence, there are two "dissenting" camps, neither of which situates any form of education privatization in relation to capital and its current drive to privatize.

There is a dissenting camp which calls for reinstatement of a welfarist state, invoking both the 1944 pre-independence Sargent Committee (CABE Committee of 1944, also known as the Sargent Commission) report and the Kothari Commission reports for a CSS, albeit with many modifications (such as bringing private schools as well within the ambit of Common Schools). Even though this apparently left camp does not directly and sharply question the character of the state, the other camp goes all out in support of a neoliberal state. The former group of intellectual-activists differentiate themselves by (1) questioning the current system; and (2) creating spaces for dissent. However, even their "struggle" gets limited to being a within-system call for certain reforms, an "action" that amounts to nothing more than an engagement in the politics of disruption, after which the ruling ideas become more firmly entrenched. The significance of their call lies in the challenge that they momentarily – but only momentarily – pose to neoliberal capital. Yet, because the "challenge" is conceptualized from the confines of a within-system acceptance of the system as "natural," this challenge lacks an anti-system basis. Consequently it becomes a group enterprise that not only cannot explain in any systematic manner the relationship between capitalism and education, but one that also oscillates between two forms of capitalism – a welfare state and a neoliberal state.

Despite their professed political differences, both camps play on the rhetoric of multiple subjectivities (such as caste, race, religion, tribe, gender, and so forth), thereby committing the same mistake of ignoring the social classes-education correlation. Left and right, in other words, present themselves as different but in actuality are a unified force against the interests of the great majority. Here it becomes essential to posit that the interactions among classes at the level of culture are determined by the location of each social class in the production process, and it is this placement that explains the relationship between them and education. This hierarchical location determines the relationship of these classes to the commodified economy within which schools, as a commodity, are placed.

At this juncture, critical educationists represent a major break in analysis when they argue that "education plays a key role in the perpetuation of the capital relation" (Allman, *et al.* 2005: 136). Their analysis becomes highly relevant to us in working to understand the Indian situation. Looking at education as an effective instrument against exploitation, Allman, McLaren, and Rikowski (2005) argue that, while "education is an aspect of the class relation," the circumstance "yields educators a special sort of social power" because education has the potential to initiate a process of radical transformation. "Education," they continue, "can be the foundation of a politics of human resistance to the capitalization of humanity" (151).

Educational transformation, the politics of co-option and the triumph of capital

When the United Progressive Alliance government took over, only one of the two issues mentioned above (the rise of right wing politics and persistent illiteracy) saw resolution: the communal Hindu religious content in curricula was questioned and deleted. However, the neoliberal principles of state withdrawal in favor of allowing the "free-play" of market forces, resulting in a two-tier education system producing vast illiteracy, continued, and in fact, Arjun Singh, the Human Resource Minister, asked the provinces to speed up their Sarva Shiksha Abhiyan (SSA) programs.[3] Any demand which could have improved the educational status of the poor classes and dalits, who lack the purchasing power to survive in the market, has been scuttled quite assiduously. The principle of private capital dictation continued unabated. In Punjab the Congress Party government decided to hand over management of government schools to private bodies (Dogra 2005), and in Delhi the Municipal Corporation of Delhi started working on a policy to hand over management of its schools to transnational capital (Jha 2005). Many schools are being seen as possible venues for a shopping mall, with one floor for the school (Jha 2004). Though the state is quite apprehensive about the possible opposition to such projects, which has in fact delayed the process, it has been moving ahead with its agenda of providing more space to private capital in different ways. For instance, the draft Approach Paper for the 11th Five Year Plan talks about implementing a voucher system because it "can help promote both equity and quality in schooling in areas where adequate private supply exists, provided that this is combined with strict requirements on private schools to give freeships to students in economic need" (GOI 2006a: 48).

A more direct understanding and commitment of the Government of India to private capital, argued in a position paper on allowing private companies in secondary education, was revealed when the Government said that "education has therefore become a commercial activity and it is time to recognize it as such. Profit making is after all not entirely undesirable. The common Indian today is willing to pay for quality education" (quoted in Kumar 2005: 20). This unrelenting support to private capital need not be a cause of astonishment because it merely indicates the direction in which capitalism moves – from a welfarist regime to a neoliberal state, which is acting in the current historical moment as the most efficient agent of private capital. And if the development of the character of the Indian state is looked at as a process, one finds a linear progressive trajectory of capitalism.

Dominant analyses of the Indian state such as those discussed have been not very convincing among many Indian educationists whose aim is actual educational equity for all. The problems raised by those analyses have not been located as emerging out of the state as an instrument serving the interests of the bourgeoisie. Consequently, the "hopes" such analyses raise are generally those of the "government's." Many have yet to realize that "the power of the state is a permanent power" (Mandel 1969: n. p.) in a society divided by class, and that moreover, as Engels (1884) argued,

> As the state arose from the need to hold class antagonisms in check, but as it arose, at the same time, in the midst of the conflict of these classes, it is, as a rule, the state of the most powerful, economically dominant class which, through the medium of the state, becomes also the politically dominant class, and thus acquires new means of holding down and exploiting the oppressed class.
>
> (n. p.)

That the power of the state is the power of the capitalist class is reflected in the unchanged institutions that remain always at the same place in a cosmetically altered way, if altered at all. The absence of such an understanding of the state not only results in the absence of identifying capitalism as the enemy insofar as it relies for its existence on a society divided by class, but it also generates a false hope that things can improve if the government desires.

Those who have been asking not to engage with the issue of the character of the state and its linkages with the policies lack the basic perceptible and readily available knowledge about how the government has been treating the social sector when it decides on its expenditure. The social sector has been the ignored sector. Despite the education cess of 2 percent that the government levied on every taxpayer, the money for the education sector has been declining (GOI 2006b: 205). Leaving aside the question of where the cess that is collected is going, one needs to ask a basic question: Why is the social sector accorded such a low priority when we all know that the poor cannot afford the market in this neoliberal age?

The government figures have pointed out how impossible it has been for people lacking purchasing power to buy this commodity called education. But those figures are seldom referred to by the experts (even the dissenting voices) to show that "poverty" and (lack of) education are directly related (GOI 2001b).

When the Government of India recently enlivened the education debate in the country, much to the chagrin of many critics, it was nothing but a simple example of farcical debates launched by the system in order to create spaces for co-option of dissent as well as to create consensus. The formation of seven committees under CABE to look at the most basic tenets of education in the country generated a hope about some profound changes that the government wished to initiate. Hopes were also generated because many of the new social movement representatives as well as many others who have been considered "secular and progressive" were nominated to these committees. Many organizations and "concerned" individuals began interacting with these committees, arguing to include elements of equal education opportunity for all Indians. Constituted towards the end of 2004, these committees have already submitted their reports and recommendations.

Right from the beginning contradictions persisted within the government. For instance, while committees were looking at the issue of the CSS, inclusive education, and education of girls, as well as to frame a Free and Compulsory Education Bill, there were strong directions from the Ministry of Human Resource Development (MHRD) to increase the pace of SSA implementation. Similarly, two simultaneous exercises of CABE committees and the National Curriculum Framework by National Council for Educational Research and Training (NCERT)[4] were underway despite them dealing with overlapping issues such as textbooks, culture education, girls' education, inclusive education, and so forth. In brief, the state has been quite forthright in its agenda. It has been pursuing its agenda without any consideration for the need to make it more equitable and democratize its access, while instituting committees to serve as eyewash. Ultimately, when the reports came out, they were endorsed in a CABE meeting, except for the Free and Compulsory Education Bill, which was stalled because some members of the CABE opposed its content and objected to the procedure followed by the Chairperson of the Committee ("Compulsory Education Bill" 2005; "Education Bill Stuck" 2005). The Chairman of the sub-committee, Kapil Sibbal, happens to be the Science and Technology Minister in the Government of India. He did not incorporate many of the points raised by some of the members in the final version of the Bill. The Bill, also, was being opposed by a section of people because it did not put any control on the private schools and continued to deny, in its proposal, the issue of quality for the poor children, who generally go to the schools.

Expectations went down with a big thud when the HRD Minister reminded towards the end of the meeting that CABE is just an advisory body, and therefore, as a subtext, not binding on the government. Thus, we are back at square one. The many voices of dissent have become part of the state apparatuses and the zeal of popular mobilization has been subdued once again, as a result of "leadership" that myopically seeks to achieve changes in basic state structures that are in actuality the terrain of well-entrenched capitalist interests.

The exercise of committees and the desire to effect long-term changes through state apparatuses goes against the logic of control and domination exercised by the capitalist state through such apparatuses. After all, the state will never allow its bodies to act against its larger mandate of facilitating private sector penetration in profit making sectors. Even if the argument is made about the possible advantages of such "opportunities" when the balance of class forces is tilted against the state, the current situation in India is clearly not such. The booming economy with the fast pace of economic growth, the expanding riches of Indian private capital, and the expansion of earning opportunities for the middle class through Business Process Outsourcing (BPOs)[5] has mediated the possibility of any crisis confronting the state. Thousands of slum dwellers are evicted from Delhi, Calcutta, Bombay and other cities, public sector undertakings are being privatized, the cost of living is becoming more and more expensive, informalization of the workforce is the order of the day, pensions are being done away with – and yet there is no movement. Even the left, on whose support the central government rests, is becoming a part of it – and then one recalls how Engels cautioned against joining governments with the bourgeoisie because ,even if the communist parties think otherwise (though many people would say that they no longer think "otherwise"), they become partners in whatever the bourgeoisie does as part of the government (Engels 1894). Though there are signs of distress at the increasing gap between the rich and the poor, it is yet to produce a crisis of such magnitude that would produce a movement capable of threatening the existence of private capital.

Hence, what we have seen historically is that, even if some committee reports have been radical for a government to digest, that government has tried to delegitimize them by instituting a review committee or by ignoring them, as in the case of the Ramamurti Committee. The Ramamurti Committee was the last breath of welfarism in Indian education that tried to put the issues of caste, class and gender justice as well as the CSS on the education agenda of the state, but the Indian State realized its mistake in appointing such a committee and got its recommendations refuted by a CABE Committee on Policy appointed in 1991 under Janardhan Reddy to review it (see Kumar 2006b).

Symptomatic of the contradictions of capital, there is an inbuilt contradiction in the whole exercise of committees – it decides policies about people without allowing their participation in the process. Even if it allows participation it is limited to the select regular crowd in the metros and state capitals. It is interesting to recall in this context that participation is seldom seen as mobilization in development discourse. The development discourse in India looks at overcoming conflicts, which include class conflict or conflicts generated as a result of the inequitable social relations that capitalism produces. Hence, even if mobilizations occur on issues of education or health issues, they try to "bridge" these conflicts and work on an agenda of harmony and peace. And the most serious flaw in this exercise is that it entices us into mistaking a small section of self-appointed intellectuals as comprising or speaking for all of the "people." There has to be a process through which all "people" – including especially the workers and peasants – become involved in the process of policy making. But this will be a difficult proposition for a system that bases itself on the ideas of a centralized power (the consolidated power of capital), exercising its whims and fancies through different mechanisms, veiling its hegemonic agenda dexterously enough to be taken as "progressive" and "democratic," while subtly pushing the agenda of dominance of private capital.

Participation essentially needs to be about engagement at the horizontal level, as a dialogue that does not deliver (because deliverance is essentially a top-down approach) but gives rise to opinions, views and actions. This horizontality is to be built in the interests of a class, though, if necessary, drawing in support from other classes as well. Such a practice might help dissolve hierarchies, create working-class unity, pressure the state and may even compel it to decommodifiy vital components of the social sector. It is a contest that bases itself in the material conditions of the participants and so the responses are more vivid.

The very idea of such a practice, however, raises the question of whether any agency actually interested in initiating such a dialogue would in fact have the various resources to be able to reach diverse sections of the population. For instance, the debates that have ensued on the National Curriculum Framework (NCF) do not have a design to reach the landless agricultural workers, those most affected by the rapaciously aggressive private capital and its education policies. As the debate fails to emerge from diverse socio-economic and geographical locations, for which not only the state (due to its character) but also agencies claiming to be their representatives are responsible, the voice of the class which accesses the instruments of info-power at various levels becomes the voice of people. For instance, when asked whether debates are generated on issues of such vital importance as the Right to Education, the state says yes because the debates are put on the website and have been circulated to the different state governments and departments. But what actually happens is something else — the majority of Indians lack access to the Internet and, secondly, the proposals such as the Draft Free and Compulsory Education Bill (FCEB) remain within the confines of a small group of administrators or educationists who have access to the documents. Those who have access to information exercise the power (but even not all have this access because the fate of the FCEB does not affect them since they operate in the market and can purchase education for their children) and decide the framework of the kind of education that India should have through NCF or FCEB. Hence, the apparent façade of a democratized exercise becomes not only conceptually but also practically problematic.

Participation in the process set in motion by the state, hence, is reduced to a miniscule section which is already represented and is largely in tune with capital's expansion plan due to its aspirations and aspiration driven actions. If mobilization is to be seen as a tool for ensuring participation and enhancing democratic capacities of people, it cannot be implemented by a neoliberal state. If, at all, people arguing for "within-system radical initiatives" believe that radical changes can be brought about by using the capitalist-interested state apparatuses, their effort will be futile unless accompanied by larger popular mobilization, which will represent the aspirations and demands of a larger population in a democratic polity. If followed with persistence and theoretical clarity, it may culminate in a horizontal dialogue instead of the current practice of a vertical dialogue, although, despite all the hullabaloo, the demand for putting the reports of CABE or NCERT to a much wider mass for debate will not be achieved because of the lack of any such guiding, proletariat class-interested framework.

The committees, for instance those appointed by NCERT to make a NCF and those appointed by CABE to look into the most fundamental aspects of Indian education, became a major source of hope and inspiration, especially in the age of decline of social movements as sources of alternatives. This decline is about the marginalization of movements that argue against the system, capitalism, and seek to ground their understanding and action in an all-sided critique of the nature of the capitalist system. We are bearing witness instead to momentous mobilizations seen many times as (and literally engaged in as) "cutting-across-class" "celebrations," as in the form of the World Social Forum and the Asian Social Forum. Yet the sense of "hope," generally touted as popular expression, represents the sentiment of a section of intelligentsia and political leaders who fail to act as leaders so that the popular mobilization is crystallized and can evolve effectively, and instead act as mediators between the working class and the state in such a way as to block all-sided mobilization. The demands emerge from this "middle ground" (constituted by these intellectual-activists) and assume the role of "wise," sensitive representatives of people. The business of delegitimization and legitimization is undertaken by these bodies. What is knowledge and what comprises knowledge is decided by sitting in committees, which further crystallizes the process of alienating the actual producers of knowledge of class – all those subject to exploitation – from their own product: all-sided knowledge of the uses to which capital puts the proletariat. This alienation is part of the strategy of the ruling elite to create structures of hegemony, the most apparent being the division between those who appropriate knowledge, as the ruling elite, and those who create it. Hence, the issue of any measure being made a Fundamental Right that would empower the actual producers of knowledge is a distant possibility.

Similarly, the processes of democratization within capitalism also have a logic that limits change. The process of democratization, created through nomenclatures of "de-centralization" and "participation," are limited and limiting. They are always designed in such a way that the benefits of democratization can at best be availed by the local elite. In the case of India over the past decade or so, there has been a devolution of power from the centralized elite at the "center" to the localized elites, all being linked and part of the larger scheme of things. It is relevant to examine the way power is structured and manifested in societies. That is one of the reasons why the discourses on participation and decentralization do not dwell on questions of class contradictions within a community which is rather portrayed as a homogeneous collective.

The concerns being raised about why the committees are not considering the principles laid down in the constitution or why they are trying to give further credence to the 86th Amendment, despite many of its drawbacks, are better explained if a historico-structural analysis of capitalist development and education policy in India is undertaken. But, quite contrarily, the tendency has been to look at the different aspects of everyday life as distinct, fragmented parts of the reality. The approach can be termed an offshoot of "functionalist" typology. Functionalism focuses on maintaining "stability in societies" and does not talk about structural change, even if certain elements become dysfunctional, which can be corrected. Every element is seen as having a role to play (Hill and Cole 2004: 145). But functionalism also entails autonomy of different elements which otherwise integrate to sustain a social system.

Hence, functionalism is about, at a much finer level, different parts having distinct functions but aimed at maintaining a particular kind of system. The parts are attributed roles and functions and represent a "within-ist" autonomy (but portrayed as an agency capable of bringing about radical social transformation) to effect change. For example, education has a role and it is seen as an autonomous element that can lead to transformations in society – but within capitalism and not outside it. "Relative autonomy," in other words, is simply another name for "autonomy within" a given totality of social relations, an autonomy that is not interested in looking at, much less transforming, the social relations of production of capitalism that constitute the conditions of possibility of "what is."

It is relevant to reflect on this typology while we try to understand the possibilities of a social movement against the state's anti-people (where "people" includes all members of the proletariat, all workers and peasants) policies. Due to the tendency to look at education as an autonomous unit, divorced from the overarching political economy of the system, we are unable to explain why the state, despite being "driven" by the "progressive" and "democratic" forces active "within" it, follows an anti-people program in the education sector. The fragmentation and "autonomy within" hamper unity, which is not only important for understanding the dynamics of capitalism and education within capitalism, but also to foster a strong movement against the system for radical transformation. The majority of Indian educationists do not realize this, because they look at education as outside the labor-capital relationship. Education has a function, to create consensus in society, but it has the capacity to produce the anti-system movement as well, and capitalism realizes this. Therefore, capitalism fragments the reality, and, through the autonomy within that develops, gradually even the oppositional forces come to agree to this fragmentation.

The capitalist system has its own mechanisms to co-opt and make the voice of dissent its own. And it is extremely difficult to stay away from this systemic impulse. Nonetheless there are people who completely denounce the system and try not to "become a part of it." But it is too complex a matter to be resolved so easily. The option available is that of maintaining a highly critical and clear approach to "participation" in the system. It is necessary to "participate" by critiquing capitalist practices and theoretical frameworks (as I am doing here) from outside the interests of capital, that is, from the standpoint of the proletariat interest in transforming capitalism. Such critique is pedagogical, raising awareness of the limits of a "within-ist" framework. Problems arise when our criticality ceases to function and we assume that the system's voice is our voice because we are inside it. And because some are "progressive" and always push for the people's agenda, it is assumed that the agenda of the state is also pro-people. This is what generally happens to people who, due to a lack of understanding of the intersections among education, the state, class, and the contradiction between labor and capital, become integrated into the system. For instance, historically, class analysis of Indian education policy has been absent. And it is this absence that leads to tendencies of a "middle-path" approach or "changing the system from within." It is in this process of co-option that the ideas of "feasibility" and "do-ability" gradually emerge as an excuse for furthering and multiplying the so-called alternatives that the system offers. Hence, in India, the SSA is taken as the only option because making formal education available to all appears impossible due to its massive cost and other logistical difficulties. The acceptance by the "progressive" and "democratic" intelligentsia of the measures by capitalism emerges from their unwill-ingness to question the system and from their understanding that capitalism, though based on rampant rule of capital, does not pose any threat to the welfare state. This group strives for within-system reform. Whatever has been happening in the Indian education sector, and the education debate in particular, brings us to a fundamental question of whether the state can be treated as a terrain of contestation or not.

Possibilities for change and the misconceptions about a "radical" capitalist state

Fighting the state from within is an argument forwarded for quite a long time and only those naïve to the functioning of the capitalist state can buy it. Such an argu-ment bases itself on a certain understanding of the character of the state, one of them being the state's ability to transform radically, even on issues which run counter to the interest of the private capital, such as taking "education" out of the ambit of the market where it is treated as a commodity. One cannot deny the possibility of such a move, but it is dependent on a variety of factors such as the nature and extent of political movement pressuring the state to do that as well as the stage of capitalist development. That the state in capitalism serves the capitalist ruling class cannot be refuted so easily, and Saad-Filho (2003) writes that

> the reasons are easy to understand. First, the state is *constitutionally* committed to capitalism by custom and law, and state institutions are geared towards, and have been historically shaped by, the development of markets, wage employ-ment and profit-making activities. Second, the staffing and policy priorities of the state institutions are heavily influenced by the interest groups represented in and through them, where capital tends to be hegemonic. Third, the reproduc-tion of the state relies heavily on the fortunes of capital, because state revenue depends upon the profitability of enterprise and the level of employment. Fourth, the economic and political power of the capitalists, and their influence upon culture, language and habits, is overwhelming, especially in democratic societies.

(10)

Another significant lacuna in such an understanding emanates from the myopic understanding about the way the state functions. It uses its various instruments to establish and sustain its hegemony. For instance, as Gramsci (2004) writes, while dealing with the issue of law

> the State must be conceived of as an "educator," in as much as it tends precisely to create a new type or level of civilisation. Because one is acting essentially on economic forces, reorganising and developing the apparatus of economic production, creating a new structure, the conclusion must not be drawn that

superstructural factors should be left to themselves, to develop spontaneously, to a haphazard and sporadic germination. The State, in this field, too, is an instrument of "rationalisation," of acceleration and of Taylorisation. It operates according to a plan, urges, incites, solicits, and "punishes" ... The Law is the repressive and negative aspect of the entire positive, civilising activity undertaken by the State.

(247)

One may change the form of capital appropriation, from aggressive to somewhat mild, after pressure generated by substantial public mobilization. Even that is extremely difficult (look at how Delhi government is showing the way in standing by private capital through privatizing road maintenance, electricity, water and public utilities, among other things, despite so much pressure from its own Member of Legislative Assemblies and its partners, the Resident Welfare Associations). Or for that matter, everyone knows how subsidies continue to be curtailed, disinvestment continues, privatization of basic necessities such as education, health, electricity and water continues unabated, and decent labor conditions and social security remain a mirage despite the pressure put up by a "progressive" left from within the alliance which is in power. There is a need to realize that, at this juncture, the limiting side effects of "revolt from within" are quite perceptible and, if the current tactics and frameworks of understanding continue to be used, will lead to nothing more than further bludgeoning of any possible resistance and deeper co-option into the system.

In fact, in India there is a section of intellectual-activists committed to an anti-liberalization project on the grounds that liberalization has brought tremendous immiseration to common people. This section, fragmented at one level, does not owe or profess any single "political allegiance" and is comprised of people from civil society organizations, members from communist parties in their individual capacities, and some independent progressive people. The voices of "dissent" in education are also "organized," if at all, on the same lines. A notable characteristic of this group is that its analysis is seldom grounded in class relation, as a result of which it remains a fluid body of "progressive" people. This dissent has certain noticeable features: (1) it does not challenge the state; (2) the state is not seen as representing the interests of a ruling class, and is, therefore, attributed a "democratic" and "impartial" imagery; (3) the state is rather seen as a change agent (through its system of committees and commissions), which would imply at a critical juncture that it would act against the interests of capital (when committees are expected to make recommendations against privatization and the state is expected to implement them); (4) (hence) it does not see the state and market as related; (5) globalization of capital is accepted but with the clause of "with a human face," as if capital will give up its aggressively expansionist and imperialist innate character; and (6) education is seen as an autonomous powerful change agent unaffected by factors such as the division of labor, or is expressly said to be located outside the labor-capital conflict.

It needs to be realized that "the emergence of the State is a product of the social division of labor" (Mandel 1969: n. p.; Engels 1884), and in capitalism today it represents the bourgeoisie carrying forward its interests. It has been generally believed by liberal and social democratic intellectuals that the state

> stands as an impartial arbiter above the selfish contention of classes and deals justly with the respective claims of diverse "interest groups." This exalted notion of a classless state presiding over a pure democracy, based on the consent of the people, rather than engaged in the defense of the property rights of the ruling class, is the core of bourgeois-democratic ideology.
>
> (Novack 1969: n. p.)

The dangers of holding a view of the state as "impartial arbiter" in the Indian context is manifested in a variety of ways. For instance, "class," in its Marxist sense as a concept that, as Lenin (1969) suggested, must involve a "response" to "*all* cases of tyranny, oppression, violence, and abuse," to "*all* aspects of the life and activity of *all* classes, strata, and groups of the population" (69) is dismissed as incapable of analyzing the so-called complex realities of multiple subjectivities such as religious, linguistic minorities, castes, tribes, etc. In actuality, as I have argued, dismissing all-sided class analysis in favor of single-interest frameworks simply fragments the proletariat into "the people," a collection of individuals with local and shifting concerns.

The state is the biased arbitrator, which, as shown by Gramsci, maintains the status quo not only through coercion but also through building consensus. It becomes extremely difficult to treat the state as a terrain of contestation with the hope of effecting radical transformations. Unless there is a crisis of capitalism[6] (and there are internal contradictions within the ruling class that come up occasionally), the discourses, debates and dialogues are merely "entertained" by the state, and that only if they do not harm the interests of capital accumulation. Hence, there are certain implicit dangers in the existing strategy. If the state is treated as the terrain of contestation it would imply that (1) the character of the state has not been explored and challenged in the ultimate analysis; (2) the "dissent" becomes a part of the discourse initiated by the state and will function within the parameters provided by it (we have ample examples in the Indian context wherein the most significant dissenters in education have become part of state bodies such as CABE or NCERT); and (3) the battle for equality (as in the case of education) will remain limited to a few selected people located near the power-center because it is not transformed into a political battle leading to social movements due to the absence of its devolution to the affected masses through the medium of radical pro-socialist groups.

While some believe in radical changes through state apparatuses, some believe that capturing state power without transforming the capitalist relations of production that produce the state as it is will resolve the problems. They forget that both methods will fail unless the effort is supplemented consistently by popular mobilization on issues informed by a critical perception of the resistance movements – itself based in the concept of class. One of the prime reasons for the failure to weed out communalism (which has primarily taken the form of religion-based conflict and has been used extensively by the right wing as well as some of the centrist political formations) in India, apart from its analytical aspects, has been the idea that it can be fought through the state. Unless anti-communalism becomes a part of popular consciousness, which is possible only through popular mobilization, communalism will be used time and again by India's ruling class. Looking at the question of fighting through the state, Sam Gindin (2002) observes that

> Conventional wisdom has it that the national state, whether we like it or not, is no longer a relevant site of struggle. At one level, this is true. If our notion of the state is that of an institution which left governments can "capture" and push in a different direction, experience suggests this will contribute little to social justice. But if our goal is to transform the state into an instrument for popular mobilization and the development of democratic capacities, to bring our economy under popular control and restructure our relationships to the world economy, then winning state power would manifest the worst nightmares of the corporate world. When we reject strategies based on winning through undercutting others and maintain our fight for dignity and justice nationally, we can inspire others abroad and create new spaces for their own struggles.
>
> (Quoted in McLaren and Jaramillo 2003: 85)

Building the contours of a movement!

The problems before the education sector in India are massive. This magnitude is reflected in the way discourses on education have been moving, transforming the knowledge agenda into a suitable instrument of sustaining the rule of capital. It is reflected in the way the curriculum is designed and pedagogy as a whole manipulated. Bourdieu (1976) demonstrated this when he argued that schooling, or what we generally term as the education process – including the concepts that initiate the process of schooling, pedagogy, the curriculum and other components and ideas that go into the making of the system – reproduces inequality through enforcing formal equity in schooling as a mere cloak. His analysis penetrates deeper into structures and processes of education when he argues that even the choices are determined by the unequal objective conditions rather than the obviousness of the taste of the students or their vocational sense. He recognized the way power imposes meanings and makes them "legitimate" through concealing the power relations, which constitute the basis of "pedagogic action" that sustains the ruling ideas. He, along with Passeron (1990), held that

> In any given social formation the cultural arbitrary which the power relations between the groups or classes making up that social formation put into the dominant position within the system of cultural arbitraries is the one which most fully, though always indirectly expresses the objective interests (material and symbolic) of the dominant groups or classes.
>
> (9)

Bourdieu stops short of clearly identifying the enemy (the social relations and its dynamics) which produce and sustain the inequality and therefore the contours of a movement are also not present in his works. Now the question to be addressed is where would the battle begin? Should we just lie back "branding" some as reformists on the grounds that unless changes are systemic in nature there is no relevance in demanding equal education opportunities for all children? Or should we become part of the efforts of the state which uses the "progressive" voices to generate images of being "democratic"? Can there be a middle path between these contradictions? I would say no because it would entail understanding the state as immutable and would also negate the possibility of struggles for systemic transformation. As Lenin (1969) argued, "there is no middle course (for humanity has not created a 'third' ideology, and moreover, in a society torn by class antagonisms there can never be a non-class or above-class ideology)" (41). What needs to be emphasized is that the struggle for equal education opportunities is the struggle against capitalism in the same way that Saad-Filho considers the struggle for democracy as struggle against capitalism (2003: 21).

The problem has become more acute after the arrival of neoliberal global capital. Commodification has pervaded all aspects of our everyday life. The downfall of the welfare state and the emergence of a neoliberal agent in the garb of democratic states needs to be countered at every juncture. The path to systemic transformation is a prolonged one and the battles for the betterment of the lives of the oppressed and exploited have to continue simultaneously with that protracted war against capital. One such battle can be to de-commodify the sectors such as health and education. A stiff resistance would emerge from capital but, depending on the strength of mobilization, such battles can be won. The participation in commissions must be undertaken only with this understanding because it would also strengthen the people's movements and expose the contradictions of the state. Indian history is witness to the fact that up to this date none of the education committees/commissions appointed by the state could do that and the reason is simple – those who become part of those bodies do not locate the problems of education in the way highlighted above. If such a thing could not emerge now, when the different state bodies with "progressives" inside could have acted in harmony with the left parties (which support the government) on demands of de-commodifying education and health sectors, not much can be expected later. But then, being part of the instruments devised by the system on grounds that at least it would provide new recommendations for the state to implement an egalitarian education system and therefore provide the popular movements an agenda to pressurize the state, has remained a futile exercise. Even if committees have recommended anything relatively progressive such as the Ramamurti Committee (because the Kothari Commission was not a very radical move), the state has just shrugged them off. Simultaneity of different modes of struggle aimed at achieving a common aim is the only possibility in such a situation.

In this scenario, it is essential that the fight against such a system, which co-opts, generates "hope" and conflict, and creates inequality as well as provides instruments to fight this inequality, is undertaken with much care and understanding. This fight is against the rule of capital and its agent – the state. In order to further the struggle it is important that we learn to historicize – to historicize the trajectory of capital and education policy in India, which will provide answers to questions such as why the Indian state had a CSS as its policy once and why it wants to shrug it off now. It helps establish the vital linkages between the movement of capital and the changing character of the state and also allows us to understand that the welfarist education policies, though ineffective, represented particular moments of history and must be seen as such.

Struggle is also about engagement with the state, which can take place simultaneously on many planes. But what is crucial to understand and acknowledge in this struggle is to realize that efforts to transform the state from within are impossible and, even if we get space within the state, it cannot be utilized unless there are simultaneous mobilizations and expansions of democratic capacity at ground level. This ground is not located elsewhere in the same way that the working class is not located elsewhere. It is everywhere. Class conflict is omnipresent, in the form of the labor-capital conflict and in a variety of other cultural forms, as commodified life systems or as direct forms of conflict in everyday life. The deception of ideas that suggest there is no working class, and the simultaneous construction of social categories such as "intellectuals" or "journalists" or management workers who are said not to be workers, must be broken. Closely related to this is the idea of aspirations giving way to beliefs of upward mobility. It is a

> myth that it is possible for everyone to move up the ranks on the basis of hard work, fortitude, and perseverance. This justifies the social division of labor and class differentiation and mystifies the agonistic relation among the classes. When we talk about "white collar" and "blue collar" workers, we hide the existence of the working class and the fact that this class has common class interests. We hinder the development of a common class-consciousness among fractions within the working class.
>
> (McLaren and Rikowski 2001: n. p.)

Education needs to be located within this larger understanding of state and class, if radical changes like a CSS, doing away with privatization, providing equal educational opportunities of good quality for all, etc. are to be achieved at all. A critical pedagogy that locates education within the context of larger politico-economic analyses can serve as a tool of effective analysis of the concrete situation.

> It is axiomatic for the ongoing development of critical pedagogy that it be based upon an alternative vision of human sociality, one that operates outside the social universe of capital, a vision that goes beyond the market, but also one that goes beyond the state. It must reject the false opposition between the market and the state.
>
> (McLaren and Jaramillo 2003: 84)

We cannot achieve the goal of equal schooling, which is being denied by the system based on the aggressive expansion of profit-seeking capital, unless we understand the character of the system and direct our resistance based on that understanding.

Notes

1 Multi-grade teaching means teaching multiple grade levels in one classroom. Today across India one finds that primary schools (for Classes I–V) have less than five rooms. For instance, "there are still around 553,179 primary schools in the country with less than five teachers" (Kumar 2006a). The absence of basic facilities such as rooms has been justified by the arguments of multi-grade teaching as supported by the World Bank's District Primary Education Programme (DPEP) and even UN documents.

2 Part III of the Indian Constitution provides the Fundamental Rights (Articles 13–35) to Indian citizens, which, if violated, can be brought to Court, whereas Part IV of the Constitution has the Directive Principles of the State Policy (DPSP, Articles 36–51), which are only directives to the State. The State cannot be taken to Court for enforcement of those principles unlike the Fundamental Rights (Dhagamwar 2006: 57–91). Article 45 of the DPSP states that "The State shall endeavour to provide, within a period of ten years from the commencement of the Constitution, for free and compulsory education for all children until they complete the age of fourteen years." The Constitution came into force on January 26, 1950 but children up to the age of 14 years were not brought into schools until January 26, 1960. It was only in 2002 that, through the 86th Amendment to the Indian Constitution, education was made a fundamental right. But even this Amendment was half-hearted because it did not fix the responsibilities on the State and left everything to be decided. Four years later there is no central legislation to put the Amendment into effect.

3 The SSA, funded by the World Bank and other international funding agencies, has become the Indian government's flagship education program. Primary education, unlike different kinds of schemes earlier managed separately, comes under one umbrella of the SSA. The policy of the government, as discussed in this paper, is anti-poor and seeks to delegitimize the government schooling structure through curtailing resource flow and making low quality provisions.

4 NCERT is run by the Government of India and prepares the curriculum guidelines for school-going children. It has been in the thick of controversies about the writing of history textbooks and altering the textbooks after the right-wing alliance led by the Bharatiya Janata Party came to power.

5 Business process outsourcing (BPO) is the act of giving a third party the responsibility of running what would otherwise be an internal system or service. For instance, an insurance company might outsource their claims-processing program or a bank might outsource their loan-processing system. Other common examples of BPO are call centers and payroll outsourcing (Alexandrou n. d.).

6 Gramsci highlighted this crisis of capitalism:

> At a certain point in their historical lives, social classes become detached from traditional parties. In other words, the traditional parties in that particular organizational form, with the particular men who constitute, represent, and lead them, are no longer recognized by their class (or fraction of a class) as its expression ... In every country the process is different, although the content is the same. And the content is the crisis of the ruling class's hegemony, which occurs either because the ruling class has failed in some major political undertaking for which it has requested, or forcibly extracted, the consent of the broad masses (war, for example), or because huge masses (especially of peasants and petit-bourgeois intellectuals) have passed suddenly from a state of political passivity to a certain activity, and put forward demands which taken together, albeit not organically formulated, add up to a revolution. A "crisis of authority" is spoken of: this is precisely the crisis of hegemony, or general crisis of the state.

(2004: 210)

Bibliography

Alexandrou, M. (n. d.) "Business Process Outsourcing Definition." Online. Available at http://www.mariosalexandrou.com/definition/business-process-outsourcing.asp (accessed September 1, 2007).

Allman, P., McLaren, P. and Rikowski, G. (2005) "After the box people: the labour-capital relation as class constitution – and its consequences for Marxist educational theory and human resistance," in P. McLaren (ed.) *Capitalists and Conquerors: a critical pedagogy against empire*, Lanham: Rowman and Littlefield Publishers, Inc.

Bourdieu, P. (1976) "The school as a conservative force: scholastic and cultural inequalities," in R. Dale, G. Esland and M. MacDonald (eds) *Schooling and Capitalism: a sociological reader*, London: Routledge and Kegan Paul.

—— and Passeron, J.-C. (1990) *Reproduction in Education, Society and Culture*, London: Sage Publications.

Census of India (2001) "Census Data Online, Socio-cultural Aspects." Online. Available at http://www.censusindia.gov.in/Census_Data_2001/Census_Data_Online/Social_And_Cultural/Lite (accessed April 10, 2008).

"Compulsory education bill: no consensus" (2005) *The Hindu* (July 15). Online. Available at http://www.hinduonnet.com/2005/07/15/stories/2005071516111200.htm (accessed July 2, 2007).

Dhagamwar, V. (2006) "Child rights to elementary education: national and international provisions," in R. Kumar (ed.) *The Crisis of Elementary Education in India*, New Delhi: Sage Publications.

Dogra, C. S. (2005) "Private lessons," *Outlook* (April 25). Online. Available at http://www.outlookindia.com/full.asp?fname=Punjab%20(F)&fodname=20050425&sid=1 (accessed April 25, 2007).

"Education Bill Stuck in CABE" (2005) *The Indian Express* (July 15). Online. Available at http://www.indianexpress.com/archive/StoryO-74434-Education-bill-stuck-in-CABE.html (accessed February 12, 2007).

Engels, F. (1884) *The Origin of the Family, Private Property, and the State*. Online. Available at http://www.marxists.org/archive/marx/works/1884/origin-family/index.htm (accessed June 4, 2007).

—— (1894) "The future Italian revolution and the socialist party." Online. Available at http://www.marxists.org/archive/marx/works/1894/01/26.htm (accessed September 12, 2006).

Gindin, S. (2002) "Social justice and globalization: are they compatible?" *Monthly Review*, 54, 2(June): 1–11.

Government of India (GOI) (1966) *Education and National Development: report of the education commission 1964–6*, Ministry of Education, New Delhi: Government of India.

—— (2000) *DPEP Calling*. Vol. VI, No. 11 (December). Online. Available at http://www.educationforallinindia.com/page154.html (accessed July 12, 2007).

—— (2001a) *The Tenth Five Year Plan*. Vol. 2. New Delhi: Planning Commission.

—— (2001b) *Literacy and Levels of Education in India 1999–2000*. Report No. 473 (55/1.0/11), National Sample Survey 55th Round, December, National Sample Survey Organization, New Delhi: Ministry of Statistics and Implementation.

—— (2004) "Report of the PPP sub-group on social sector public private partnership," New Delhi: Planning Commission (November).

—— (2006a) *Towards Faster and More Inclusive Growth: an approach to the 11th five year plan*. (Draft for circulation and comments. This has yet to be approved by the Planning Commission), Planning Commission, New Delhi: Government of India (June 14).

—— (2006b) Economic Survey 2005–6, Economic Division, New Delhi: Ministry of Finance.

Gramsci, A. (2004) *Selections from the Prison Notebooks*, Chennai: Orient Longman.

Hill, D. and Cole, M. (2004) "Social Class," in D. Hill and M. Cole (eds) *Schooling and Equality: fact, concept and policy*, London and New York: RoutledgeFalmer.

International Institute for Population Sciences (IIPS) and ORC Macro (2000) *National Family Health Survey (NFHS-2), 1998–9*. India, Mumbai: IIPS.

Jha, L. K. (2004) "Municipal school at G. B. Road may be dismantled," *The Hindu* (December 27). Online. Available at http://www.thehindu.com/2004/12/27/stories/2004122703370400.htm (accessed July 12, 2007).

—— (2005) "Coca Cola municipal schools coming," *The Hindu* (January 3). Online. Available at http://www.thehindu.com/2005/01/03/stories/2005010311240300.htm (accessed July 15, 2007).

Kumar, K., Priyam, M. and Saxena, S. (2001a) "Looking beyond the smokescreen: DPEP and primary education in India," *Economic and Political Weekly*, 36, 7: 560–8.

—— (2001b) "The trouble with para-teachers," *Frontline* (November 9). Vol. 18, Issue 22. Online. Available at http://hinduonnet.com/fline/fl1822/18220930.htm (accessed July 8, 2007).

Kumar, R. (2005) "Education, State and Class in India: Towards a Critical Framework of Praxis," *Mainstream*, XLIII, 39: 19–26.

—— (2006a) "When *Gandhi's Talisman* no longer guides policy considerations: market, deprivation and education in the age of globalisation," *Social Change*, 36, 3: 1–46.

—— (2006b) "Equality, quality and quantity: mapping the challenges before elementary education in India," in R. Kumar (ed.) *The Crisis of Elementary Education in India*, New Delhi: Sage Publications.

—— (2006c) "Educational deprivation of the marginalized: a village study of Mushar Community in Bihar" in R. Kumar (ed.) *The Crisis of Elementary Education in India*, New Delhi: Sage Publications.

—— and Paul, R. (2006) "Institutionalising discrimination: challenges of educating urban poor in neoliberal era," in S. Ali (ed.) *Managing Urban Poverty*, New Delhi: Council for Social Development and Uppal Publishing House.

Lenin, V. I. (1969) *What Is To Be Done? Burning Questions of Our Movement*, New York: International Publishers.

McLaren, P. and Jaramillo, N. E. (2003) "Critical pedagogy as organizational praxis: challenging the demise of civil society in a time of permanent war," *Revista Praxis*, 3(November): 71–103.

McLaren, P. and Rikowski, G. (2001) "Pedagogy for revolution against education for capital: an e-dialogue on education in capitalism today," *Cultural Logic*, 4, 1. Online. Available at http://clogic.eserver.org/4–1/mclaren%26rikowski.html (accessed May 12, 2007).

Mandel, E. (1969) "Marxist theory of the state." Online. Available at http://www.marxists.org/archive/mandel/1969/xx/state.htm (accessed January 10, 2005).

Mukherjee, A. (2002) *Imperialism, Nationalism and the Making of the Indian Capitalist Class 1920–47*, Delhi: Sage Publications.

Nambissan, G. (1995) "Human rights education and dalit children," *PUCL Bulletin* (April). Online. Available at http://www.pucl.org/from-archives/Dalit-tribal/education.htm (accessed October 23, 2007).

—— (2004) "Integrating Gender Concerns," *Seminar*, No. 536 (April). Online. Available at http://www.india-seminar.com/cd8899/cd_frame8899.html (accessed February 3, 2006).

—— (2006) "Terms of inclusion: dalits and the right to education," in R. Kumar (ed.) *The Crisis of Elementary Education in India*, New Delhi: Sage Publications.

National Sample Survey Organisation (NSSO) (2001) "Literacy and levels of education in India 1999–2000," NSS 55th Round, July 1999–June 2000, Report No. 473 (55/1.0/11), Ministry of Statistics and Programme Implementation, New Delhi: Government of India.

Novack, G. (1969) "Foreword," in E. Mandel *Marxist Theory of State*. Online. Available at http://www.marxists.org/archive/mandel/1969/xx/state.htm (accessed October 5, 2007).

Saad-Filho, A. (2003) "Introduction," in A. Saad-Filho (ed.) *Anti-Capitalism: a Marxist introduction*, London and Sterling: Pluto Press.

Tilak, J. B. G. (1996) "How free is 'free' primary education in India?" *Economic and Political Weekly*, 31, 4–5: 275–82.

4 Class, "race" and state in post-apartheid education

Enver Motala and Salim Vally

Abstract

The elision of social class as an analytical category impoverishes social analyses and has profound implications for social transformation. Social class analysis has been largely ignored in analytical taxonomies in post-apartheid South Africa.

When social class is referred to in education analyses it is all too often understood as a descriptive term rather than an explanatory concept. As a descriptive term, it is used mostly to recognize the social location of students as "poor," or "disadvantaged," to evoke characterizations of the conditions prevalent in "poor" and "disadvantaged" communities, and to provide testimony for the rigors of school life, the intractability of the problems of access, the grinding incapacities and effects on the lives and potential opportunities for the children of the "poor." These descriptions make graphically evident the educational symptoms that typify the conditions under which the majority of South Africans learn, but do not address the cause of these conditions – the capitalist system. This chapter attempts to correct this limitation by "restoring" the value of class analysis.

We argue that the absence of class analysis leads to a debilitating failure to appreciate the deeper characteristics of society; de-links poverty and inequality from the political, economic and social system – capitalism – which underpins them; obscures the class nature of the post-apartheid state; renders ineffective social and educational reforms; and denies the importance of class struggle and the agency of working communities in the struggle for social transformation.

While this chapter reaffirms the previously dominant discourse in the movement against apartheid which recognized the salience of class and valued class analysis, it also examines the relationship between class, "race" and gender under racial capitalism historically and in contemporary South Africa. Finally, the chapter discusses the orientation of political organizations of the left to issues of class and the impact of the negotiated settlement prior to 1994.

Introduction

Over the last few years a number of important texts have been written about the post-apartheid education system in South Africa. These have dealt with a wide variety of topics, relating mainly to the progress of the reform policies and the initiatives of the post-apartheid state. They have included writings on educational management, school governance, curriculum, language, assessment, equity, teacher education, early childhood development, adult basic education, and many other issues involving the process of educational reform in post-apartheid South Africa. These texts have also dealt with external influences on the education system and system change arising from the wider remit of state policies such as the financing of education and the democratic state's orientation to educational investment, labor markets and globalization (Sayed and Jansen 2001; Motala and Pampallis 2002; Chisholm 2004; Fiske and Ladd 2004).

Questions about social and historical disadvantage, marginalization, exclusion, poverty and inequality and other such abiding social phenomena are invariably referred to in the texts about education in South Africa, and without exception, nearly every critical commentary or analytical writing on educational reform refers explicitly to the implications of these characteristics of the educational system. These writings are at pains to point out, quite rightly, that the educational system is characterized by deep inequalities, especially noticeable in relation to poor communities, even more so in rural communities, and that there are considerable backlogs arising from the discriminatory and racist history of South African education and the deliberately distorted distribution of educational expenditures to favor white people. They emphasize, often convincingly, that the interests of the "poor and marginalized" must be the foundation on which the post-apartheid educational system has to be built and that there are constitutional and other imperatives to achieve a just, fair, equitable and humane social order. Even the mélange of official policy texts looks impressive at face value.

Yet few of these texts and policies have dealt specifically with the existence of social classes for the unfolding reform process in the aftermath of the pre-1994 negotiations. Where class is referred to, as in the case of Chisholm (2004),[1] the discussion is essentially about the *effects* of educational reform on social class formation in the post-apartheid period. Class formation is understood in its complexity as "having both a social and economic phenomenon and class is understood as having both cultural and material dimensions" (Chisholm and Sujee 2006: 144). Soudien (SADTU 2006), in a chapter titled "Thwarted access: 'race' and class," comprehensively shows how working-class communities, because of their vulnerable economic and cultural situations, feel alienated from the state's education reform process and how the provision of education continues to be structured on racial and class lines. This is of course very important, especially to show that, despite the best intentions of the reform process, there is evidence of the growth of social bifurcation through education.

Our concern here is not only about the *effects* of the reform initiatives, nor is it about issues that are endogenous to educational systems, important as these might be in themselves. An analysis of the social class effects or of how social class gets "done" is necessarily limited for our purposes even though it is of great importance otherwise, since it is concerned with issues of policy and practice, with how the resources of the state are socially distributed and who is privileged by this, and also how social class divisions are related to educational practices. These approaches to class do not – because that is not their intention – draw attention to the question of why such *effects* or processes of social reproduction are visited on some social classes more than on others in the first place and whether this is related in any way to the even more fundamental structural and relational attributes of capitalist societies.

These points of departure in the framing of educational analysis are significant but do not explain these differentiations as inherent to the forms of capitalist development in South Africa and their *a priori* implications for social systems, including education. In our view the recognition of class as an analytical category inherent in South African capitalism would provide greater clarity to social analysis and to strategic interventions. It can reveal the relationship between social class and reform and show how reform processes are constrained by the existence of particular structural conditions in society. Even if better policy choices are made, their effects are likely to be muted by the underlying characteristics of such societies where material and objective conditions define questions of access in a pre-emptive way. Analyses that do not recognize the intrinsic nature of these characteristics and the constraints they impose on reform processes will remain limited.

The absence of rigorous and complex social analysis has profound implications at another level. If the condition of poverty is not analyzed and understood as an enduring and inherent characteristic of societies at a particular stage of their historical development, in this case, as a phenomenon of capitalist development in South Africa, then the necessary interventions of social reform will be weak. This is so because such interventions are likely to be regarded as the interventions made by a "caring" welfarist state, out of a benevolent concern for the "most disadvantaged" and as a "helping hand" to such communities within the framework of "their" disadvantage. Such an approach to social policy is both patronizing and ineffectual over the long term since it does not provide any basis for mobilization against the causal basis of poverty and the deeply entrenched structures of social differentiation, nor does it address the question of social agency and the ability of such communities to use their historical experience, knowledge and traditions to deal with social disadvantage in an empowering way. This failure results largely from a "deficit" view of such communities, regarding them as being struck by the inescapable conditions of lacking the basic resources for their survival. The role of the state in such a case is inevitably conceived of not as a facilitative democratic state, in which the primacy of social agency for change is recognized, but merely as a "charitable" and social welfare state. Worse still is the fact that these deficit descriptions about the abiding characteristics of poverty are damaging because they reinforce conceptions of social change from above. In this approach, social interventions of a charitable nature are the solution to the "problem," since the "poor will always be with us."

Class analysis would enhance our knowledge of specific local school communities both individually and in relation to the society as a whole. Class analysis also implies the ability to listen critically to the voices of the most oppressed social classes because through these voices greater clarity might be achieved about the challenges of development. The praxis of some initiatives in the education field is beginning to engage democratically with working-class communities in recent times in South Africa. This dialogical interaction is an important development and must be extended methodologically and theoretically. It also has broader implications for the discourse of "development" which itself invites greater clarity through class analysis. Possibilities around "development" imply that our analysis takes account of the social pathologies, divergent interests and inherent contradictions of capitalism in South Africa. Development as an idea is an area of considerable ideological contestation and unless the many aspects of the concept of development (including how it is related to different class interests) are openly acknowledged, more is hidden than revealed in the use of the concept of development (Motala and Chaka 2004).

The absence of class analysis or in relation to other deeply inured social structures of differentiation such as gender leads to a debilitating failure in our understanding of the deeper characteristics of society and disables policy actors from seeking more penetrative social interventions in education and social policy in general. The failure to provide such analysis in education could be attributed to several factors. Firstly, it could be argued that the limitations of extant educational analysis result from the pre-occupation with a range of education policy-related matters. Analysts have concentrated largely on the state's educational reform processes and more recently on the vexed question of "implementation," sometimes de-linked from policy matters because policy itself is often regarded as unproblematic. This in turn is related to the issue of the "capacity" of government to implement policies. In our view it is not possible to view the reform of education in post-apartheid education without reference to the unfolding dynamic of the negotiation process that took place before 1994. An analysis of this process would have revealed for educational analysts the conditioned nature of reform especially in regard to its implications for working-class children.

Thirdly, while there is a wide range of references to "race" and "gender" and a great deal of statistical information of value relating to these social characterizations, they remain de-linked from any conscious appreciation of the impact of social class and its deeper structural implications on the very communities of the "poor" and "disadvantaged" which is the subject of educational theory, policy and practice. For instance, the report produced by the Nelson Mandela Foundation, *Emerging Voices* (2005), contains rich and evocative testimonies of the social conditions affecting learning in poor rural communities in South Africa. It speaks about the desolate and inhospitable conditions for children in rural schools and from communities that are severely impoverished by the circumstances of their past history in which "race" was the defining characteristic of state provision, and indeed of the trials visited upon the daily lives of young women and girl learners in communities where gendered roles are definitive. It speaks about the lack of the fundamental resources for a meaningful social life and of the difficult conditions under which learning is expected to take place. These descriptions of the conditions of "disadvantage" do not, however, set out to explain the socially relational nature of "race" and gender to class in the context of rurality, that is, their existence as expressions of much deeper, more profound and obdurate attributes of societies in which social divisions (among other divisions) are both inherent and egregious.

Fourthly, and this is understandable, greater emphasis has been placed on analyzing the state's reform initiatives within the classroom and there is quite a large body of work relating to issues of the financing of education, global influences and the privatization of public education. But as we have argued, there is a paucity of analysis regarding the non-educational "externalities" that affect classroom practice.

The project here is a modest one; it is to "restore" the value of class analysis in the traditions of South African social theory even if that is done by abandoning some of the more reductionist approaches to class analysis. It does not pretend to resolve all the historical debates about class-based analysis. It sets out only to argue why in South Africa at this time any social analysis that does not pay attention to questions of class will be impoverished by that failure.

We accept that there is much other causality for explaining social fragmentation. These causes give rise to social differentiation, incoherence, prejudice, religious and other divisions, marginalization and even violent conflicts. Ideological and political issues, too, play a huge role in defining historical conjunctures and these must be seen in a complex interplay with issues of class, "race" and gender. We therefore do not accept class reductionist approaches as adequate explanations about these conflicts, although we have no doubt that these conflicts are likely to be exacerbated by the underlying contradictions of capitalism either within nation states or globally. Nor do we, on the other hand, deny that even such conflicts might well be an expression of conflicts over social resources and wealth, conflicts germane to much class analysis. Other research is necessary to understand the nature of these conflicts, which express themselves in factionalist, sectarian, religious, territorial, ethnic and other forms of division, and we make no claim to examining all these contingent and conjunctural factors here.

The importance of "class" in social analyses

The main argument of this paper is that, while many educational analyses about South African education have great merit, they have largely ignored any direct reference to or analysis of the social pathologies and structures created by racial capitalism in South Africa and have consequently not provided any theoretical (or practical) basis for understanding the continuing and pervasive phenomena of class and its relevance to analyses of school reform in South Africa. These social pathologies are an expression of the more fundamental social cleavages that exist in society and unless understood and analyzed more fully, interventions in the schooling system alone (which are necessary and critically important) will have only a limited effect. The idea of "class" represents much more than a gradational approach to material inequality and speaks rather to the inherent consequence of a particular form of production as constitutive of class in political economy. This means that the social category of "class" represents an important expression of the historical, structural, ideological and largely refractory barriers to social mobility which characterizes class-ridden societies.

The best hopes of educationists to address these impediments through policy interventions are constrained by their very intractability and their effects on large parts of society. Our view is that no amount of educational policy or practice can, by itself, overcome these deeply entrenched and fundamental attributes of capitalist societies, and that, unless they are properly understood and analyzed, policy interventions can become no more than the capricious hopes of politicians, bureaucrats and social reformers. The latter, despite their good intentions, face, for instance, the dilemma that "legally and politically sanctioned demands and guarantees remain unreconciled to exigencies and capacities of the budgetary, financial and labor market policy of the capitalist economy" (Offe 1974: 37).

The analysis here will also show how the category of "class" is significant not only in itself but relationally in its connectedness to questions about "race" and gender, and that educational analysis in South Africa about these categories is rarely connected with questions of class. "Race" in particular is examined largely in relation to the achievement of greater "race" equity and the quantification of improvements in relation to it. Where "race" is used for analytical purposes, moreover, its use is explained as historically necessary given the policies and practice of the apartheid state in the allocation of resources and the continuing existence of racially defined school cohorts. Its justification is therefore largely about questions of output and measurement, for evaluating the progress of reform and the achievement of the goals of equity.

Very little, if any, attention is paid to the social construction of racial identities (more especially in relation to their differing social class locations), and their pervasive effects on the lives of learners, on the curriculum, on the struggles of learners and their communities in regard to education, and in relation to educational policy and practice.[2] These socially relevant categories of analysis (class, "race" and gender) must be used in an integrative way to produce a more diverse and complex yet more illuminating picture about the combination of forces that shape educational policies and practice. This is because their combination as social and historical factors has had particularly devastating effects on working-class communities.

Back in 1999 it was argued that the shadow of apartheid ideology continued to cast its Stygian gloom, not any longer through racially explicit policies, but by proxy and exclusions on the basis of social class (Vally and Dalamba 1999). It was understood that a study of post-apartheid racial integration in schools had first to acknowledge racism as linked to capitalism in South Africa and to understand it in its historical context. Racism is woven deeply into the warp and woof of South African society and nothing short of transformation of the social totality can overcome it. The authors of the South African Human Rights Commission report supported the view that racial inequality in schools was not merely an aberration or an excrescence, but structurally linked to wider social relations and the economic, political and social fabric of society. The apartheid education system engineered "race," class, gender and other categories to serve and reinforce the political economy of the racial capitalist system. Present-day racism in education in South Africa has to be understood with reference to this history and to contemporary political and economic disadvantage and patterns of inequality in society. Racism in education does not constitute an autonomous form of oppression, but rather is inextricably linked to power relations and reproduced in conjunction with class, gender and other inequalities.

Social class as an analytical and conceptual category has been a casualty of the post-apartheid period. Initially, the post-1994 period signaled a pre-occupation with the immediacy of the reform process in which "consensus," "mediation" and "social compact" were given primacy, and because of the relationship between these reform processes and the ideological ascendancy of particular globally hegemonic capitalist approaches to "modernization" and "development." Postmodern theory, in vogue during this period, was used as a justification for the retreat from class, made even more seductive by its coincidence with the negotiated settlement and the illusionary "miracle of the New South Africa." It could be argued that intellectuals in South Africa have themselves been complicit in the elision of class as an analytical category, quite often consciously and disparagingly. There is also the possibility of timidity in the face of the avalanche of academic and public voices representing capital, which have made any reference to class seem both archaic and "ideological," as though these voices are themselves not ideological. The epic histories of class struggles and the associated political, social and economic analyses representing the viewpoint of Marxism appear to be transcended in this period by other "free-from-class" analytical paradigms, both in South Africa and elsewhere. In our view, this is consistent with the decline of the scholarship which represented the strength of such analyses, itself a victim of the self-censorship imposed by scholars on any work that overtly recognized the importance of social class.

We support the assertion of Saul (2006) in a chapter titled "Identifying Class, Classifying Difference" that class analysis and class struggle imply

> a crucial demand to transcend the structural and cultural limits of capitalism that is too easily lost to view, not only by post-modernists but also within the commonsensical hegemonies and glib universalisms that currently haunt us. It is a discourse that is both central to human emancipation and essentially non-co-optable either by liberalism or reformism.
>
> (88)

Class and "race" in South Africa

The events of the last two decades of apartheid, especially the importance of working-class mobilization around specifically class issues (in conjunction with more general issues of political and social rights) and the vigorous contestation around the relationship between such forms of mobilization and the "national question," could hardly have been irrelevant to an understanding of the apartheid state and its demise, nor indeed of the particular form of post-apartheid compromise and social compact. Analysis which does not pay careful attention to the interaction between class and the "national question" in the last decades of apartheid is likely to represent a truncated version of South African history and should not be taken seriously.

In South Africa itself, and throughout the period of the 1970s and 80s, debate about class analysis characterized a vast array of writings including historical studies, sociology, political science and economic analysis in particular (Lipton 1986; Legassick 1973; Wolpe 1988; Fine 1990). There is evidence of similar analyses in earlier writings too (Roux 1964; Simons and Simons 1969). A number of these analyses attempted to explain the relationship between "race" and class in South Africa and how this relationship is conceptualized as critical to an understanding of the struggle against apartheid.

For instance, in an interview with Callinicos (1992), Alexander talks about how "pre-existing social relations" were transformed by the development of mining capitalists at the end of the nineteenth century, drawing a necessary connection between the development of capitalism and racism. The consequence for him was that it was not possible to get rid of racism without dealing with its "capitalist underpinnings in South Africa." He refers to Wolpe's (1988) writing on the subject approvingly as clarifying the "contingent" relationship between racism and capitalism:

> At certain times racial ideology was and is functional for the accumulation of capital, whereas at other times it could be dysfunctional. So there is no necessary connection, it is a contingent one ... This is of course a different thesis from the liberal thesis, which is that racism is allegedly dysfunctional in regard to capital accumulation.
>
> (115–16)

In a more recent article on the subject, Alexander (2004) deals specifically with the question of how "race" is understood outside the domain of human biology where its "invalidity" is acknowledged but where "inherited perceptions" remain:

> The articulation of race science and stereotypes deriving from perceptions of racial difference is a manifestation of the social constraints on the integrity of academic and professional practices. Nonetheless, as a social construct, race is real and has obvious pertinent material effects. On these matters, there is more than sufficient consensus in the social sciences today.
>
> (1)

Alexander (2004) relates these perceptions to colonial conquest and particularly to the second British occupation of the Cape. For him, "race theory in South Africa is not the excrescence of Afrikaner nationalism in the first instance. The prime suspects are in fact British soldier-administrators, missionaries and other organic intellectuals of British imperialism" (3).

Alexander (2004) questions both "idealist and economic reductionist" theorizations of racism and argues for a "historical materialist" analysis of the causal factors explaining racism. In regard to the relationship between "race" and "class" he argues that it could be reasonably generalized

> that conservative and liberal-pluralist approaches have tended to attribute to the category of "race" an independent causal value, however different the levels of sophistication of individual analysts might be. On the other hand, radical approaches have tended to veer in the direction of broadly economic reductionist or, more narrowly, class reductionist, explanations. Political developments in the world and in South Africa during the last 15 years of the 20th century left their influence in the form of a kind of paradigm drift that affected all these schools of thought. On all sides, there has been a shift to a much more pragmatic stance

in social science scholarship. In the case of some formerly avowed Marxist approaches, one is tempted even to speak of a return to empiricism.

(5)

Du Toit (1981) too sees apartheid as an integral part of capitalism in South Africa. He too regards the struggle against apartheid as inseparable from that against capitalism in South Africa and refers to Legassick's (1973) view that "National oppression is simply a *form* of social oppression, but a form which calls forth its own anti-thesis: 'national liberation'" (Du Toit 1981: 461). In a similar vein, in his introduction to *Race, Class and the Apartheid State*, Wolpe (1988) complains about the "undeveloped" nature of South African analyses of the state and politics. For Wolpe, the preoccupation with racial concepts in the definition of the "society" in South Africa results in a perspective on the state which treats that state "as the instrument of oppression of Whites over Blacks but (precisely because class relationships are not normally included in the analysis) as neutral in the relationship between classes" (7). He makes this complaint in the context of the increasing political conflict of the 1980s in South Africa in which the apartheid state was confronted by a militant organization intent on its overthrow. These challenges threw up a number of important theoretical questions. They raised questions about how the relationship between "race and class" was conceived and how the relationship between the "political structure" and the "capitalist economy" was understood. Clarification on these issues was important not only for theoretical purposes but also to inform political perspectives and objectives.

Wolpe (1988) argued that where "race" is given primacy in the analysis of apartheid, the state would be regarded as "exclusively a racial order." Against this he ascribes to the African National Congress and South African Communist Party (SACP) the view that is informed by the theory of South Africa as a colony "of a special type," a theory based "on a conception of linkages between race and class, ... which accords to the black working class a leading role in the overthrow of the apartheid system" (1).

For Wolpe (1988), "race" and class stand in a "contingent relationship" to the South African capitalist economy and "white domination," and the idea that racism was functional and necessary to capitalist development, forecloses any analyses of the "uneven, asymmetrical, contradictory and unstable" nature of the relationship between capitalism and "race."

Wolpe (1988) uses the concept of "class" in a Marxist sense, while "race" is used strictly to refer to social categorizations. In his critique of Wolpe's *Race, Class and the Apartheid State*, Fine (1990) argues that Wolpe regards class, in the South African context, as an "abstraction," while regarding race as a "concrete social reality" (1–118). Fine (1990) attributes Wolpe's analysis to Wolpe's "economistic" conception of class, which "Reduces the relation between capital and labour to a merely economic relation removed from all juridic, cultural, sexual and political dimensions ... and leads directly to a reification of race despite all warnings against 'race reductionism'" (92).

Indeed, Fine (1990) argues that this approach to "race" and class prepares the ground for Marxists to endorse nationalism. For Fine, the very idea of race in South Africa is the "critical ideological glue" that underwrites the social order and power relations. The idea of "race" confronts the population as though it is real while in fact it is "the ideological expression" of the particular form of exploitation. He argues that "the state demands that people behave as if race is, whatever they actually believe in their heart of hearts." The consequence of this is that "people reproduce the lie as reality" and by so doing they are not only oppressed by apartheid but reproduce its lies and "hypocrisy" in their daily lives (93). For Fine "race" is not "real." It is, in his words, "the illusion of those who exercise power and seek profit at the expense of life. It is the triumph of abstraction over reality, the lie over truth" (94).

We are not persuaded by Fine as to the "unreal" and "hypocritical" nature of the concept of "race" because it oversimplifies the complex relation between "race" and class. The view of the Trinidadian Marxist C. L. R. James, quoted in Walter Rodney's seminal work *How Europe Underdeveloped Africa* (1983), is apposite here:

> The race question is subsidiary to the class question in politics, and to think of imperialism in terms of race is disastrous. But to neglect the racial factor as merely incidental is an error only less grave than to make it fundamental. (100)

While "race" is not an adequate explanation for exploitative processes or for the structural attributes of capitalist political and economic systems, that does not automatically imply that it has no explanatory value in relation to "class" and the process of exploitation. Indeed, it is precisely because racist policies and strategies have come to be used in societies, both for capitalist accumulation and for engendering social conflict, and by the ruling class of global hegemonic states like the US to advance their global exploitative interests, that ideas about "race" (and other such discursive categories such as "civilization" and "culture") have such powerful meanings in the public consciousness, in global politics and ultimately in the control over resources. Although the US does not use explicitly racial language in its ideological discourses, it has been cogently argued that its discourse and practice is racist nonetheless. This is because it is premised on false conceptions about "modernity" and "pre-modernity," the "clash of civilizations" and "culture talk" and such ideas which mask its underlying imperialist intentions (Ali 2002; Mamdani 2004).

The last two decades have shown how pervasive the impact of racist stereotyping has been in the orientation of Western institutions and states towards the people of the Middle East[3] in this phase of "accumulation by dispossession" (Harvey 2003). The pervasiveness of the impact means that, despite the seeming "modernity" and "rationality" of Western governments and their ideologues together with international agencies like the World Bank, the International Monetary Foundation and the World Trade Organization, these entities continue to define societies, whole continents and civilizations in racialized terms. This reality can hardly be explained away as signifying nothing more than "hypocrisy," even though it is true that the idea of "race" is not sustainable from any scientific perspective and has limited explanatory value for the purpose of understanding political economy and capitalist forms of exploitation.

The history of post-colonial Africa, where deep divisions based on constructions of "race," "ethnicity," religion and other affinities have wreaked havoc over many societies, is testimony to the impact of this reality. While these conflicts may sometimes be attributable to conflicts over resources, they are not easily explained away by that alone. Simply rejecting these deeply embedded social norms, practices and histories, often developed over many centuries preceding the advent of capitalist accumulation, as "hypocrisy" is disarming and does not provide a basis for understanding them. In other words, the idea that "race" (or other such conceptions and practices) is a social construct does not automatically imply that it has no explanatory value especially about how power is constituted through racist categories and/or gender to reinforce the structural attributes and impediments of working-class lives. The explanatory value of "race" and gender lies in the power to reveal the relationship between these social constructs and class without suggesting that they provide a better explanation of "exploitation."

The fact that "race" alone is less able to explain the objective and material basis of exploitation in relation to the law of value is therefore not simply a reflection of the underlying material basis of exploitation. It is in fact a concrete expression of and inseparable from the racist forms of control over the labor process in capital accumulation in South Africa. It is not simply imagined. "Race," in certain historical conjunctures, provides the particular form, defines the content of exploitative relations by giving it such a form (historically, especially outside Europe), and defines the modalities for the extraction of surplus value. The entire edifice of legal norms and repressive legislation predicated on racial forms has no meaning unless it is understood as the developed expression of capitalist exploitative practices and controls over the working class.

Understanding the role of ideology fully and its construction of forms of subjectivity that reinforces class domination are essential. Ideology allows capitalist relations to be concealed, blocked from being grasped conceptually, by the empirio-experiential actuality of racist practices. And because the empirio-experiential trumps the theoretical, the root cause of inequity is accepted as and ascribed to the empirical – to "race," in this case – rather than to capitalist relations. Ideology is rooted in and impacts on the material and cannot be reduced to falsehood.

The limited understanding of ideology also goes to the root of how knowledge is accessed – epistemic questions. An unintended consequence of reductionist conceptions of class is the effacing of the concrete and lived experiences of the working class and of women in racialized societies. This also explains the failure to pay attention to the impact of racism within advanced Western capitalist societies themselves, and the view that it has a limited impact in such societies. In reality deeply racist practices continue to abide in these societies because of the nature of their predatory relationship with countries of the Majority World whose resources they largely control. The necessity for these controls is no less an objective basis for, and an expression of, racist and globally hegemonic, even if contradictory, relations that pertain between advanced capitalism and the rest of the world.

Regrettably, even many left-leaning scholars and activists, especially those who are schooled in Marxism in the West, continue to be dismissive of racism as intrinsic to global capital's agenda and therefore do not fully understand the relationship between "race" and exploitation on a world scale. As a consequence, they do not understand the specificities of accumulation in developing societies as these are affected by globally organized structures in which forms of difference – "cultural," "racial," "religious," etc. – are fundamental to capitalist accumulation.

How the relationship between "race" and class is conceptualized is, therefore, of great epistemological value because it speaks to the privileging or the denial of particular experiences. In South Africa, the struggles against apartheid are also testimony to the developed consciousness of working-class organizations in their understanding of "race" and other forms of division. A great deal of emphasis was placed by these organizations on policies and campaigns about how racism must be dealt with in practice in the struggles against apartheid capitalism. Without these experiences, the ideas and values of intellectuals unschooled in the context of racialized working-class struggles become increasingly dominant.

While "race" alone is not adequate to explain relations of production and the process of exploitation, it has huge explanatory value in the analysis of the particular forms of power – state, legal systems and dominant ideologies – which class analysis *alone* does not do. Marxist approaches to theorization are considerably more enriching and explanatory of the complex relationship of the forms of capital accumulation and power in developing societies. To wit, the experiences of racialized and gendered workers are important as a source of knowledge of the processes of exploitation and the state and cultural practices that reproduce an inequitable hierarchy of racialized and gendered workers, and these experiences need to be understood in the framework of the social relations of production.

The argument here can be exemplified by reference to the debates between Critical Legal Theorists and Critical Race Theorists in the US where issues of "race" and class have a similar resonance in social analysis. There the adherents of a school of thinking described as "new left" activists at the Conference on Critical Legal Studies had argued that liberal and conservative approaches to the law regarded the law as separate from politics. This untenable distinction between law and politics was based on the idea that legal institutions are based on "rational, apolitical and neutral discourse with which to mediate the exercise of social power." Politics, they argued, was embedded in legal categories with the very "doctrinal categories with which law organized and represented social reality." This meant that the political character of judicial decision making was obscured by technical discussions about "standing, jurisdiction and procedure" based on such concepts as "rules, standards and policies" (Crenshaw, *et al.* 1995: xviii).

This critical tradition was a precursor to what came to be known as Critical Race Theory. It drew on Critical Legal Theory and the civil rights movement and was intent on developing and enriching the former by adding a "race intervention into left discourse" and a "left intervention into race discourse" (Crenshaw, *et al.* 1995: xviii.). Its perspective that law was not neutral was useful and "formed the basic building blocks of any serious attempt to understand the relationship between law and white supremacy" (xxii). For it, "race and racism functioned as central pillars of hegemonic power" in the US and it saw the "rights" discourse as legitimating "the social world by representing it as rationally mediated by the rule of law" (xxiii).

Critical Race Theory speaks to the "embeddedness" of the practices and values of racism, despite these not being formally manifested. It argues that the forms of power which existed prior to the formal and legal recognition of discriminatory policies continue to exist through the distribution of resources and power and that concepts of merit continue to obfuscate the reality of privilege and power in favor of those who determine the very meaning of "merit." The ostensibly neutral "baseline" is in reality heavily laden with particular distributions of power and privilege. Critical Race Theory would therefore "neither apologize for affirmative action nor assume it to be a fully adequate political response to the persistence of white supremacy" (Crenshaw, *et al.* 1995: xxx). It also argues that the failure of liberal (and even left) efforts at understanding questions of racial ideology and power truncates its approach to global politics – and, what Claude Ake, cited in Crenshaw, *et al.* (1995), called, the "hierarchization of the world" (xxviii)

Matsuda (1995), in a chapter in Crenshaw, *et al.* (1995), too, is critical of the "unsophisticated rights-thinking that can be a seductive trap for those on the bottom" (64). For Matsuda it is important that the oppressed themselves are skeptical of the claim that the law is free from value, politics, or historical conditions, believing that the skills of interpreting social questions are enhanced by the direct experience of oppression. Matsuda suggests that

> Those who have experienced discrimination speak with a special voice to which we should listen ... the perspective of those who have seen and felt the falsity of the liberal promise ... can assist critical scholars in the task of fathoming the phenomenology of law and defining the elements of justice.
>
> (63)

We might add that the experience of racism can enhance an understanding of class and the particular forms of capitalist power in those parts of the world subjected to the most brutal and racialized forms of exploitation and oppression and that such experience and reflecting upon it would augment the power of class based analysis.

According to Ruccio, Resnick and Wolff (1991), "class" also has great relevance in the context of global capitalism. The changes now characteristic of global capitalism through the activities of multinational corporations, the rapid changes in national stock and capital markets, and the existence of rapid transmission information networks were preceded by similar sea changes in the production system at the turn of the last century. Does the rapid development of capitalism beyond the confining limits of the nation state "mean that we are also beyond class, as proclaimed in so many quarters," they ask. Their unequivocal answer is that they do not think so:

> We argue that the tendency of class to be de-emphasized (or forgotten altogether) in analyses of global capitalism loses something very important for understanding critical issues in the world today – from calls for protecting national markets or, alternatively, for "belt-tightening" in the face of international competition to debates about the contours of postmodernism.
>
> (26)

After reviewing competing orientations to the problem of how class is situated in this nexus of national and international dimensions of capitalist development, Ruccio, Resnick and Wolff (1991) conclude that there are serious limitations in these approaches to understanding the import of class analysis against the background of such international development. Although in the approaches they review, class is recognized, "a problem from our perspective arises when class is made secondary to those other processes and therefore is displaced from the centre of analysis or from analysis altogether" (28). Against this, their proclaimed purpose is to address "some of the important space (and time) dimensions of class processes" in understanding the relationship between nation-states and international relations and to examine "international value flows" from a class perspective defined in terms of "surplus labour"(29). In their view, the increasing role of international economic activities requires that analyses should foreground the class dimensions of society if change is to be achieved. This is especially important for conceptions of social justice and democracy that include the notion of collective public participation in the "production, appropriation, and distribution of the surplus labours they perform" (37).

This approach to globalization would be enriched by also focusing (together with class) on the particular "non-class" strategies adopted by imperial powers, for instance, the manipulation by them of "political Islam" and other social fractures to advance the interests of global capitalism.

National Democratic Revolution

As we argued earlier, questions about class (and "race") are not only of theoretical value. They also have great relevance to the question of political practice, the orientation of political organizations of the left to issues of class formation, class alliances and compromises, and the very strategies and tactics formulated in struggles for revolutionary social change. The analytical usage of class in South Africa is closely linked to conceptions of the National Democratic Revolution (NDR). In this paper we cannot traverse the wide literature about the NDR, which has been the subject of considerable debate for many decades in relation to the liberation movement's strategy. More recently – in the post-1994 period – the issue of the NDR has been raised in the conferences of the African National Congress (ANC), South African Communist Party (SACP) and the Congress of South African Trade Unions (COSATU). It is clear that the content of the NDR remains contentious and will continue to be the subject of discussion and debate, and that it is profoundly linked to the question of the leadership of the NDR and class alliances, class struggle and the outcomes of the transformation process in South Africa.

At a 2005 conference of COSATU, a key paper (COSATU 2005) complained about the absence of class analysis in post-apartheid South Africa and posited the view that, for the SACP, the main task of the "post-liberation" period was that of advancing the NDR "whose main content is the liberation of black people in general, and African people in particular, from the oppression of colonialism, racism and apartheid" (1). It argued that this implies more than "formal political liberation" and the existence of formal institutions of political democracy and insisted that it include the idea of socioeconomic liberation which would free the "black majority from the socio-economic legacy of poverty, underdevelopment, exploitation and inequality." Moreover, this liberation was to be achieved by the actions of a "bloc of class forces among the historically oppressed, with the working class playing a leading role." It recognized the influence of different class forces on the unfolding of the NDR and reasserted the importance of understanding the dynamics of class struggle (2).

The COSATU paper's analysis refers to shifts in the state's recent orientation to interventionist policies, its adherence to the idea of a "developmental state," the recognition of market failure and realization of the weaknesses of neoliberal prescriptions. The document attributes these shifts largely to the ANC's engagements with its mass base driven by electoral concerns more than any "major breakthrough" at the level of policy and the agreement "among all the class and strata forces represented in the ANC on the need for a more interventionist policy, a developmental state, etc. – all of this in a context of greater tolerance for this in the global conjuncture" (COSATU 2005: 13).

Many of the issues reflected in the debate on the nature of class construction in the apartheid period have an obvious resonance with the issues that have arisen in the context of a discussion of the NDR today and it would be foolhardy to pretend that the positions adopted within the alliance foreclose on other approaches to the "national question" which are not traversed here. For instance, in criticizing Wolpe's position on the NDR, Buroway (2004) speaks specifically of the view which he attributes to Wolpe and which it can be argued is substantially that of the SACP (despite his disagreements about the "colonialism of a special type" thesis). Buroway criticizes Wolpe's position because Wolpe

> could not imagine separating the socialist project from the national bourgeois project. At most he saw this as a clash of the short term and long term interests so that the National Democratic Revolution would be the first stage and the socialist revolution the second stage. He didn't see what Frantz Fanon saw: two very different, opposed projects that existed side by side, that vied with each other within the decolonization struggle. If the national bourgeois road were taken then, according to Fanon, hopes for a socialist road would be ground to zero.
>
> (22)[4]

In a prescient talk given in 1992, Neville Alexander (1994) argued that "the present strategy of the ANC never was and does not have the potential to become the continuation of a revolutionary strategy for the seizure of power" (66). Alexander predicted that the eventual settlement would be for a power-sharing arrangement between Afrikaaner and African nationalism in which the *denouement* would be at the expense of the urban and rural poor.

Factors which persuaded the ANC–SACP leadership to probe a historic compromise in about 1986–7 included the collapse of the Soviet Block; the destabilization policies in Southern Africa; the fatigue and exhaustion of the struggles of the 1980s; and the "overt and subtle arm-twisting by the liberation movement's imperialist 'benefactors'" (Alexander 1994: 86). The political registers of the ANC and the fundamental outline of post-apartheid South Africa all became negotiable. Alexander agreed that all negotiations imply compromise but responded to this banal statement by arguing that, "if the purpose is to place oneself in control of the levers of the state power within a capitalist framework, one has to realize and accept that the end effect will be to strengthen, not to weaken and much less destroy, that system" (87).

After the negotiated settlement in South Africa, the state tried to convey itself as a neutral force and as the promoter of a "fraternity of common purpose." It did this through its "stakeholder" representation in the policy making process, which led many to assume that there were no conflicting interests in establishing policies once consensus had been reached. The eagerness to overcome the legacy of apartheid, coupled with overwhelming public enthusiasm, shielded the policy making process from scrutiny. As a result, policy development churned ahead under the assumption that there were no conflicting interests once consensus was reached.

While policies were being introduced into schools, some also came out denounc-ing the national and provincial departments for "not promoting the interest of working-class communities by addressing inequalities in the education system" (South African Democratic Teachers Union [SADTU] 1998: 1). They criticized the government for failing to prevent overcrowding; failing to prevent additional costs of financing education being passed on to schools and consequently to parents; and failing to create a funding mechanism to address the disparities between the previously advantaged and the previously disadvantaged. Vally and Spreen (1998) argue that it is no longer credible to blame the crisis on poor implementation alone and suggest that the technically rational search for best practice innovations which were "cost-effective" did no more than tinker with the fundamental educational and social problems in question and ignored the mainsprings of a system and its policies that maintained, reproduced and often exacerbated inequalities. They sardonically comment that South Africa's neoliberal macroeconomic strategy is to be blamed for "the Scylla of a blurred vision and the Charybdis of obstructed implementation" (3). This does not mean that there are no feasible and practical reforms which make a difference or address issues of inequality, an area that cannot be done justice in this chapter.

Significantly, the mediatory role of the ANC-led government founded on the basis of its consensus-seeking mandate has given considerable legitimacy to its educational policy decisions. False assumptions about democracy and consensus have clouded the policy process. Furthermore, South Africa's negotiated settlement, the Truth and Reconciliation Commission, the Bill of Rights clauses in the Constitution and the establishment of institutions such as the South African Human Rights Commission, the Commission for Gender Equality, and the Public Protector have provided a fairy tale façade, often serving to disguise the often vicious nature of the society we live in (Felice 1996). The language of rights that masks privation by presenting values that are unattainable for the majority obscures this reality. These values are then meant to be the pillars upon which South African society is constructed. A single mother in a township compared to a well-heeled corporate executive cannot be said to have the same power of political persuasion or opportunity. These are real distinctions that give some people advantages and privileges over others. The fiction that promotes the view that real social differences between human beings do not affect their standing as citizens allows relations of domination and conflict to remain intact.

Locating and understanding the present reality, including inequalities in schooling, means locating and understanding the straightjacket of dominant class relations and the class formation of the present state. The ANC government came to office in 1994 on the back of promises to prioritize the redistribution of natural and human wealth/resources as the means to achieve equality. The years since have witnessed the state's clear, even if at times contested, political and ideological acceptance of the broad framework of a globally dominant, neoliberal political and economic orthodoxy. Many recent writers on the political economy of the post-apartheid South African state have concluded that, rather than an aspirational developmental state saddled with "two economies", we have neoliberalism twinned to liberal bourgeois democracy – that is, two "right wings." A reluctance to delineate this and developments leading to this outcome as the cause of generalized inequality in our society hinders the search for solutions to the egregious inequalities plaguing the schooling system.

It will be clear from the conclusions drawn that our approach to class is not simply about pointing to the effects of education policy and practice on different social classes. What we deal with here, though, is more fundamental – it is about the conceptual categories used in social analysis and the value of class analysis as critical to social and organizational thinking. In summary:

1 Extant educational analysis is limited in its explanatory power because it does not deal with the deeper implications of social class and other characteristics of developing societies and their meanings for educational reform.

2 Class analysis is critical to the question of leadership in social transformation, changing class relations, class alliances, strategy and tactics.

3 Class analysis has value for re-examination of the idea that democratic societies are identifiable through the guarantees they provide to "rights bearing citizens"; that everybody is "equal before the law"; that everyone has the same "opportunities"; and that learners are indistinguishable except by their schooling abilities. Invoking class requires a more rigorous analytical platform in which the social basis underlying the material conditions of life of education constituencies are examined so that the relations of power, consciousness and other questions also come into view.

4 Approaches to class that do not appreciate its specificities in the context of racist forms of accumulation are both reductionist and less meaningful for practice, and for understanding the way in which struggles against the specific form of capitalism in South Africa bore the imprint of its structural and other attributes. And the same can be said of the question of gender. It is not enough to analyze capital in general as though the law of value has a universal form applicable to all exploitative contexts. Put another way, the forms of exploitation (based on its historical development, including the struggles against it) prevalent in Europe, the US and other advanced capitalist systems are different from that in the developing world, and the experience of workers in these systems are very

different from each other, although surplus value is derived from exploitative relations in all instances. In this paper we have shown the relational nature of class and "race" in South Africa as intrinsic to a historical view of the process of capitalist development in South Africa. Space constraints preclude a similar analysis of the relationship between class and gender, which is also necessary.[5]

5   Although we have dealt with the relationships among issues of class, "race," gender and globalization fleetingly, there are clear relationships. Policy development that does not take this into account is likely to fail, given the implications of global change on the role of nation-states. It has been convincingly argued that there is a strong relationship between "state logic" and the role of capital in the global political economy. This has had important implications for how the nation-state is conceptualized and how class relations are constituted as a consequence. Class cannot be understood in the context of nation-states alone, since, as Tabb (2005) has argued, national policies need to speak to global issues also.

> "Policy failure" needs to be theorized in the context of the goals of policy makers, what class interests they represent, and so how "bad" policies may be the best policies available given the contradictions of capitalism. It is an economic and political system structured not only by class domestically but by North-South relations put in place by colonial and neocolonial power symmetries.
>
> (50)

6   Class analysis is inseparable from issues of class struggle. Although not dealt with here, class struggle remains the most important motive force for social change in history. The implications of this for democratic South Africa, in which the state has a critical role in mediating the effects of capitalism, need to be carefully analyzed in relation to the question of agency and social change in democratic societies.[6]

In our view, therefore, class analysis continues to have great relevance to social enquiry. It is important not only for theory but also for practice – based on clear theory and analysis. The absence of analysis based on class, especially in relation to its related categories of "race" and gender in South Africa, impoverishes our social analysis, theorization, strategies and practice. The weaknesses of any analysis invariably give rise to poor and sometimes failed strategies. Class analysis has salience in a reforming South Africa since it too is marked by the contradictions of capitalist development even while undergoing the process of social reform. Capitalist development cannot avoid these contradictions which arise from the forms of ownership and control over capital and other productive resources and the share of these resources accruing to capital and labor. An analysis of the processes of reform in South Africa must reckon with these contradictions if it is to have any explanatory value. Such analysis would indeed be ideological and not neutral and not pretend to be objective. The proponents of such analysis must declare their acceptance of the underlying tenets of their analysis based on a critique of political, social and economic systems and the underlying causes of social division and conflict.

Notes

1 Chisholm's (2004) work is an important exception in this regard. For Chisholm, the title of her book *Changing Class* "suggests both the active process of effecting change within social classes and classrooms and the nature and process of that change" (2). The major conclusion of the book relates to how present policies favor an "expanding, racially-mixed middle class" (7).

2 Analyses of gender are generally much more developed since they often speak to the social class and racial location of gendered roles and how these roles are socially constructed.

3 For instance, see the massive study of 900 films by Jack Shaheen (2001) titled *Reel Bad Arabs: how Hollywood vilifies a people.*

4 Indeed, there are other writings in the same vein which include those of Alexander, strongly critical of the SACP's approach to the "national question." Moreover, his views are derived from the important formative debates about socialist construction that took place at the turn of the nineteenth century, especially between the leaders of the Russian and European revolutionary movements of the time, and important subsequent debates around Trotsky's formulation of a Theory of Permanent Revolution. See in particular Legassick (2007).

5 Chisholm and September (2005) is a useful text for making such an analysis. It speaks about the "patchwork of patriarchies" that was structured by "race" and class in the lives and experiences of women under racial apartheid and provides rich material about the construction of gender and women's struggles in South Africa.

6 Although we do not deal with this here, there is no question about the importance of class struggle in any analysis of social change or "transformation," although this too has vanished from the language of social analysis, largely because it has been substituted by "statist" conceptions of social change which replace the agency of social movements and societies with that of the state *alone.*

Bibliography

Ali, T. (2002) *The Clash of Fundamentalisms: crusades, jihads and modernity*, London: Verso.

Alexander, N. (1992) "Interview," in A. Callinicos (ed.) *Between Apartheid and Capitalism*, London: Bookmarks.

—— (1994) *South Africa: which road to freedom?* San Francisco: Walnut Publishing Co.

—— "An introduction to perceptions and conceptions of 'race' in South Africa," Paper presented at the University of Cape Town, October 2004.

Buroway, M. "From liberation to reconstruction: theory and practice in the life of Harold Wolpe," Paper presented at the Harold Wolpe Memorial Lecture, Harold Wolpe Trust, Cape Town, 2004.

Callinicos, A. (ed.) (1992) *Between Apartheid and Capitalism*, London: Bookmarks.

Chisholm, L. (ed.) (2004) *Changing Class: education and social change in post-apartheid South Africa*, Cape Town: Zed Books and HSRC.

Chisholm, L. and September, J. (eds) (2005) *Gender Equity in South African Education, 1994–2004*, Conference Proceedings, Cape Town: HSRC.

Chisholm, L. and Sujee, M. (2006) "Tracking racial desegregation in South African schools," *Journal of Education*, 40: 141–55.

Congress of South African Trade Unions (COSATU) (2005) "Class struggles in the National

Democratic Revolution (NDR): the political economy of transition in South Africa 1994–2004, a discussion note," in *COSATU Conference to Celebrate Ten Years of Democracy, Commission on Political Transformation: labour and ten years of governance*, Book 1, Johannesburg, March 2005.

Crenshaw, K., Gotanda, N., Peller, G. and Thomas, K. (eds) (1995) *Critical Race Theory: the key writings that formed the movement*, New York: The New Press.

Du Toit, D. (1981) *Capital and Labour in South Africa, Class Struggle in the 1970s*, London: Kegan Paul International Ltd.

Felice, W. F. (1996) *Taking Suffering Seriously*, New York: State University of New York Press.

Fine, R. (1990) "The antinomies of neo-marxism, a critique of Harold Wolpe's *Race, Class and the Apartheid State*," *Transformation*, 11: 1–118.

Fiske, E. B. and Ladd, H. F. (2004) *Equity, Education Reform in Post-apartheid South Africa*, Cape Town: HSRC Press.

Harvey, D. (2003) *The New Imperialism*, Oxford and New York: Oxford University Press.

Legassick, M. (1973) "Class and nationalism in South African protest: the South African Communist Party and the 'Native Republic' 1928–1934," *Eastern African Studies*, XV: 1–67.

—— (2007) *Towards Socialist Democracy*, Durban, South Africa: UKZN Press.

Lipton, M. (1986) *Capitalism and Apartheid, South Africa 1910–1986*, London: Wildwood House.

Mamdani, M. (2004) *Good Muslim, Bad Muslim: America, the Cold War and the roots of terror*, New York: Pantheon Books.

Matsuda, M. J. (1995) "Looking to the bottom: critical legal studies and reparations," in K. Crenshaw, *et al.* (eds) *Critical Race Theory: the key writings that formed the movement*, New York: The New Press.

Motala, E. and Pampallis, J. (eds) (2002) *The State, Education and Equity in Post-Apartheid South Africa: the impact of state policies*, Sandown: Heinemann.

Motala, E. and Chaka, T. (2004) *The Case for Basic Education*, Occasional Paper 4, Johannesburg: CEPD.

Nelson Mandela Foundation (2005) *Emerging Voices: a report on education in South African rural communities*, Cape Town: NMF and HSRC Press.

Offe, C. (1974) "Structural problems of the capitalist state, class rule and the political system: on the selectiveness of political institutions," *German Political Studies*, 1: 31–57.

Rodney, W. (1983) *How Europe Underdeveloped Africa*, Harare: Zimbabwe Publishing House.

Roux, E. (1964) *Time Longer than Rope*, Wisconsin: The University of Wisconsin Press.

Ruccio, D., Stephen, R. S. and Wolff, R. (1991) "Class beyond the nation state," *Capital and Class*, 43: 25–43.

Saul, J. S. (2006) *Development After Globalisation: theory and practice for the embattled South in a new imperial age*, London: Zed Books.

Sayed Y. and Jansen J. (eds) (2001) *Implementing Education Policies: the South African experience*, Cape Town: University of Cape Town Press.

Shaheen, J. G. (2001) *Reel Bad Arabs: how Hollywood vilifies a people*, Northampton, Mass.: Interlink Publishing Group.

Simons, H. J. and Simons, R. E. (1969) *Class and Colour in South Africa – 1850–1950*, Baltimore: Penguin Books.

South African Democratic Teachers Union (SADTU) (1998) "Memorandum from SADTU to the National Economic, Development and Labour Council," April 10.

—— (2006) *A Review of the State of Education in South Africa Ten Years After 1994*, Final Report, Johannesburg: Centre for Education Policy and Development.

Tabb, W. K. (2005) "Capital, class and the state in the global political economy," *Globalizations*, 2, 1: 47–60.

Vally, S. and Dalamba, Y. (1999) "Racism, racial integration and desegregation in South African public secondary schools." A report on a study by the South African Human Rights Commission, Johannesburg.

Vally, S. and Spreen, C.A. (1998) "Education policy and implementation developments," *Quarterly Review of Education and Training in South Africa*, 5, 3: 3–22.

Wolpe, H. (1988) *Race, Class and the Apartheid State*, London: James Currey.

5 Racism and Islamophobia in post 7/7 Britain

Critical Race Theory, (xeno-)racialization, empire and education – a Marxist analysis[1]

Mike Cole and Alpesh Maisuria

Abstract

In Part 1 of this chapter, we begin by suggesting that Critical Race Theory (CRT)'s prioritizing of "white supremacy" is misleading and incomplete. We go on to argue that its valorizing of "race" over class makes it unable to connect to modes of production, and thus renders it limited in explaining various manifestations of racism, which we believe are related to moments and developments in the capital accumulation process. In Part 2, we commend the Marxist concept of racialization as having more purchase in explaining and understanding racism in contemporary Britain than "white supremacy." We go on, in Part 3, to examine British imperialism and its aftermath in terms of ongoing racialization, before looking at the connections between old and new imperialisms in the light of the increase in Islamophobia in Britain since the London bombings of July 7, 2005 (7/7). We then address, in Part 4, the upping of the barometer of xeno-racism – non-color-coded racism – and xeno-racialization, since contemporary enlargements of the European Union (EU). In Part 5, we offer an alternative vision of education to the current one, driven by the burgeoning influence of business on schools and universities, and post one from a Marxist perspective, which involves critiquing existing dominant ideas and theories in the quest to create an anti-racist learning experience for students of all ages.

Introduction

Neoliberal policies have intensified the massive disparity in wealth between the richest and the poorest. At the same time, in order to ensure the smooth continuation of the capital accumulation process, the ruling class (and well-off strata of the working population) need to keep the white, Asian, black and other minority ethnic working class conditioned for the "war on terror" and the new Imperialism (Cole 2004a). Ruling-class success in maintaining hegemony in the light of the disparity of wealth and the imperial quest was displayed in England during the 2006 Soccer World Cup by the number of St. George flags signifying a solid patriotism in run-down (white) working-class estates, on white vans, on dated cars exhibiting a "proud to be British" display. In addition, as economically active migrant workers from Eastern Europe enter the UK (a great benefit for capital, and for the middle strata who want their homes cleaned or renovated cheaply), the (white) working class, who spontaneously resist neoliberalism by resisting working for low wages that will increase their immiseration, need to be assured that they "still count." Hence the ruse of capital is to open the markets, and the role of sections of the tabloid media is to racialize migrant workers to keep the (white) working class happy with their lot with the mindset that "at least we are not Polish or Asian or black, and we've got our flag and, despite everything, our brave boys in Iraq did us proud."[2]

This chapter does not and cannot deal with the multiple complexities of racism. Instead our remit is simpler: to use the Marxist concepts of racialization and xeno-racialization[3] to show the limits of CRT in explaining the increase in Islamophobia in Britain since the London bombings of July 7, 2005 (7/7) and the upping of the barometer of xeno-racism in the context of the recent enlargements of the EU.

Part 1: two tenets of Critical Race Theory (CRT) and their limits

According to Darder and Torres (2004), CRT is grounded in "the uncompromising insistence that 'race' should occupy the central position in any legal, educational, or social policy analysis" (98). Given this centrality, for CRT "'racial' liberation [is] embraced as not only the primary but as the most significant objective of any emancipatory vision of education in the larger society" (Darder and Torres 2004: 98). The two central tenets of CRT are that "white supremacy" better describes oppression based on "race" in certain contemporary societies than does the concept of "racism"; and that "race" rather than social class is pre-eminent.[4]

Tenet I: "white supremacy" as a central and extensive form of racism

The idea that "white supremacy" captures the essence of deep-seated racism is not a new idea in the US. Indeed as Gillborn (2005) points out, it was adopted by leading US black intellectual and activist, bell hooks, in preference to racism, many years ago. As she put it in 1989:

> As I write, I try to remember when the word racism ceased to be the term which best expressed for me exploitation of black people and other people of color in this society and when I began to understand that the most useful term was white supremacy.
>
> (112; cited in Gillborn 2005: 485)

This line of argument was taken up in the late 1990s (e.g. Mills 1997) and has recently been revisited (e.g. by Gillborn 2005). "White supremacy" is reconceptualized in a way "that goes beyond the usual narrow focus on extreme and explicitly racist organizations" (Gillborn 2005: 485–6), with Critical Race Theorists arguing for the existence of "a central and extensive form of racism that evades the simplistic definitions of liberal discourse" (492), one that "is normalized and taken for granted" (486).

"White supremacy" signifies "a deeply rooted exercise of power that remains untouched by moves to address the more obvious forms of overt discrimination" (492) to which the concept of "racism" usually refers. In other words, "white supremacy" is considered more useful in certain contexts than the concept of "racism" alone because the concept of "racism" tends to put the focus on overtly racist practices that "are by no means the whole story" (491). The influence of "extreme and obviously racist positions" usually denoted by the term "white supremacy" thus "risks obscuring a far more comprehensive and subtle form of race politics" (491) – one which, it is said, is best captured by the CRT usage of "white supremacy." As Gillborn (2005: 496) argues in relation to education, "white supremacy" involves "the routine assumptions that structure the system" and "encode a deep privileging of white students and, in particular, the legitimization, defence and extension of Black inequity."

We argue, however, that the Marxist concept of racialization, in connecting to modes of production, provides a more useful analysis of racism than does the concept of "white supremacy." For example, while it is manifestly the case, as argued in this paper, that racism is widespread in UK society, as it is in societies around the globe, one significant problem with the use of the term "white supremacy" is that it homogenizes all white people together in positions of power and privilege.

This homogenization of all white people is suggested by advocacy of "white supremacy" in conjunction with the idea that we should reject the "commonsense (white-sense?) view of education policy and the dominant understanding of the functioning of education in Western societies" in favor of "the recognition that race inequity and racism are central features of the education system," and that they "are not aberrant nor accidental phenomena that will be ironed out in time," but "fundamental characteristics of the system" (Gillborn 2005: 497–8). While we agree that racism is a fundamental characteristic of the system, we will argue that the Marxist concept of racialization better explains racism both historically and contemporaneously than does the concept of "white supremacy."

The presumption that all white people are in positions of privilege, as CRT suggests, is, simply, factually incorrect. Moreover, while it is undoubtedly true that racism and xeno-racism have penetrated large sections of the white working class, resulting in racist practices that contribute to the hegemony of whites, and while it is clearly the case that members of the (predominantly though not exclusively) white ruling class are the beneficiaries of the common sense view of education policy, it is certainly not white people as a whole who hold such "power" to "structure the system." For example, sections of the white working class in England have voted for the fascist British National Party (BNP) at recent elections *precisely* because they feel that they are treated with less equality than others (Cruddas, *et al.* 2005). In addition, as we argue below in relation to xeno-racism, not all whites are in this hegemonic position.

Thus, while we would agree that the notion of "commonsense" should be rejected (as we argue below in relation to the Marxist concept of racialization), we would disagree that "commonsense" in any way equates with "white-sense" insofar as this equation claims that all whites are in positions of power and privilege.

Gillborn's conclusion that *"education policy is an act of white supremacy"* (2005: 498, italics in original) is, we would argue, misleading and incomplete. The limits to this argument are symptomatic of the narrow formulation of racism as a set of practices articulated, as it was in the days of the British Empire (for example), to biological features – "white" and "black" skin color – that signified overall biological superiority or inferiority. The Marxist concepts of racialization and xeno-racialization, discussed below, provide an explication that embraces the complexities of racism, with the latter concept facilitating an explanation of a form of racism that is not primarily color-coded.

Tenet II: valorizing "race" over "class"

The CRT position on the centrality of "race," with its concomitant lack of social class analysis or analysis of capitalism, has been articulated as follows:

> CRT offers a challenge to educational studies more generally, and to the sociology of education in particular, to cease the ritualistic citation of "race" as just another point of departure on a list of exclusions to be mentioned and then bracketed away. CRT insists that racism be placed at the centre of analyses and that scholarly work be engaged in the process of rejecting and deconstructing the current patterns of exclusion and oppression.
>
> (Gillborn 2005: 27)

For Marxists, while recognizing the crucial significance of identities other than social class, it is nevertheless class exploitation and class struggle that are constitutive of capitalism. Furthermore, in capitalism's current neoliberal form, class antagonism is greater than ever before. Racialization, we will argue, needs to be understood in terms of the role that racialization plays in the retention and hegemony of capitalism. The chief problem with CRT is that it does not frame its analyses within the context of capitalism – it does not connect with the mode of production. Indeed, the suggestion that "commonsense (white-sense?)" "structure[s] the system" inequitably (Gillborn 2005: 496) is idealist. It ignores, as Marx and Engels argued, that "life is not determined by consciousness, but consciousness by life" (Marx and Engels 1845: n. p.). A major strength of Marxism is that it does make the connection between "sense" (consciousness) and the material relations of production that (re)produce conditions in society.

Marx noted that the fundamental relation of capitalism is the relation of exploitation between the two major classes: capitalists – who own the means of production and exploit workers for surplus value (profit); and the working class – those who own only their labor power (capacity to work). Cheaper labor power by means of greater exploitation of workers means greater profits for the capitalist class, and since the rate of profit has a tendency to fall (Marx 1894), the capitalist class is always in pursuit of cheaper labor power. The capitalist class is interested in practices that (re)produce racism as a means of legitimating and justifying capital's need for cheap labor power.

The importance of the Marxist perspective is that it explains the role of racism in capitalist societies and in explaining this role indicates what it is that needs to be transformed if racism is to end: the social relations of production. In contrast, Gillborn's "white supremacy" is merely descriptive. As Gillborn himself claims, "white supremacy is actually a wholly apt descriptor of the functioning and structure of contemporary education" (2005: 498). As a "descriptor" (as we have argued, an inaccurate descriptor), it cannot explain *why* racism is continually reproduced, and therefore cannot serve as a guide for anything other than reformative, rather than transformative, practice. "White supremacy" can merely describe racism as an effect that has consequential effects.

This does not mean that CRT cannot provide insights into racism in capitalist societies; for example, its emphasis, that "people of color" need to be heard, to provide meaningful analyses of racism, is useful and particularly illuminating for those whose life experiences are restricted to monocultural settings in multicultural societies (Delgado 1995). Racism and the process of racialization can best be understood, however, by a combination of listening to and learning about the life histories and experiences of those at the receiving end of racism, and by objective Marxist analysis. The integration of objectivity with subjectivity is not yet another attempt to blur or hybridize the objective relations of production and thus take the focus away from them. There is a richness to be gained from this theoretical technique, which facilitates a synthesis of lived experience through the lens of Marxist theory and traces the "how" of life experience back to the "why" of capitalist class practices – which is always rooted in shifts in the relations of production aimed at more profit for the few, more immiseration for the many. There is thus considerable purchase in Zeus Leonardo's attempt to "integrat[e] Marxist objectivism and race theory's focus on subjectivity" (2004: 483), a move that works to ensure that the CRT concept of "voice" does not drift into postmodern "multivocality" (multiple voices) where everyone's opinion has equal worth and therefore "voice" becomes thoroughly depoliticized (Maisuria 2006).

In summary, the insistence of CRT to valorize "race" over class is significantly incomprehensive. On the other hand, Marxism has the crucial benefit of contextualizing practices in capitalist relations of production. Marxism gives priority to the abolition of class society because, without its demise, racism (as well as other forms of discrimination) is likely to continue in its various guises.

Part 2: the Marxist concept of racialization

We have flagged the Marxist concept of racialization a number of times in the preceding analysis. It is now time to define it, and to explain its relevance. Robert Miles (1989) has defined racialization as an ideological[5] process that accompanies the exploitation of labor power, where people are categorized into the scientifically defunct notion of distinct "races." Racialization, like racism, is socially constructed. In Miles's (1989) words, racialization refers to "those instances where social relations between people have been structured by the signification of human biological characteristics in such a way as to define and *construct* differentiated social collectivities" (75; our emphasis). For Miles (1987), racialization is essentially a Marxist concept. As he puts it:

the process of racialisation cannot be adequately understood without a conception of, and explanation for the complex interplay of different modes of production and, in particular, of the social relations necessarily established in the course of material production.

(7)

Whereas for postmodernists, *discourse* refers to the way in which different meanings are constructed by the readers of texts, for Marxists, all discourses are products of the society in which they are formulated. While such products can, of course, be refracted and disarticulated, dominant discourses (e.g. those of the government, of big business, of large sections of the media, of the hierarchy of some trade unions) tend to directly reflect the interests of the ruling class rather than "the general public." Racialization connects with popular consciousness, however, via "common sense." "Common sense" is generally used to denote a down-to-earth "good sense" and is thought to represent the distilled truths of centuries of practical experience, so that to say that an idea or practice is "only common sense" is to claim precedence over the arguments of left-wing intellectuals and, in effect, to foreclose discussion (Lawrence 1982: 48). Antonio Gramsci differentiated between "good sense" and "common sense." For him, the latter

> is not a single unique conception, identical in time and space. It is the "folklore" of philosophy, and, like folklore, it takes countless different forms. Its most fundamental characteristic is that it is ... fragmentary, incoherent and inconsequential.
>
> (1978: 419)

The rhetoric of the purveyors of dominant discourses aims to shape "common sense discourse" into formats that serve their interests. From a Marxist perspective, in order to understand and combat racism, we must relate it to historical, economic and political factors that shape the construction of "common sense" in the direction of racism rather than a critique of capital. It is these interconnections, which we will demonstrate henceforth, that make the concept of racialization inherently Marxist.[6]

The intensity of racialization has increased since 7/7 (and, for different reasons, since the enlargement of the EU – see below). Events such as these have provided a pretext – a "war" situation – in which it becomes justifiable to be more ruthless than ever before. For example, on the international stage, "friendly fire" that injures, maims or kills "soft targets," often unarmed citizens, becomes justifiable in the context of "war."

Tales of racist torture have become commonplace on both sides of the Atlantic. At the time of writing (February 2008), horrifying allegations of torture and killings, involving mutilation of genitalia, limb severing and eye gouging carried out by the British Army in southern Iraq have emerged.

Based on statements from witnesses, death certificates and video evidence, lawyers have claimed that 22 people were killed in British custody following an unequal firefight, about 100 miles northwest of Basra, on May 14, 2004. The lawyers allege that nine more people survived torture and abuse.

Shiner told Reuters

> This incident, if proven, is off the scale for abuse committed by either British or American troops serving in Iraq. If these harrowing allegations are proven, then you'd be pushed to be able to put it in context – it would be the worst conduct by the British army in the last 100 years.

(James 2008)

Similarly, in Britain, human rights and civil liberties, especially for Muslims and people perceived to be Muslim, are being revoked with counter-terror raids on a massive scale acting on what appears to be consistently flawed "intelligence." Two most recent examples include the tragedy of Brazilian Jean Charles de Menezes who was shot dead by the police, and of the two young British Muslim men, Mohammed Abdulkayar and Abul Koyair, where the former was also shot in the Forest Gate area of East London. Abdulkayar said, when he began to plead for mercy, one of the police officers kicked him in the face and kept telling him to "shut the fuck up" (Muir 2006: n. p.). Whereas CRT might view these actions as normal acts of white supremacy, a Marxist interpretation would relate the events to ongoing processes of state racialization.

It is important to note that racialization post 7/7 needs to be seen in the context of the convergence of the legacy of British Imperialism and current US imperialism, including the so-called "war on terror," as do xeno-racism and xeno-racialization. Xeno-racism and xeno-racialization have festered in Britain, in the context of the enlargement of the EU, and the ongoing capitalist quest for cheaper and easier to exploit human labor. The net result of these processes is that in contemporary Britain all *Others* are racialized.

We would argue that, in making these connections, racialization has more purchase in explaining and understanding racism in contemporary Britain than "white supremacy." Indeed, we would maintain that, if social class and capitalism are not central to the analysis, explanations are ambiguous and partial.

Part 3: British imperialism and its aftermath

In the old Imperial era, in order to justify the continuance of "the strong arm and brave spirit ... of the British Empire" (Bray 1911; cited in Hendrick 1980: 166), and the ongoing and relentless pursuit of expanding capital accumulation, the African subjects of the colonies were racialized in school textbooks as "fierce savages" and "brutal and stinking" (Glendenning 1973: 35), while freed West Indian slaves were described as "lazy, vicious and incapable of any serious improvement or of work except under compulsion" (Chancellor 1970: 240). When the British "race," and therefore Empire and global capital expansion, was seen to be under threat at home, foreign Jews were described at the same time by the media as "semi-barbarous," unable or unwilling to "use the latrine," depositing "their filth" on "the floor of their rooms" (Holmes

1979: 17) and involved in world conspiracy (thus directly threatening British Imperial hegemony): "whenever there is trouble in Europe," as the Independent Labour Party paper, *Labour Leader*, put it, "you may be sure a hook-nosed Rothschild is at his games" (Cohen 1985: 75).

In the post-World War II period, not surprisingly given British colonial history, the British Cabinet racialized many of the African-Caribbean community as "accustomed to living in squalid conditions and hav[ing] no desire to improve" (Whitfield 2004: 18) while their children were described by one local education authority (LEA) as "physically robust and boisterous, yet mentally lethargic." At the same time the same LEA perceived there to be "very real problems" with the "domestic habits and personal hygiene of the Asiatics" as well as "the problem of [their] eating habits" (Grosvenor 1989: 34–5). Children from minority ethnic groups (not a source of cheap labor, as were their parents) were racialized as "problems" to be dealt with in these postwar years.

Anti-black racism

The racialization of black people in British society continues, and while this occurs sometimes in "seemingly positive" forms (e.g. prowess in sport and music),[7] *obviously* negative racism continues unabated. As far as permanent exclusion from school is concerned, for example, recent figures (Department for Education and Skills [DfES], 2006) show that 0.29 percent of black Caribbean, black African and black other students are in this situation as compared with 0.14 percent of white students.

According to extensive research by Marian FitzGerald, which underlines the connection between "race" and social class, yearly crime figures only reinforce the negative stereotype of young black men as "a problem" to society.

FitzGerald, Stockdale and Hale (2003; see also FitzGerald 2006) argue that street crime is unrelated to ethnicity but has everything to do with poverty and social circumstances. FitzGerald's research led her to conclude that the education system (primary school to General Certificate in Secondary Education [GCSE]) was letting down black children, especially in poor areas. As she puts it:

> In discussion, I'd see kids who were unmistakeably bright but when I got them to fill in a short survey at the end of class, it was obvious they were being sent out into the world with a standard of literacy which was lower than that of my 8 year old granddaughter even though they were nearly twice as old and just as bright. This meant their job prospects were poor; so their chances of legitimately earning the things they aspired to were very limited. Yet, as I knew only too well, those in the poorest areas were surrounded by crime and opportunities for crime. Also very few of them were white but that was simply because these were areas that most whites had long-since abandoned.
>
> (FitzGerald 2007)

It would be easy to overlook this important social class dimension in conventional CRT analysis.

Islamophobia

Islamophobia is a key facilitator of racialization by connecting aspects of the Old (British) to the New (US) Imperialism in capitalism's ongoing quest for global profits. The racist term, "Paki," co-exists with the racist term of abuse, "Bin Laden," and Islamic head scarves – hijabs – are now a symbol for a "cause for concern," with some *educational* institutions now forbidding students to wear them, thereby negating any notions that Britain has become a genuine multicultural society.

These connections between the old and new imperialisms are particularly obvious, for example, in discussions surrounding the case of British detainees of Pakistani origin at Guantanamo Bay (see below).

According to the Commission on British Muslims and Islamophobia (CBMI), Britain is "institutionally Islamophobic," with hostility towards Islam permeating every part of British society (Doward and Hinsliff 2004). The CBMI states that, since 9/11, there has been a sharp rise in attacks, some violent, on perceived and actual followers of Islam, and symbols that are Islamic in appearance. The attacks intensified after the London bombings exemplified by the *London Metro* newspaper, which led with an unequivocal front-page headline "Faith Hate Crimes Up 600% After Bombings" (Austin 2005). The report accompanying this title noted:

> [t]he number of attacks ... have soared ... There have been 269 faith hate crimes reported since the suicide blasts, compared to just 40 in the same three-and-a-half weeks last year [2004]. In the first three days after the attacks, there were 68 religious hate crimes in the capital. There were none in the same period 12 months ago [2004].
>
> (1)

The backlash from 7/7 has also meant that Hindus have suffered as a consequence of racialization. Although no figures are collated to differentiate ethnic groups, there is evidence to suggest that Hindus and Hindu buildings have suffered aggression (Bennetto 2006).

In addition to being targeted by individual racists, people perceived to be Muslims have seen an increase in police attention. The Police and Criminal Evidence Act (1984) permitted stop and search measures on civilians only if there was "reasonable suspicion." "Reasonable" is a contentious word that does not have a normative reference point, but controversially it was legislated. However, racialization has increased dramatically under the Terrorism Act 2000 (section 44), which, against much opposition, introduced new powers that allow stop and search on a random basis without suspicion, intelligence, prior information or accountability. The Act legitimizes racial profiling, and thus racialization, by stating that "[t]here may be circumstances ... where it is appropriate for officers to take account of a person's ethnic origin in selecting persons to be stopped in response to a specific terrorist threat" (Kundnani 2006: 2). People who appear to be of Islamic faith, wearing a veil, sporting a beard, or even carrying a backpack (see Austin 2006: 21), are immediately identified as potential terrorists and are five times more likely to be stopped and searched than a white person (Dodd 2005). It is important to underline here the fact that Islamophobia is not primarily triggered by skin color, but rather by one or more (perceived) symbols of the Muslim faith.

In 2003, more than 35,000 Muslims were stopped and searched, with fewer than 50 charged for non-terrorism related and minor offenses (Doward and Hinsliff 2004). After the July attacks in London, the number of Asian and black people likely to be stopped and searched without reasonable suspicion in London increased by more than twelve times from 2004 when 100 people were stopped each day (Kundnani 2006: 2–3). In London, just two months after 7/7, 10,000 people were stopped and searched, and none were charged nor arrested (Kundnani 2006: 2–3). Between July 7 and August 10, 6,747 Asian people accounted for 35 percent of the people stopped and searched (Dodd 2005), one being one of the authors of this chapter. There can be no doubt that racial profiling is being adopted by the authorities and state-sanctioned racialization is being instituted, since Asian people constitute 12 percent of London's population against 63 percent white people, meaning that there is huge disparity in the ratio of the population and those who were targeted by police for the application of the Terrorism Act 2000 (section 44). What is clear is that "stop and searches" cannot be justified by the conviction rate for terrorism offenses. The result of these measures to combat the potential of attacks has led to the racialization of huge numbers of Muslim people, or people perceived to be Muslim.[8]

Old and New Imperialisms

Much of the world in the twenty-first century is imbued with the vestiges of the Old (British) and the New (US) Imperialism. Thus there co-exist images of primitive barbarism and violence. As living testimony to the two Imperialisms, Benjamin Zephaniah (2004) states:

> when I come through the airport nowadays, in Britain and the US especially, they always question me on the Muslim part of my name. They are always on the verge of taking me away because they think converts are the dangerous ones.
>
> (19)

Zephaniah's experience was by no means an isolated one with thousands of Asian people being given "special" attention at security checkpoints. The actors in the highly acclaimed film *The Road to Guantanamo* were stopped at an airport after returning to England from Germany where the movie had been awarded the Silver Bear Award. They were treated with intimidation about making further "political" movies, refused access to legal aid, had personal belongings, including a mobile phone, confiscated, and were verbally abused (BBC 2006).

Islamophobia, like other forms of racism, can be cultural or it can be biological, or it can be a mixture of both. Echoing the quote from the school textbooks, cited above, where Asia was denigrated as "a continent of dying nations rapidly falling back in civilisation," and where reference was made to "the barbaric peoples of Asia," the former Archbishop of Canterbury defended a controversial speech in which he criticized Islam as a faith "associated with violence throughout the world" (Reynolds 2004: n. p.). At the Gregorian University in Rome he said that Islam was resistant to modernity and Islamic societies had contributed little to world culture for hundreds of years, thus choosing to subscribe to the notion that Asia is overrun by "mad Mullahs" and "Islamic fundamentalists," and failing to acknowledge the fact that there are fundamentalists in all faiths and religions, not least his own.

A more biological Islamophobic racism is revealed by Jamal al-Harith, a British captive freed from Guantanamo Bay. He informed *The Daily Mirror* that his guards told him "You have no rights here." al-Harith went on:

[a]fter a while, we stopped asking for human rights – we wanted animal rights. In Camp X-Ray my cage was right next to a kennel housing an Alsatian dog.

He had a wooden house with air conditioning and green grass to exercise on. I said to the guards, "I want his rights" and they replied, "That dog is member of the US army."

(Prince and Jones 2004: n. p.)

Such treatment is sustained by racialization. Indeed, the *a priori* racialization of Muslims as sub-humans and terrorists serves to facilitate and legitimize torture, rape, humiliation and degradation. US soldier Lyndie England, serving at the Abu Ghraib camp in Iraq, was charged with seriously abusing detainees by forcing them to stack naked in a human pyramid. The BBC (2004) reported that there "were numerous incidents of sadistic and wanton abuse ... Much of the abuse was sexual, with prisoners often kept naked and forced to perform simulated and real sex acts" (n. p.). This is particularly humiliating for Muslims who place importance on covering and not exposing flesh. The New Imperialism, of course, exacerbates such abuse and dehumanization.

Racialization, under conditions of imperialism, is fired by what Dallmayr (2004: 11) has described as "the intoxicating effects of global rule" which anticipates "corresponding levels of total depravity and corruption among the rulers." Global rule, of course, is first and foremost about global profits and serves to relate Old and New Imperialisms. This connection to capital, national and international is outside the remit of CRT, thereby rendering its use as a tool for analysis significantly lacking.

Part 4: xeno-racialization and skin color

It is not only Muslims and people perceived to be Muslims who have been racialized. Indeed, Miles (1987) makes it clear that, like racism, racialization is not limited to skin color:

The characteristics signified vary historically and, although they have usually been visible somatic features, other non-visible (alleged and real) biological features have also been signified.

(75)

Following Cole (2008), we would like to make a couple of amendments to Miles's position. First, consistent with our preferred definition of racism (see above), we would want to add "*and cultural*" after "biological." Second, the common dictionary definition of "somatic" is "*pertaining to the body*," and, given the fact, as noted above, that people can be racialized on grounds of symbols (e.g. the hijab), we would also want this to be recognized in any discussion of social collectivities and the construction of racialization.

With respect to refugees, economic migrants and asylum-seekers,[9] Sivanandan (2001; see also Fekete 2001: 23–4) has coined the term xeno-racism to describe the process whereby people thus labeled (often white) become racialized. Sivanandan defines xeno-racism as follows:

> [T]he "fear or hatred of strangers" ... the defence and preservation of "our people," our way of life, our standard of living, our "race." If it is xenophobia, it is – in the way it denigrates and reifies people before segregating and/or expelling them – a xenophobia that bears all the marks of the old racism, except that it is not colour-coded. It is a racism that is not just directed at those with darker skins, from the former colonial countries, but at the newer categories of the displaced and dispossessed whites, who are beating at western Europe's doors, the Europe that displaced them in the first place. It is racism in substance but xeno in form – a racism that is meted out to impoverished strangers even if they are white. It is xeno-racism.
>
> (2)

There is substantial evidence of xeno-racism (although it is not labeled as such) both outside and within the education system in the UK (e.g. Rutter 1994; Richman 1995; Rutter and Jones 1998; Geddes 2004; Guild 2000; Save the Children Scotland and Glasgow City Council 2002; Hewitt 2003; Rutter 2003; Cole 2004b; Watts 2004; Rutter 2006). This includes xeno-racism directed at people from the newly joined countries of the EU (e.g. Fekete 2002; BBC News 2005a–b, 2007; Belfast Today 2006). In Britain in 2007, the enlarged EU provides an abundance of cheap Eastern European labor. As noted above, one of us (Cole 2004b) has defined the process by which refugees, asylum-seekers and certain migrants from the newly joined countries of the EU become falsely categorized as belonging to distinct "races" as xeno-racialization (for an analysis, see Cole 2004b, 2008).

Capitalism benefits from cheap Eastern European labor. It also benefits from "illegal" labor power, from outside the EU, which is even cheaper. As Alex Callinicos (2006) puts it, "the interests of capital are best served by controls that are weak enough to allow immigrants in, but strong enough to keep illegal workers vulnerable and therefore easy to exploit." (n. p.). As David Renton (2006) argues, business welcomes migration, but on its own terms, with migrant workers "insecure, unpopular: a class of people who will remain as long as possible marginal and poor" (12). As he puts it, "[e]conomically, they will not feel confident to demand the same rights as the settled population" (12–13), while the non-migrant majority is encouraged to see migrant workers as a threat.

Given the widespread existence of xeno-racism and accompanying xeno-racialization (Cole 2004b), it is important that, in the current era as well as through history, racism directed at people with "white skins" remains firmly on the agenda.

In focusing on issues of color and being divorced from matters related to capitalist requirements with respect to the labor market, CRT is ill-equipped to analyze the historical material causes of the discourse of xeno-racism and processes of xeno-racialization.

Part 5: the role of education

In contemporary societies, we are in many ways being globally miseducated. The Bush and Blair administrations' propaganda war about "weapons of mass destruction," aimed at masking New Imperialist designs and capital's global quest for imperial hegemony and oil, is a key example.

Conditioning the discourse is only half the story. "Education" has become a key component in the profit-making process itself. Tied to the needs of global, corporate capital, "education" worldwide has been reduced to the creation of a flexible workforce, the openly acknowledged, indeed lauded (by both capitalists and politicians) requirement of today's global markets (Cole 2007). Corporate global capital is in schools, both in the sense of determining the curriculum and exercising burgeoning control of schools as businesses.

An alternative vision of education is provided by Peter McLaren. Education should, McLaren argues, following Paulo Freire, put "social and political analysis of everyday life at the center of the curriculum" (McLaren 2003: xxix). Racism should be a key component in such an analysis. Following through the thrust of this chapter, we argue that, in order for racism to be understood, and, in order for strategies to be developed to undermine it, there is a need first to reintroduce the topic of imperialism in British schools; second to initiate in schools a thorough analysis of the manifestations of xeno-racism and xeno-racialization. We will deal with each in turn.

The reintroduction of the teaching of imperialism in schools[10]

Reintroducing the teaching of imperialism in schools, we believe, would be far more effective than CRT in increasing awareness of racism, and crucially linking racism to capitalist modes of production. British imperialism was taught for a number of years in British schools in ways that exalted the Empire (e.g. Cole and Blair 2006). If we are to return to the teaching of imperialism, past and present, with integrity in British schools and universities, the syllabus must, we would argue, incorporate a critical analysis of the actual events of imperialism themselves. In addition to this, we would argue for the implementation without delay of the following further inputs to the curriculum.

First, we believe that it is helpful for today's students to understand how British imperialism was taught in the past, *and* why. This will enable them to make connections between the treatment meted out to those in the colonies and the experiences of Asian, black and other minority ethnic communities in Britain from World War II onwards.

Second, and allied to the above, students need media awareness. They need the critical faculties to critique pro-British imperialist and/or racist movies and/or TV series, still readily available in the age of multiple channel, digital TV. They also need to be able to understand manifestations of nationalism, racism, xeno-racism and xenophobia, such as that engendered and fostered by the media hype surrounding popular events, such as international football where nationalism is implicated in the coverage.

Third, at a national level, students are entitled to a critical awareness of how British imperialism relates to and impacts on racism and racialization, both historically and in the present. The curriculum should include contemporary racism directed at both the Asian, and the black, and other minority ethnic communities, encompassing both "seemingly positive" but potentially racist images of black people (e.g. in the media, pertaining to popular music and sport).

Fourth, at a global level, students will need skills to evaluate the New Imperialism and "the permanent war" being waged by the United States with the acquiescence of Britain. Boulangé (2004) argues that it is essential at this time, following the inauguration of the Bush and Blair "war on terror," and Islamophobia worldwide reaching new heights, for teachers to show solidarity with Muslims, for "this will strengthen the unity of all workers, whatever their religion" (Boulangé 2004: 24), and this will have a powerful impact on the struggle against racism in all spheres of society, and education in particular. In turn, this will strengthen the confidence of workers and students to fight on other issues.

According to neoconservative Niall Ferguson (2003):

> Empire is as "cutting edge" as you could wish ... [It] has got everything: economic history, social history, cultural history, political history, military history and international history – not to mention contemporary politics (just turn on the latest news from Kabul). Yet it knits all these things together with ... a "metanarrative."
>
> (n. p.)

For Marxists, an understanding of the metanarrative of imperialism, past and present, does much more than this. Indeed, it encompasses but goes beyond the centrality of "racial" liberation in CRT theory. It takes us to the crux of the trajectory of capitalism from its inception right up to the twenty-first century, and this is why Marxists should endorse the teaching of imperialism, old and new. Of course, the role of education in general, and teaching about imperialism in schools in particular, has its limitations and young people are deeply affected by other influences and socialized by the media, parents/carers, and by peer culture (hence the aforementioned need for media awareness). The question of reintroducing in the British education system a historically all-sided evaluation of imperialism presents a choice: that between a continued enslavement by an ignorance of Britain's imperial past, or an empowered acknowledgment of it. Such awareness would also begin a process of understanding the New Imperialism currently being waged in earnest. Unlike Marxism, CRT does not explain why Islamophobia, the "war on terror" and other forms of racism are necessary to keep the populace on task for "permanent war" and the accumulation of global profits.

The manifestations of xeno-racism and xeno-racialization

Marxism most clearly connects the Old and New Imperialisms with capitalism. It also provides an explanation for xeno-racism and xeno-racialization. While CRT certainly reminds us that racism is central in sustaining the current world order, and that we must listen to the voices of people oppressed on grounds of racism, it does not and cannot make the necessary connections to understand and challenge this racism. Indeed its advocacy of "white supremacy" as an explanatory metanarrative is counter-productive, particularly, we would argue, in the school and university context, in the struggle against racism.

Xeno-racism and xeno-racialization in the UK and the rest of Europe need to be understood in the context of the origins of the EU, and globalization generally. With respect to the EU's current enlargement, connections need to be made between the respective roles of (ex-)imperial citizens in the immediate post-World War II period, and migrant workers from Eastern Europe today (both sources of cheap labor). An analysis of the way in which the media portrays asylum-seekers and refugees on the one hand, and migrant workers on the other, would also foster an awareness of the processes of xeno-racism and xeno-racialization.

Education does not have a merely institutional dimension; it is also about formal and non-formal self-education, resistance and struggle. According to Marxism, in this collective struggle, education achieves its true potential and its ultimate emancipatory purpose with nothing less than the demise of global neoliberal capitalism and imperialism, and its replacement by a new world order based on human need and not on corporate profit. Only then do the conditions exist for the final eradication of racism and racialization.

Notes

1 This chapter draws heavily on Cole (2008), in particular Chapter 9. For a comprehensive Marxist critique of CRT, see Cole (2009). For a discussion of the origins of CRT in Critical Legal Studies, see Chapter 1 of Cole (2009).
2 For a discussion of the success of the state apparatuses in instilling the message that neoliberal global capitalism is "natural," and imperialism is unavoidable, see Cole (2008).
3 The concept of xeno-racialization was first developed in Cole (2004b).
4 CRT tended to be confined to academic discourse and this has led to a reappraisal of the significance of social class. Richard Delgado, one of CRT's founders, has put forward a materialist critique of the discourse-focused trend of recent CRT writings. Delgado's paper was the subject of a symposium entitled, Going Back to Class: The Re-emergence of Class in Critical Race Theory, February 4–5, 2005, sponsored by the University of Michigan Law School. Charles Mills, leading Critical Race Theorist and a symposium panelist, said he agreed with Delgado on the belief, central to CRT, that class structure keeps racial hierarchy intact. The working class is divided by "race," Mills said, to the advantage of the upper class, which is mainly composed of white elites (Hare 2005). At the same symposium, Angela Harris argued that CRT is essential in exposing how

interconnected class, "race" and sex are (Hare 2005). As an example, she referenced the affirmative action disputes in higher education. The often-cited argument that working-class whites are being rejected in favor of middle-class blacks and Latinos – who, the argument goes, have a better chance of acceptance regardless of "race" – is looking at class based solely on income (Hare 2005). "What CRT exposes is that class also needs to be looked at in terms of access to wealth and the racialization of class" (Hare 2005: n. p.). As for the future of CRT, Delgado envisions a new movement of CRT theorists to recombine discourse and political activism. "I'm worried that the younger crop of CRT theorists are enamored by the easy arm-chair task of writing about race the word and not race in the world," Delgado concluded. "A new movement is needed" (Hare 2005: n. p.). For Marxists, these are promising developments and point towards a possible alignment between CRT and Marxism.

5 As Hill (2001: 8) has pointed out, the influence of ideology can be overwhelming. He cites Terry Eagleton (1991), who has written, "[w]hat persuades men and women to mistake each other from time to time for gods or vermin is ideology" (xiii). The efficacy of this observation resonates throughout this chapter.

6 In adopting Miles's definition of racialization, we should make it clear that there are a number of non-Marxist applications of the concept of racialization. Indeed, the concept is a contested term which is widely used and differently interpreted (for an analysis, see Murji and Solomos 2005).

7 All stereotypes of ethnic groups are invariably problematic and, at least potentially, racist (Cole 2004c, 2008).

8 In many ways, the Muslim communities of Britain are being scapegoated in similar fashion to "black youth" in the 1970s and 1980s (see Cole 1986) and, previously, the Irish settlers.

9 We recognize the problematic nature of the terms "asylum-seeker" and "refugee." They form part of a "discourse of derision" (Ball 1990: 18) in the media, and in the pronouncements of certain politicians. However, given the legal status of "asylum-seeker" and "refugee," we will continue to use the terms. "Forced migrants" (Rutter 2006) might be a more appropriate term.

10 This part of the chapter draws on Cole (2004d).

Bibliography

Austin, S. (2005) "Faith hate crimes up 600% after bombings," *London Metro* (August 3), 1.

Austin, S. (2006) "9/11 Cinema goer is mistaken for terrorist," *London Metro* (June 9), 21.

Ball, S. (1990) *Politics & Policymaking in Education*, London: Routledge.

BBC News (2004) "Chaos and violence at Abu Ghraib." Online. Available at http://news.bbc.co.uk/1/hi/world/americas/3690097.stm (accessed July 19, 2007).

—— (2005a) "Three suffer unprovoked beating." Online. Available at http://news.bbc.co.uk/1/hi/england/tees/4710011.stm (accessed July 19, 2007).

—— (2005b) "Polish student assaulted by gang." Online. Available at http://news.bbc.co.uk/1/hi/endland/dorset/4713593.stm (accessed July 19, 2007).

—— (2006) "Guantanamo actors held at airport." Online. Available at http://news.bbc.co.uk/1/hi/entertainment/4736404.stm (accessed July 19, 2007).

—— (2007) "Poles in Redditch hit by racism." Online. Available at http://www.bbc.co.uk/herefordandworcester/content/articles/2007/03/22/breakfast_polish_racism_feature.shtml (accessed January 18, 2008).

Belfast Today (2006) "Polish man hurt in vicious attack." Online. Available at http://www.belfasttoday.net/ViewArticle2.aspx?SectionID=3425&ArticleID=1532979 (accessed July 19, 2007).

Bennetto, J. (2006) "Hindus caught in backlash after July 7 terror attacks." *The Independent* (January 4). Online. Available at http://news.independent.co.uk/uk/crime/article336392. ece (accessed July 19, 2007).

Boulangé, A. (2004) "The hijab, racism and the state," *International Socialism*, 102, Spring: 3–26.

Callinicos, A. (2006) "Capitalism Fails Without Cheap Migrant Labor," *Radical Left* (April 12). Online. Available at http://www.radicalleft.net/blog/_archives/2006/4/12/1879534.http (accessed February 20, 2008).

Chancellor, V. (1970) *History for their Masters*, Bath: Adams and Dart.

Cohen, S. (1985) "Anti-semitism, immigration controls and the welfare state," *Critical Social Policy*, 13, Summer: 73–92.

Cole, M. (1986) "Teaching and learning about racism: a critique of multicultural education in Britain," in S. Modgil, G. Verma, K. Mallick and C. Modgil (eds) *Multicultural Education: the interminable debate*, Lewes: The Falmer Press.

—— (2004a) "US imperialism, transmodernism and education: a Marxist critique," *Policy Futures in Education* 2, 3–4: 633–43. Online. Available at http://www.wwwords.co.uk/ pfie/content/pdfs/2/issue2_3.asp#15 (accessed July 19, 2007).

—— (2004b) "F*** you – human sewage: contemporary global capitalism and the xeno-racialization of asylum seekers," *Contemporary Politics* 10, 2: 159–65.

—— (2004c) "'Brutal and stinking' and 'difficult to handle': the historical and contemporary manifestations of racialisation, institutional racism, and schooling in Britain," *Race, Ethnicity and Education*, 7, 1: 35–56.

—— (2004d) "'Rule Britannia' and the New American Empire: a Marxist analysis of the teaching of imperialism, actual and potential, in the British school curriculum," *Policy Futures in Education*, 2, 3–4: 523–38. Online. Available at http://www.wwwords.co.uk/ pdf/viewpdf.asp?j=pfie&vol=2&issue=3&year=2004&article=7_Cole_PFIE_2_3–4_ web&id=81.111.108.255 (accessed July 19, 2007).

—— (2007) "Neo-liberalism and education: a Marxist critique of New Labour's five year strategy for education," in A. Green, G. Rikowski and H. Raduntz (eds) *Renewing Dialogues in Marxism and Education: Volume 1 – Openings*, Basingstoke: Palgrave Macmillan.

—— (2008) *Marxism and Educational Theory: origins and issues*, London: Routledge.

—— (2009) *Critical Race Theory and Education: a Marxist response*, New York and London: Palgrave Macmillan.

—— and Blair, M. (2006) "Racism and education: from Empire to New Labour," in M. Cole (ed.) *Education, Equality and Human Rights: issues of gender, "race," sexuality, disability and social class*, 2nd edn, London: Routledge.

Cruddas, J., John, P., Lowles, N., Margetts, H., Rowlands, D., Shutt, D., and Weir, S. (2005) *The Far Right In London: a challenge for local democracy?* York: Joseph Rowntree Reform Trust. Online. Available at http://www.jrrt.org.uk/Far_Right_REPORT.pdf (accessed February 18, 2008).

Dallmayr, F. (2004) "The underside of modernity: Adorno, Heidegger, and Dussel," *Constellations*, 11, 1: 102–20.

Darder, A. and Torres, R. D. (2004) *After Race: racism after multiculturalism*, New York and London: New York University Press.

Delgado, R. (1995) *The Rodrigo Chronicles: conversations about America and race*, New York: New York University Press.

Dodd, V. (2005) "Asian men targeted in stop and search. Huge rise in number questioned under anti-terror laws." *The Guardian* (August 17). Online. Available at http://www. guardian.co.uk/attackonlondon/story/0,16132,1550470,00.html (accessed July 19, 2007).

Department for Education and Skills (DfES). (2006) *Priority Review: Exclusion of Black Pupils: Getting it right* (September). Department for Education and Skills (DfES). Online. Available at http://www.standards.dfes.gov.uk/ethnicminorities/resources/PriorityReviewSept06. pdf (accessed February 20, 2008).

Doward, J. and Hinsliff, G. (2004) "British hostility to Muslims 'could trigger riots'," *The Guardian* (May 30). Online. Available at http://www.guardian.co.uk/race/story/ 0,11374,1227977,00.html (accessed July 19, 2007).

Eagleton, T. (1991) *Ideology*, London: Verso.

Fekete, L. (2001) "The emergence of xeno-racism," Institute of Race Relations. Online. Available at http://www.irr.org.uk/2001/september/ak000001.html (accessed July 19, 2007).

—— (2002) "Evictions against xeno-racist neighbours," Institute of Race Relations. Online. Available at http://www.irr.org.uk/europebulletin/united_kingdom/extreme_right_ politics/2002/ak000003.html (accessed July 19, 2007).

Ferguson, N. (2003) "Prince and empire are the key to history," *The Sunday Times* (July 6). Online. Available at http://www.timesonline.co.uk/tol/news/article1099497.ece (accessed February 19, 2008).

FitzGerald, M. (2006) "Lies, damned lies and 'ethnic' statistics: some challenges for British criminology," Paper presented at British Society of Criminology Conference, December 6, 2006.

—— (2007) "Re: Is this you I am quoting?" Email (April 19, 2007).

——, Stockdale J. and Hale C. (2003) *Young People and Street Crime*, London: Youth Justice Board.

Geddes, A. (2004) *The Politics of Migration and Immigration in Europe*, London: Sage.

Gillborn, D. (2005) "Education policy as an act of white supremacy: whiteness, critical race theory and education reform," *Journal of Education Policy*, 20, 4: 485–505.

—— (2006) "Critical race theory and education: racism and antiracism in educational theory and praxis," *Discourse: studies in the cultural politics of education*, 27, 1: 11–32.

Glendenning, F. J. (1973) "History textbooks and racial attitudes: 1804–1969," *Journal of Educational Administration and History*, 5: 35–44.

Gramsci, A. (1978) *Selections from Prison Notebooks*, London: Lawrence and Wishart.

Grosvenor, I. (1989) "Teacher racism and the construction of black underachievement," in R. Lowe (ed.) *The Changing Secondary School*, Lewes: The Falmer Press.

Guild, E. (2000) "The United Kingdom: Kosovar Albanian Refugees", in J. van Selm (ed.) *Kosovo's Refugees in the European Union*, London and New York: Pinter.

Hare, B. (2005) "Law symposium to feature black racial theorists," *The Michigan Daily* (April 2). Online. Available at http://www.michigandaily.com/media/paper851/news/2005/02/04/ News/Law-Symposium.To.Feature.Black.Racial.Theorists-1428501.shtml?norewrite&so urcedomain=www.michigandaily.com (accessed July 19, 2007).

Hendrick, H. (1980) "A race of intelligent unskilled labourers: the adolescent worker and the debate on compulsory part-time day continuation schools, 1900–1922," *History of Education*, 9, 2: 159–73.

Hewitt, R. (2003) *Asylum-Seeker Dispersal and Community Relations*, Swindon: Report to the ESRC.

Hill, D. (2001) "Equality, ideology and education policy," in D. Hill and M. Cole (eds) *Schooling and Equality: fact, concept and policy*, London: Kogan Page.

Holmes, C. (1979) *Anti-Semitism in British Society 1876–1939*, London: Edward Arnold.

hooks, b. (1989) *Talking Back: thinking feminist, thinking black*, Boston MA: South End Press.

James, S. (2008) "British Army accused of 'off the scale' abuses in southern Iraq," World

Socialist Web Site (8 February). Online. Available at http://www.wsws.org/articles/2008/feb2008/iraq-f08.shtml (accessed February 19, 2008).

Kundnani, A (2006) "Racial profiling and anti-terror stop and search," Institute of Race Relations. Online. Available at http://www.irr.org.uk/2006/january/ha000025.html (accessed July 19, 2007).

Lawrence, E. (1982) "Just plain common sense: the 'roots' of racism," in Centre for Contemporary Cultural Studies (ed.) *The Empire Strikes Back: race and racism in 70s Britain*. London: Hutchinson.

Leonardo, Z. (2004) "The unhappy marriage between Marxism and race critique: political economy and the production of racialized knowledge," *Policy Futures in Education*, 2–4: 483–93. Online. Available at http://www.wwwords.co.uk/pfie/content/pdfs/2/issue2_3.asp#4 (accessed July 19, 2007).

McLaren, P. (2003) *Life in Schools: an introduction to critical pedagogy in the foundations of education*, 4th edn. Boston: Pearson Education.

Maisuria, A. (2006) "A brief history of the British 'race' politics and the settlement of the Maisuria Family," *Forum: for promoting 3–19 comprehensive education*, 48, 1: 95–101.

Marx, K. (1894) *Capital*. Vol. III, Ch. 13, "The Law As Such." Marxist Internet Archive. Online. Available at http://www.marxists.org/archive/marx/works/1894-c3/ch13.htm (accessed July 19, 2007).

—— and Engels, F. (1845) *The German Ideology*, Ch. 4, "The Essence of the Materialist Conception of History Social Being and Social Consciousness". Marxist Internet Archive. Online. Available at http://www.marxists.org/archive/marx/works/1845/german-ideology/ch01a.htm (accessed July 19, 2007).

Miles, R. (1987) *Capitalism and Unfree Labour: anomaly or necessity?* London: Tavistock.

—— (1989) *Racism*, London: Routledge.

Mills, C. (1997) *The Racial Contract*, New York: Cornell University Press.

Muir, H. (2006) "He looked at me and shot. As soon as he had eye contact, he shot me," *The Guardian* (June 14). Online. Available at http://www.guardian.co.uk/terrorism/story/0,1796915,00.html (accessed July 19, 2007).

Murji, K. and Solomos, J. (eds) (2005) *Racialization: studies in theory and practice*, Oxford: Oxford University Press.

Prince, R. and Jones, G. (2004) "My hell in Camp X-ray". Online. Available at http://www.commondreams.org/headlines04/0507–05.htm (accessed July 19, 2007).

Renton, D. (2006) "Does capitalism need racism?", Paper presented at the *Racism and Marxist Theory Workshop*, University of Glasgow, September 7–8, 2006.

Reynolds, P. (2004) Preventing a clash of civilisations, BBC News (March 29). Online. Available at http://news.bbc.co.uk/1/hi/world/americas/3578429.stm (accessed July 19, 2007).

Richman, N. (1995) *They Don't Recognise Our Dignity: a study of the psychosocial needs of refugee children and families in Hackney*, London: City and Hackney Community NHS Trust.

Rutter, J. (1994) *Refugee Children in the Classroom*, Stoke-on-Trent: Trentham Books.

—— (2003) *Supporting Refugee Children in 21st century Britain: a compendium of essential information*, Stoke-on-Trent: Trentham Books.

—— (2006) *Refugee Children in the UK*, Buckingham: Open University Press.

—— and Jones, C. (eds) (1998) *Refugee Education: mapping the field*, Stoke-on-Trent: Trentham Books.

Save the Children Scotland and Glasgow City Council (2002) *Starting Again*, Glasgow: Save the Children Scotland.

Sivanandan, A. (2001) "Poverty is the New Black," *Race and Class*, 43, 2: 1–5.

Whitfield, J. (2004) *Unhappy Dialogue: the metropolitan police and black Londoners in postwar Britain*, Devon: Willan Publishing.

Watts, M. F. (2004) "Telling tales of torture: repositioning young adults' views of asylum seekers," *Cambridge Journal of Education*, 34, 3: 315–29.

Zephaniah, B. (2004) "Rage of Empire," *Socialist Review*, 281: 18–20.

6 Marxism, critical realism and class

Implications for a socialist pedagogy[1]

Grant Banfield

Abstract

Against the impulse of contemporary social theory and social science this chapter presents a materialist view of history as indispensable to radical critique. It will show why, and in what ways, (1) assertions that historical materialism is determinist, teleological and reductionist are to be taken as false and (2) social theories that do not position class as an essential and deep-real feature of capitalist societies lack sufficient explanatory power for radical action. To these ends, the chapter draws on assistance from outside Marxism in the form of a movement in philosophy known as critical realism. As a philosophy of science, critical realism offers a general meta-theory of the stratification of nature of which the Marxian base/superstructure arrangement – the source of much of the contention with which this chapter deals – can be seen as an example. In bringing critical realism to work for Marxism, a "strong historical materialism" is advanced where class relations within capitalism are understood as being rooted, essentially but non-reductively, in material bases consisting in both human and non-human mechanisms. The concluding sections draw on Marx's dialectical method to show how "strong historical materialism" can be used as a practical frame for socialist pedagogy: the development of class consciousness through the deliberate teaching of Marxist critique.

Introduction

This chapter takes Marx's materialist view of history as a science and not simply a philosophy or world-view. Furthermore, it describes Marx as a scientific realist *par excellence* who understood the objects of science (and the objects of revolutionary transformation) as deep-real structures irreducible to their phenomenological forms. In stark contrast to positivism and the vulgar materialism – against which Gramsci (1971), for example, applied the full weight of his historicist critique – this chapter shows Marx's materialist view of history to be founded on a non-reductionist ontology of which class is base-ic. It is argued that this insight is (1) compatible with an emergentist base-superstructure model and (2) indispensable to radical transformative politics generally and to socialist pedagogy in particular.

Claims that class relations are essential to capitalism and that the base/superstructure model has metaphorical adequacy for historical materialism are contentious.

Indeed, even within some versions of Marxism, such expressions of "classical" Marxism sit as quaint ideas from a past long gone. For example, within the field of Marxist Sociology of Education the base-superstructure metaphor has always held a problematic place. Ever since Bowles and Gintis' (1976) interjection into the field of educational sociology with the release of their *Schooling in Capitalist America*, the metaphor has been associated with the twin evils of economism and class reductionism.

The purpose of this chapter is to show why, and in what ways, declarations that historical materialism is set in determinist, teleological and reductionist casts are to be taken as false. The chapter's method will be to draw on assistance from outside Marxism in the form of a movement in philosophy known as critical realism. Importantly, however, the intent will not be to replace Marxism or to offer critical realism as yet another philosophy of Marxism. Rather, it will be to bring critical realism to work *for* Marxism. The role of critical realism is that of an underlaborer at the level of philosophy – or more precisely, the philosophy of science.

The challenge of elaborating a Marxist philosophy of science will begin by considering the base/superstructure "metaphor" and its implications for theorizing social class.[2] Given the metaphor's close association with "classical" Marxism, this initial elaboration will be advanced through a brief sketch of Marx's materialist view of history. Next, attention will turn specifically to critical realism, which will be shown to offer a general meta-theory of the stratification of nature of which the base/superstructure arrangement can be seen as an example. In particular, the critical realist concepts of "emergence" and "stratification" will be explored, emphasizing their importance to the development of an anti-positivist naturalism for the social sciences. By showing how critical realism charts a realist path between the reductionism and empiricism of positivist science and the anti-naturalist, anti-foundational tendencies within conventionalism, the ground will have been prepared for a return to a consideration of historical materialism. Here critical realism is put to work for Marxism by attending to two sources of much conjecture: the primacy theses of base over superstructure and forces of production over relations of production. In this move, a case will be put for a "strong historical materialism" that recognizes that natural relations exist at a deeper ontological level than social ones. The argument will be that while class relations are essential to capitalism they are rooted, non-determinantly, in a material base consisting in human and non-human mechanisms.

The concluding sections begin to draw out the implications of a "strong historical materialism" for socialist pedagogy. Here Marx's dialectical method is employed to show how a "strong historical materialism" can be used as a guiding conceptual frame for socialist pedagogy and revolutionary practice.

Class and the materialist view of history

Class is of central importance to Marxist theory and practice. It was the class structure of early capitalism, and the struggles in this form of society, which constituted the main reference point for a Marxian materialist theory of history. Accordingly, "all hitherto existing societies" (Marx and Engels 1969: 108) since primitive communism have been characterized by struggles over productive surpluses and conflicts over wealth appropriation. In order for people to live and "make history" their need for material necessities such as food, shelter and clothing must be satisfied. Before anything else, the material requirements for survival and reproduction must be met. Indeed, the "first historical act" is the production of the means to satisfy such needs: "the production of material life itself" (Marx and Engels 1976: 47).

While Marx saw the foundation of human history lying in production, he did not understand it simply in terms of the satisfaction of material needs. Production was also social involving cooperation and organization. As such, Marx distinguished between the material factors of production (the objects of production, the instruments of production, and labor power) and the social relations through which it is orientated. These two dimensions – the forces of production and the relations of production – are understood to comprise the foundation of all human societies. However, it is the particular way in which the means of production and labor are brought together that differentiates one society or "economic epoch" from another. In class societies the nature of this union is such that control over productive resources rests in the hands of non-producers. Separated from the means of production, direct producers are forced to labor for a privileged minority. At the heart of class societies is exploitation: the appropriation of labor and the extraction of a surplus from one class by another. How this exploitation is achieved defines a particular class society. In slave economies, surplus labor is appropriated by the master who owns the direct producers in the same way as any instrument of production. Slaves have no claim to the fruits of their labor. Under feudalism, the serf or peasant may own some instruments of labor but not the objects of labor such as land. The surplus labor left over, after producing for the material needs of the family, is given to the lord.

Within slave and feudal societies, exploitation is obvious and the threat of physical violence ever-present. Under the capitalist mode of production things *appear* different. On the surface, labor and capital come together as equals in the labor market to negotiate a "fair day's work for a fair day's pay." Unlike the slave or serf, the capitalist worker is "free" to sell, withdraw or withhold their labor power as they wish. In the apparent absence of physical domination there is no direct compulsion for the worker to exchange their labor for a wage. However, this freedom has a "double sense." As Marx explains, the wage laborer is

> free from the old relations of clientship, bondage and servitude, and secondly free of all belongings and possession, and of every objective, material form of being, *free of all property*; dependent on the sale of [their] labour capacity or on begging, vagabondage and robbery as its only source of income.
>
> (Marx 1973: 507)

Marx's point here is that within the capitalist mode of production exploitation is concealed. As Rick Kuhn has bluntly put it: "Capitalism is the first class system in history that pretends not to be one" (Kuhn 1996: 145). For the worker, the alternatives to selling their labor power to capital are poor: if not starvation, they be "begging, vagabondage or robbery." Beneath the appearance of freedom, rests the essence of un-freedom experienced by slaves and serfs: their separation from the means of production. However, unlike other class societies, capitalist exploitation is exercised predominately through economic power. But, as Mandel notes, its force is ever present:

> under capitalism, labour is fundamentally *forced* labour. Whenever possible, capitalists prefer hypocritically to cloak the compulsion under a smokescreen of 'equal and just exchange' on the 'labour market'. When hypocrisy is no longer possible, they return to what they began with: naked coercion.
>
> (Mandel 1976: 49)

Here we see a stark contrast with, for example, Weberian sociology, where class is disconnected from its roots in property and production and tied to the phenomenal appearances of market exchange and consumption (see Callinicos 1999: 146–78). Class, in other words, functions as a descriptive category. Conversely, Marx's materialist view of history is an explanatory theory. It posits a stratified ontology of the natural and social worlds where superficial appearances can hide more fundamental mechanisms. The explanatory essence of historical materialism is captured in the base/superstructure metaphor where out of the material mechanisms of a particular social formation emerges its politico-ideological superstructure. It is the superstructure that, in turn, sanctions, regulates and normalizes the existing social relations of production. Since (and during) the days of Marx and Engels, this metaphor has occupied the minds of Marxist theoreticians as well as providing ammunition for the dismissal of Marxism as determinist and economically reductionist. The oft-quoted passage from the *Preface* presents the essence and elements of historical materialism succinctly:

> In the social production of their existence, men inevitably enter into definite relations, which are independent of their will, namely relations of production appropriate to a given stage in the development of their material forces of production. The totality of these relations of production constitutes the economic structure of society, their real foundation, on which arises a legal and political superstructure and to which correspond definite forms of social consciousness. The mode of production of material life conditions the general process of social, political and intellectual life. It is not the consciousness of men that determines their existence, but their social existence that determines their consciousness. At a certain stage of development, the material productive forces of society come into conflict with the existing relations of production. [...] From forms of development of the productive forces these relations turn into their fetters. Then begins an era of social revolution.
>
> (Marx 1970: 20–1)

From a first glance reading of this passage it is perhaps easy to see how charges of economic determinism can be made against "classical" Marxist thought.[3] With its apparent insistence that certain inevitabilities occur "independent of will," that the economic structure of a society is its "real foundation," and that social existence determines consciousness, it is understandable that the "superstructure" can be interpreted as simply a passive effect of the economic "base." However, even in the days of Marx before Marxism, Marx warned against reducing his work to some historicist formula blind to the concrete realities of particular circumstances. He appealed to friends and critics alike not to "metamorphose [his] historical sketch of the genesis of capitalism in Western Europe into a historico-philosophic theory of the general path every people is fated to tread, whatever the historical circumstances in which it finds itself" (Marx 1977: 572).

As is well known, mechanical interpretations of the base-superstructure relation have not been left unchallenged within Marxism. For example, Althusser's work is to be understood as an attempt to transcend the economic reductionism of "vulgar" Marxism. For Althusser (1996), reality was "overdetermined" with social forms existing in "relative autonomy": the economic base is determining only "in the last instance." Also, the rise of humanist or "Western" Marxism can be understood as a movement against the perceived positivism of dialectical materialism with its elevation of Marxism to the status of a universal science of history and nature. For the likes of Lukács, Sartre and Gramsci, for example, social reality was to be grasped, in Hegelian fashion, as an "expressive totality" where each "moment" contains the whole. These Marxian movements emphasized drawing the categories of culture, class consciousness and subjectivity into Marxism where, rather than being exhausted by science, they claimed to offer a critique of bourgeois ideology and cultural life. The adequacy of such claims will be the focus of upcoming sections. However, before this can be done consideration will be given to the potential of critical realism to act as an underlaborer for Marxist theory and practice.

Critical realism and an emergentist ontology

Critical realism is a movement in philosophy largely associated with the work of British philosopher Roy Bhaskar. Its starting point can be located in 1978 with the publication of Bhaskar's *A Realist Theory of Science* (Bhaskar 1978). From this work, where Bhaskar set out to establish a transcendental realist philosophy for natural science as a viable alternative to positivism, Bhaskar moved to extend his transcendental realism to a second phase: the development of a critical naturalist philosophy for social science. First released in 1979, it was in *The Possibility of Naturalism* that Bhaskar set out to explore the extent to which social objects could be studied in the same way as natural ones (see Bhaskar 1998). The substantive focus of this work centered on the problem field of positivism and hermeneutics. His solution was a qualified anti-positivist naturalism: one that recognized the natural and social sciences to be unified in a transcendental realist method but distinguishable by virtue of the nature of the objects they study. In this, his early work, Bhaskar acknowledges the influence of Marx. According to Bhaskar "there is an elective affinity between critical realism and historical materialism, in that ... critical realism is a heterocosmic instance of the emancipatory transformation socialism aspires to achieve" (1991: 143). It is on Bhaskar's transcendental realism and critical naturalism, where he establishes the possibility of an emancipatory philosophy for the human sciences, that this chapter centers its attention.

Bhaskar's critically naturalist meta-theory of stratification provides a particularly useful philosophical backdrop to the examination of social class through the problem of the base-superstructure relation and the issue of the relation between the forces and relations of production. In *A Realist Theory of Science*, Bhaskar shows that for science to be both possible and necessary, its object must be stratified and differentiated. After all, if reality is exhausted in actuality (what appears to us, or what we directly experience, is all there is) then there would be no point to science. Using a transcendental argument (i.e. asking "what must be the case for x to be possible?") Bhaskar enquires how material objects, like sticks and stones, are able to be handled. His response: "it is because sticks and stones are solid that they can be picked up and thrown, not because they can be picked up and thrown that they are solid" (1998: 25). While it might be taken as obvious, or at least intuitively correct, that the physical constitution of sticks and stones is not dependent upon events or our experiences (and conceptualizations) of them, this ontological realism rubs uncomfortably against the hegemony of positivist science and its core assumptions resting in Humean causality. According to Bhaskar, Humean empiricism works counter intuitively to reduce knowledge to that of individual events (captured in sense experience) and then identify those events as constituting the nature of the world. Thus, within the doctrine of empirical realism, causal laws are taken as simply the constant conjunction of events. In contrast to Humean empirical realism where empirical regularity is a necessary (or, at least, a sufficient) condition for causality, Bhaskar takes the constant conjunctions of events to be both extremely rare in nature and "praxis dependent" (see especially Bhaskar 1986: 27–50). It is within closed, not open, systems where constant conjunctions obtain. Rather than being given in experience and simply captured through sense-perception – as per the "positivist illusion" – facts consist in the activities of causal agents (Bhaskar 1986: 224–308). They comprise, what Bhaskar calls, the "transitive" dimension of science. Importantly, however, recognizing science and its practices as socio-historical products does not deny the existence of praxis independent structures and mechanisms: the "intransitive" dimension of science (Bhaskar 1978). To conflate the transitive products of science with its intransitive objects is to reduce ontology to epistemology and fall to, what Bhaskar claims is, one of Western philosophy's great and persistent errors: the "epistemic fallacy."[4] Contra positivism, generality in nature consists in things not conditions (Bhaskar 1978: 233).

Distinguishing the objects of science from its products (i.e. holding the intransitive and transitive domains separate) facilitates the description of scientific laws as tendencies: transitive statements of "a real generative mechanism at work" (Bhaskar 1978: 183). However, the existence of a mechanism does not guarantee the realization of a particular event or outcome. Events may be out of phase with structures or, indeed, the latter may be unexercised. Also, events can occur independent of our experience or knowledge of them. Bhaskar's point here is that the very intelligibility of science is the ontological distinction between mechanisms and structures; the events those mechanisms and structures generate; and the experiences humans have – and the sense they make – of events, mechanisms and structures. A critical realist depiction of the stratification of nature can be represented as in Table 6.1.

Table 6.1 Ontological domains

Real	Actual	Empirical, Subjective
Experiences/Concepts	Experiences/Concepts	*Experiences/Concepts*
Events	*Events*	
Mechanisms		

(Adapted from Hartwig 2007: 401)

In critical realist terms, the stratification of nature consists in three domains where the "Actual" and "Empirical, Subjective" attend only to surface features of the "Real." It is the recognition of underlying mechanisms that distinguishes the "Real" from the "Actual" and "Empirical, Subjective." Depth realism insists that passive observation and "objective" description of the world are not good enough to understand it. In open systems, where multiple mechanisms are co-determining, events are not predictable and must be understood as "conjunctures." Contrary to philosophical nominalism where only particulars are understood to exist and predicates are seen simply as descriptors in classificatory schemas, depth realism insists that

> predicates [such as] 'natural, 'social', 'human', 'physical', 'chemical', 'aerody-namical', 'biological', 'economic', etc. ought not to be regarded as differentiating distinct kinds of events, but as differentiating distinct kinds of *mechanisms*. For in the generation of an open-systemic event several of these predicates may be simultaneously applicable.
>
> (Bhaskar 1978: 119)

In open systems it is an array of mechanisms that co-determine the realization and possible experience of events or "conjunctural occurrences." The relations between these mechanisms are also stratified. For example, the predicate "social" presupposes the "natural." Likewise, biological mechanisms would be impossible without chemical ones. The reverse, in both instances, does not hold. Rather, we can say that the "social" is emergent from the "natural"; the "biological" from the "chemical"; or the "aerodynamical" from the "physical."

It is the realist concept of emergence that provides the basis of critical realism's non-reductive ontology. Within transcendental realism, emergentism takes the mechanisms operating at one ontological stratum to be irreducible to those at lower – or deeper – strata. It also asserts that higher order mechanisms set the boundaries and the conditions upon which lower order mechanisms operate. In this way, higher-level mechanisms are seen as being "rooted" in underlying ones and, as such, cannot be accounted for by simply referring to laws governing more basic strata. For example, in the case of water, we know that, separately, hydrogen and oxygen have certain powers (e.g. flammability). But in combination they exhibit quite different properties (e.g. the potential to extinguish fire). The new (or "emergent") powers of water, while rooted in the properties of oxygen and hydrogen, exist at different strata and, as such, are not reducible to them. More generally, in critical realist terms, we can say that given the ontological stratification of the natural world, the existence of powers at one level presupposes mechanisms operating at deeper strata but cannot be explained away in terms of them. In this way, transcendental realism is understood to stand in opposition to both pluralism and reductionism where the former claims higher strata exist independent of – or "relatively autonomous" from – lower ones, and the latter take higher strata as mere reflections of – or are determined by – more basic strata.

Drawing on his emergentist view of stratification established for the natural sciences, Bhaskar moved to develop a non-reductive naturalism that would underlabor the human sciences. In *The Possibility of Naturalism*, Bhaskar attended to the task of resolving the problem of naturalism in social science: the extent to which society can be studied in the same way as nature. For Bhaskar, the problems of social science stem from an inadequate account of science and an erroneous view of its relation to natural science. In contrast, the critical realist position holds that knowledge can be gained of the social world, like that of the natural world, by studying it scientifically: in a social process whose "essence lies in the *movement* at any one level from knowledge of manifest phenomena to knowledge of the structures that generate them" (Bhaskar 1998: 13). However, recognizing that natural science with its success in generating facts about the world cannot be taken and directly applied to the social, Bhaskar charted an alternate route. He employed a transcendental realist argument to deduce the properties that societies and people must possess if they are to be possible objects of knowledge. This involved holding to a distinction between ontology and epistemology – but one that gave priority to the ontological. This is different, for example, from Kant's transcendental idealism where, according to Bhaskar, in attempting to "save the empirical character of our knowledge" Kant "involutes" ontology "within the transcendental subjectivity of the mind." This results in a "radical de-ontologizating of the world": the price Bhaskar believes that Kant pays for accepting Humean empirical realism (Bhaskar 1994: 204).

Within transcendental realism, it is only after establishing the ontological properties of societies that an understanding of how social science must proceed can be grasped. To put it simply, human knowledge is possible only because humans exist in the world. The qualities of natural or social objects exist independently of human knowledge or experience of them. Not knowing an object is solid until it is picked up or, for example, being unaware of the injurious effects of class relations until one loses her job, does not deny the pre-existence of things like sticks, stones or capitalism. Rather, the reality of both natural and social things consists in their deep structures and generative mechanisms. Their natures not only determine the ways in which humans can interact with them but they are also contingent conditions for knowledge of them.

The problem Bhaskar sets out to confront here is well known in social science: how to reconcile what Callinicos calls the "orthodox conception of agents" "– which takes persons seriously as initiators of action – with the idea that social structures (for example, social relations of production) have causal powers" (2004: xix). It is also a problem well-known within Marxism. For example, it surfaces in Thompson's famous rejection of Althusser's anti-humanism (Thompson 1978), which subsequently opened the door to Nietzschean pluralism and Weberian methodological individualism (see Callinicos 1999; Elliot 2006). In the former with its "post"-ing of Marx, relations of production are lost in heterogenous struggles for power. While in the latter "neo"-ing causal powers of both agents and structures are left as a mystery. Bhaskar's solution to the problem of structure and agency is to recognize them as an analytic dualism: that there is "an ontological hiatus between society and people" (Bhaskar 1998: 37). Both structures and agents have distinct causal powers and effectivities: each are emergently real. Bhaskar recognizes that reductive social atomism touches an assumed ontological truth: society only consists of people and their actions. But the "truth" glimpsed by methodological individualism is only a partial one. For Bhaskar, individualists are correct to affirm that society is made up of people and that social changes are always related to people's actions. However, what escapes voluntarists is a truth captured by methodological collectivists: social structures are imposing and determining. As social theorists have long recognized, both models cannot be true to the exclusion of the other and, as Bhaskar observes, it has been "tempting to try and develop a general model capable of synthesising these conflicting perspectives" (1998: 32). Bhaskar describes such efforts to accommodate both voluntarism (typical of Weberian hermeneutics) and reification (typical of Durkheimian positivism) in a coherent social theory as "conflationist." The essence of conflationism takes individuals as both, *simultaneously*, creatures and creators of their social worlds. Bhaskar recognizes that conflationism has some kind of immediate common sense appeal. In the concrete complexity of everyday life, the activity of agents and the social structures they make can *appear* indistinguishable.

However, for Bhaskar, rather than solving the problems of voluntarism where "there are actions, but no conditions" and structuralism where there are "conditions, but no actions" (1998: 37), conflationism only succeeds in amalgamating the problems. In contrast, critical realism takes "individuals" and "structures" as ontologically (and analytically) distinguishable and stratified. In other words, societies (which preexist people) are not agents and people (who make societies) are not social structures. The properties possessed by, and the mechanisms consisting in, one are different from the other. According to Margaret Archer, it is Bhaskar's insight into "the *pre-existence* and *autonomy* of social forms [that] marks a real turn of the tide" (1995: 138) in theorizing the relation between structure and agency. Furthermore, Bhaskar's insistence that "the genesis of human actions, lying in the reasons, intentions and plans of people ... and the structures governing the reproduction and transformation of social activities" (1998: 35) can be distinguished also has a common sense appeal. As he insists, "we do not suppose that the reason why the garbage is collected is necessarily the garbage collector's reason for collecting it (though it depends upon the latter)" (Bhaskar 1998: 37). In acknowledging Marx, Bhaskar draws attention to the "ontological hiatus" between people and societies by insisting that "people, in their conscious activity, for the most part unconsciously reproduce (and occasionally transform) the structures governing their substantive activities of production" (Bhaskar 1998: 35). On this point, Bhaskar might well have quoted Marx directly:

> Men make their own history, but they do not make it just as they please; they do not make it under circumstances chosen by themselves, but under circumstances

directly encountered, given and transmitted from the past. The tradition of all the dead generations weighs like a nightmare on the brain of the living.

(Marx 1969: 398)

Reconsidering historical materialism: emergent Marxism and the base/superstructure metaphor

Holding to an emergentist ontology, a critical realist meta-theory of stratification can assert that relations between levels of generative mechanisms in open systems do not conform to laws of simple correspondence. Higher-level mechanisms are rooted in lower ones: existing by virtue of, but not reducible to them. If, as I argue, we can take the Marxian view of history as an emergent one, the very materiality of the "economic base" and the "forces of production" places them at deeper ontological levels than the "superstructure" and "relations of production." With social being rooted in the material, we can say, in critical realist terms, that the "superstructure" and "relations of production" are emergent forms of the "economic base" and the "forces of production." Material and social mechanisms exist in vertically stratified but non-reductive relations. As Marx (1973) has put it, the material is "pre-dominant" – and not functionally determinant. In his dialectical interpretation of historical materialism, Hunt (1998) – without recourse to critical realism – makes a similar point. Taking forces and relations of production, and base and superstructure, as consisting in a "unity of opposites," Hunt understands their interactions as reciprocal and mutually defining but not symmetrical. The base and forces of production have overall "orchestrating" roles. For example, referring specifically to the primacy of the forces of production, Hunt notes that

> When Marx says that production is the "predominant moment" when compared with consumption, he can be understood as claiming that in any clash between ends and means, specifically between our wants and our capacity to provide for them through production, the means of action we possess have a more powerful effect on the outcome than our desires have. It is easier in the short run for us to adapt our wants to our circumstances than it is to adapt our means of action to our wants. The objective standpoint is the correct one because reality is relatively intractable.
>
> (1998: 172)

Following Marx, Hunt argues that whatever the particular interests or wants might be they are more likely to be realized where conditions shaping the means to act are favorable. In the end, those conditions are materially rooted in a hierarchy of human interests where "interest in material well-being is a more powerful spring of action than loyalty to existing forms of ownership and control over production" (1998: 173). The great contradiction of capitalist production arises from the historical fact that it is not organized to meet such interests. Indeed, its relations of production are not geared to satisfy even the most basic of human *needs*: to fulfill its "first historical act," as Marx put it, directed to the "production of material life itself" (1976: 47). Rather, capitalist production is – first and foremost – organized to extract surplus value from the producing class such that economic production "comes to a standstill not at the point where needs are satisfied, but rather where the production and realization of profit impose this" (Marx 1981: 367). From this we can deduce, as Michael Lebowitz (1992) does, that implicit in the "primacy of the forces of relations" thesis are deeper mechanisms resting in the reality of human needs rooted in but not reducible to the laws of motion of the natural world. Accordingly

> no one would suggest that capitalist relations of production sheepishly step aside to let the new era begin ... people *recognise* the inadequacy of capitalist relations and do away with them ... social change occurs when the existing structure of society no longer satisfies the needs of people formed in that society; it occurs when the relations of production prevent the development of productive forces *in a way which conforms to the particular needs of definite human beings.*
>
> (Lebowitz 1992: 127)

The acknowledgment of human needs and the human powers to consciously change material circumstances to realize those needs brings active human beings to the fore. History requires agents. But agents – as ontologically distinct from, and rooted in, social and natural forms – are never unfettered. While emphasizing the human power to consciously and actively transcend relations, the "primacy of need" *also* recognizes, in this instance, capital's tendency to the "constant generation of new social needs for commodities, the production of new links in the golden chain which binds workers to capital" (Lebowitz 1992: 127). In concert with a realist ontology of emergence, a non-reductive materialism holding to a "primacy of need" can explain why relations of production, and superstructural mechanisms, may be dominant at times – and over time – while simultaneously allowing, as Bhaskar would insist, reasons having causal efficacy. Acknowledging the rootedness of the "mental" and "social" in the "material" allows for the rejection of crude mechanistic causality while asserting the existence of a mind independent reality. As Marx said of "society": it "must always be envisaged ... as the pre-condition of comprehension" (1970: 207). The material needs of human beings, and the particular way a society organizes its productive capacities to meet those needs, conditions – ether-like – all other societal relations and forms of social consciousness:

> In all forms of society there is one specific kind of production which predominates over the rest, whose relations thus assign rank and influence to the others. It is a general illumination which bathes all the other colours and modifies their particularity. It is a particular ether which determines the specific gravity of every being which has materialised within it.
>
> (Marx 1973: 106–7)

Marx's imagery of a "particular ether" washing over and modifying particulars draws us to Bhaskar's understanding of deep mechanisms and the autonomy of the intransitive dimension of science. In critical realist terms, the experiences, events and concepts that comprise the Domain of the Actual are contextually sensitive emergent features of the Deep Real (see Table 6.1).

Consequently, ontological stratification must be between generative mechanisms (captured conceptually in predicates such as "economic," "political" and "ideological") and not between particular entities, events or experiences that belong in the Domain of the Actual. As such, particular social institutions like schools, for example, consist in a multiplicity of interacting mechanisms and perform a variety of (economic, political and ideological) functions. They are not simply, as Althusserians might have it, "ideological apparatuses" but mechanisms of "many determinations" operating within and between ontological levels. In his critical realist explanation of historical materialism, Collier (1989) describes these as "horizontal" and "vertical" causal relations. As we have seen in Hunt's explication, the former refers to mechanisms operating conjointly while the latter involves a relation in which a higher order mechanism is determined by a lower one. To consolidate his point about the nature of stratification in open systems, Collier provides an instructive concrete example. Drawing attention to the workings of a factory he notes that the "factory will work when the laws of physics and economics permit, but either a mechanical breakdown or a recession will stop it" (Collier 1989: 49).

Here Collier points to physical and economic mechanisms co-determining events. While the laws of physics govern the structure and material possibilities for the factory, economics govern the social relations of production. However, this is not the end of it. The laws of physics and those of economics exist in an asymmetrical, or vertical, relation of determination. While physics is not dependant upon economics, economic mechanisms cannot operate outside physical laws. No matter how much a capitalist might want to intensify the working day or cut back on essential machine maintenance to increase profits, there comes a point where human beings and machines break down. Equally, an economic system that works on the assumption that its laws operate at a more basic stratum than those of physics, biology or ecology will (in the end) be unsustainable.

Here we are reminded that the Domain of the Real consists in more than *social* mechanisms. Consistent with Marx and Engel's ontological materialism, social forms are rooted in *non*-social strata. As Marx insisted, the natural world is "man's inorganic body": "Nature is his body and he must maintain a continuing dialogue with it if he is not to die" (Marx 1975: 328). However, such a dialogue is difficult – and uniquely so – when the capitalist mode of production is predominant:

> It is not the *unity* of living and active humanity with the natural, inorganic conditions of their metabolic exchange with nature ... which requires explanation or is the result of historical process, but rather the *separation* between these inorganic conditions of human existence and this active existence, a separation which is completely posited only in the relation of wage labour and capital.
>
> (Marx 1973: 489)

It is to this "separation" of "active humanity" and its "inorganic condition" that

Foster (2000) draws our attention in his call for a "strong historical materialism," one that explicitly recognizes the "metabolism of man and society" (Marx 1976).[5] For Foster, echoing Marx, it is only by "connecting materialism ... to the natural/physical conditions of reality ... [that] such fundamental issues as life and death, reproduction, dependence on the biosphere ... [can] be addressed" (2000: 8).

In his development of a critical realist "emergent" Marxism, Creaven (2000) also suggests a "wider application" of the base-superstructure metaphor to include more base-ic mechanisms. It is useful for us to consider it here. Creaven presents a tripartite model consisting in "substructural," "structural" and "superstructural" levels where the latter two have a close correspondence to the traditional understandings of "base" and "superstructure." As such, ideological forms in addition to social and cultural relations comprise the "superstructure." Economic and class relations comprise the "structure" stratum. Creaven's "substructure" – the level with the greatest ontological presupposition – contains "humanity's biologically-given needs and capacities" (Creaven 2000: 60).

However, Creaven's model does not completely satisfy the criteria for a "strong" historical materialism that Foster (2000) might claim that Marx and Engels would advocate. While "emergent Marxism" emphasizes the essentiality of human biology, the natural conditions in which that biology is rooted remain implicit. Recognizing the natural conditions of capitalist production reveals what O'Connor aptly refers to as the "second contradiction of capitalism": "the general contradiction between capitalism and nature ... the contradiction between self-expanding capital and self-limiting nature" (1998: 10). A reconstructed base/superstructure model capturing a "strong" historical materialism can be represented as in Figure 6.1.

Strong historical materialism reflects the non-reductive ontology advanced by Marx in his critique of political economy. It takes the natural and social worlds as co-existing in a stratified, differentiated and dynamically emergent totality. Contra

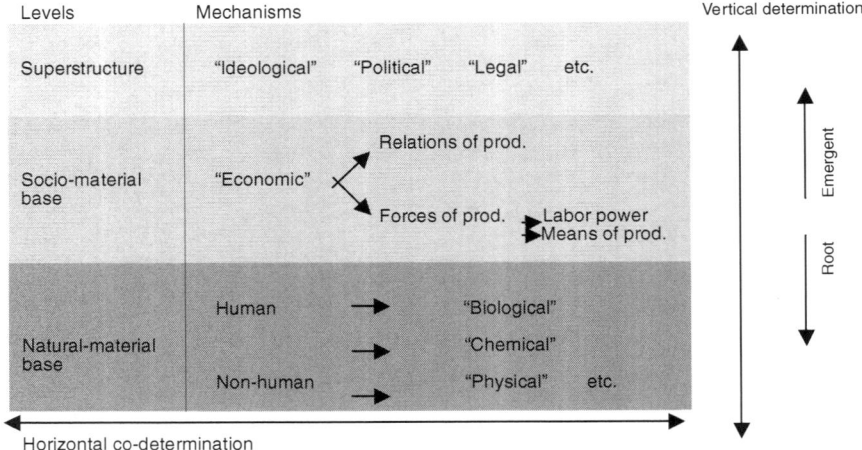

Figure 6.1 Strong historical materialism.

nominalism and conceptualism, where only particulars are understood to exist or where universals are seen as consisting only in concepts, Figure 6.1 emphasizes that generative mechanisms are predicable of particular objects. We see that it is these mechanisms – not objects, events or ideas – that exist in stratified (vertically determined) and differentiated (horizontally co-determined) relations. As such, we can say that Marx's historical materialism is a species of immanent realism where universals are intrinsic to particulars (see Niiniluoto 2002; Timpanaro 1975). The dynamism of the world is not the result of external (super-natural) force. Rather, change is immanent to it.

Figure 6.1 captures the idea of immanent dynamism in its co-representation of stratification and differentiation. Firstly, in relation to stratification, this particular dynamism extends vertically downwards beyond the "economic" base – or, rather, the "Socio-Material Base" – to ontologically deeper biological, chemical and mechanical mechanisms. This "Natural-Material Base" includes Creaven's substructural level of "human biology and its natural powers" (2000: 59) as well as the non-human world of living and non-living things. The vertical extension of the material base serves to emphasize the rootedness of the social in the deep-material and, for example, the importance of understanding the inter-relations between social and ecological systems.

Secondly to the dynamism of differentiation, it is to be noted that at particular times and under certain conditions some mechanisms will remain un-activated – but nevertheless still real. For example, while "Socio-Material" contradictions will vertically emerge at the "Superstructural" level in unpredictable ways, they will also horizontally co-determine events with other local and contextually dependent mechanisms. Claiming class relations are essential to capitalism does not mean that all events will be determined by them. Actual concrete events have to be understood as complex determinations of structured interacting mechanisms. This means grasping the predominant – and contextually novel – relations between class and, for example, other forms of oppression. In this way it makes sense to talk of the classed nature of "race," gender or whatever form of "social disadvantage" to which sociologists might refer.[6] Here we come close to Althusser's use of "overdetermination." According to Althusser, "the overdetermination of a contradiction is the reflection in it of its conditions of existence within the complex whole ... its uneven development" (1996: 253).

Indeed, we might ask, as Collier has: "What is this 'overdetermination' but 'multiple determination?'" (1989: 64). But Collier's question is a rhetorical one. He insists that, in Althusser's hands, "overdetermination" operates – unlike Bhaskar's "multiple determination" – at such a high level of generality "so as to *lose* specificity" (1989: 61). Althusser never explicitly drew out the nature of the relationship between base and superstructure. It is one thing to assert, for example, that "there are different practices that are really distinct, even though they belong organically to the same complex totality" (Althusser 1996: 167), but this does not substitute for social theory. In effect, what Althusser left was "the gesture of an intention but hardly a substantive theory" (Geras 1978: 264). This lacuna in his work has had significant repercussions for social theory generally and the development of Western Marxism in particular. According to Bhaskar, it was Althusser's conflation of the transitive and intransitive dimensions of science together with his "unrelenting hostility to ontology" (1989: 207–8) that made his formulations of, for example, "overdetermination" and "relative autonomy", attractive to neo-Kantians:

> Althusser's failure to give any apodeictic status to the real object rendered it as theoretically dispensable as a Kantian thing-in-itself and helped lay the ground for the worst excesses of post-structuralism.
>
> (Bhaskar 1989: 188)

Up to this point in the chapter I have put the case for a "strong historical materialism": one that endorses Engelsian naturalism (Engels 1969) and insists upon a stratified, emergent, ontology. Against bourgeois assertions, class does not simply evaporate if it does not appear in ways predicted or if it fails to conform to preconceived epistemological categories. The flat actualist ontology assumed by pluralism and empiricism is not only inadequate for an understanding of the deep-real nature of capitalist class relations but a manifestation of those relations. Likewise, strong historical materialism provides little comfort to reductionist and mechanical Marxist accounts of history. In this sense, "overdetermination" and "relative autonomy" theorists are right to insist that there is no direct relation between economic mechanisms and social change. However, this does not legitimate a structurally disengaged (non-emergent and ontologically flat) fascination with the local and the particular. As we will see in the following sections, such fascinations prove inadequate guides for revolutionary practice.

Marx's dialectic method: ruthless critique for revolutionary practice

> Up to now the philosophers had the solution of all riddles lying in their lectern, and the stupid uninitiated world had only to open its jaws to let the roast partridges of absolute science fly into its mouth ... But if the designing of the future and proclamation of ready-made solutions for all time is not our affair, then we realize all the more clearly what we have to accomplish in present – I am speaking of a *ruthless criticism of everything existing*, ruthless in two senses: The criticism must not be afraid of its own conclusion, nor of conflict with the powers that be.
>
> (Marx 1978: 13)

Unlike bourgeois economists whose intentions rest in description and prediction, Marx's purpose was to understand capitalism as a dynamic system and analyze it in its very movement. Rather than setting out to develop economic laws to direct human beings on how to live within capitalist relations, Marx was to show through "a ruthless criticism of everything existing" the necessity of transcending those relations in order to live humanly. According to Ollman, what is most distinctive about

Marx's method of critique was the way his abstractions "focus on and incorporate both change and interaction ... in the particular forms in which these occur in the capitalist era" (1993: 28).

In his introduction to the *Grundrisse*, Marx (1973) provides a succinct outline of his method. It is here that we learn, in general terms, that Marx abstracts from the "real concrete" to the "thought concrete." But Marx insists that it is not immediately obvious what the "real concrete" is. Nevertheless, "it seems to be correct" in economics to start with "the population" as the "real precondition": "the real and the concrete" (100). However, as it turns out, "population" itself is an abstraction if the classes which comprise it are ignored. And, in turn, classes are but an "empty phrase" (100) if wage labor, capital, value, price and profit remain out of focus. In short, beginning with "population" is to start with "a chaotic conception of the whole" (100). So, the movement of Marx's abstraction proceeds from the "imagined concrete" through "ever thinner abstractions" (100) to the "simplest determinations" only to return again to the "population." But upon return, the "population" is no longer a "chaotic conception." Rather, it is appropriated in thought as a "rich totality of many determinations and relations" (101). Here we can see Marx holding to what we recognize as the intransitive/transitive distinction in critical realism. Keeping separate the real objects and the thought objects of science Marx seeks to avoid the Hegelian illusion of idealism "of conceiving the real as the product of thought concentrating itself, probing its own depths, and unfolding itself out of itself, by itself" (Marx 1973: 101).

Marx's critique of Hegelian dialectics and his summation that it required a complete inversion "in order to discover the rational kernel within the mystical shell" (1976: 103) did not mean that he rejected it *in toto*. While jettisoning Hegel's idealist metaphysics, both Marx and Engels adopted his dialectical method. This meant taking from Hegel the understanding that the world is to be grasped in its essence: as an internally contradictory totality existing in a constant process of change (see Rees 1998, Chapter 2). But in contrast to Hegel, "external" reality was not to be taken as a projection of human consciousness whose contradictions could ultimately be resolved in thought. For Marx and Engels, it is in the material world, as the manifestation of human productive activity, where contradictions are confronted and fought out.

Illustrative of the way Marx abstracts is the manner in which he holds, and uses, the distinction between "production" and "production in general." At times Marx refers to "production" as it occurs "at a definite stage of social development – production by social individuals" or indeed, more specifically to a "particular branch of production – e.g. agriculture, cattle raising, manufactures etc." (Marx 1973: 85, 86). At other times production is given an extension across time and location or abstracted for ontological depth to grasp, in general, the natural necessity of production and productive labor itself. Ollman (1993) refers to these two moves as "modes of abstraction": the first being an "extension" and the second a "generality." An abstraction of extension represents a spacio-temporal stretch across the horizontal co-determination of mechanisms identified in Figure 6.1. On the other hand, generality strives for ontological reach into the vertical stratification of Being , as we also saw in Figure 6.1. The inter-relation of these modes of abstraction can be represented as in Figure 6.2.

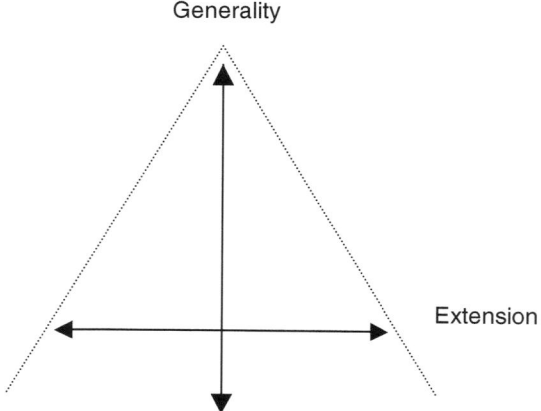

Figure 6.2 The dimensions of spacio-temporal extension and ontological generality.

Here we see that with each vertical abstraction comes a horizontal move and vice versa. As Ollman puts it, in "acquiring an extension, all Marx's units of thought acquire in the same act of abstraction a level of generality" (1993: 56). The double arrows indicate movement back and along the planes of extension and generality. Furthermore, the dotted lines joining the two modal movements define the territory brought into potential focus by the pairing of abstractions. Significantly, abstractions that either narrow spacio-temporal stretch or constrain ontological reach seriously limit emancipatory critique and the possibility of revolutionary practice. The former (i.e. the narrowing of stretch) tends to monism where the assumption of pre-destined futures makes politics and class struggle irrelevant. The latter tends to actualism that offers, in its heterogeneous depthlessness, not new horizons but, as Bhaskar has aptly put it, "an actualist blanket suffocating hope" (1994: 107).

Marxian abstractions are wide and deep. However, the simple recognition of this fact is not enough to grasp *how* Marx actually worked to appropriate in thought the "rich totality" of determining and co-determining mechanisms. Nor is this recognition sufficient to understand *how* a dynamic totality can be analyzed in its movement. But if, as I have argued, critical realist underlaboring clears some conceptual ground around this matter, one thing is clear: a "building block" approach, as Harvey has described it, "so typical of bourgeois social science" (2006: 3) with its Humean assumptions of causation, will be grossly inadequate – not only for understanding Marxian dialectics but also as a basis for emancipatory critique and revolutionary practice. Rather than isolating the likes of events, experiences and concepts from their social conditions, Marx moved systematically and deliberately from one aspect – or a necessary condition of an aspect – to another in the "totality." To effect such movement Marx employed what Ollman calls the "abstraction of vantage point": the application of a particular perspective that "colors everything that falls into it, establishing order, hierarchy, and priorities, distributing values, meanings and degrees of relevance, and asserting a distinctive coherence between the parts" (1993: 68).

Together with the abstractions of extension and generality, vantage point operates like a focus control on a microscope bringing clarity to some things while blurring or completely ignoring others. Moving from one vantage point to another Marx was able to show what particular vistas reveal – or indeed what they conceal. For example, the material realities of working-class life bring with them certain vantage points. The abstractions which workers use "to make sense of their society [is] likely to include 'labour' ... which puts the activity that is chiefly responsible for social change at the front and centre of their thinking" (Ollman 1993: 69). In contrast, capitalists are likely "to start making sense of their situation with the aid of 'price', 'profit', and other abstractions drawn from the market-place" (Ollman 1993: 70). Figure 6.3 depicts the incorporation of vantage point into a representation of Ollman's three modes of abstraction.

It is to be stressed that, in Marx's hands, "vantage points" are not abstract imaginings. They are *a posteriori* positionings drawn from knowledge of natural kinds and empirical evidence. Marx does not impose his abstractions on the world. Social class is not simply a conceptual invention – a sociological category or mere adjective. Unlike bourgeois social science, "classical" Marxism does not take social class to refer to groups of people or events, but deep-real mechanisms. Even amongst theoreticians broadly sympathetic to the revolutionary impulse of Marxism this is not well understood. In a final move to bring the arguments of this chapter into focus and point to the possibilities of socialist pedagogy, it is to one such "sympathetic" source that the chapter turns: the post-structural "discourse" theorizing of Gibson-Graham (1996).[7]

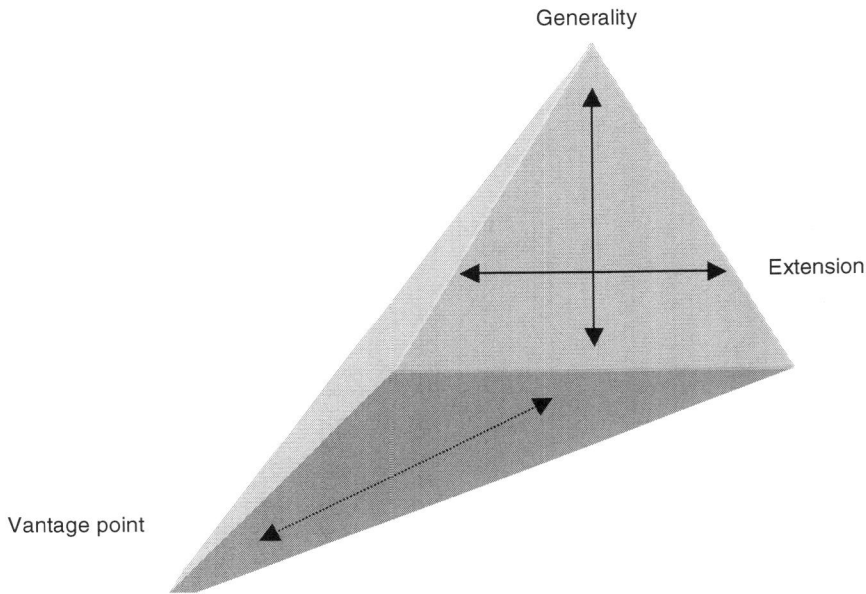

Figure 6.3 The three-dimensional modal operation incorporating vantage point.

The case of Gibson-Graham and the possibility of socialist pedagogy

Gibson-Graham's book, *The End of Capitalism (as we knew it): A Feminist Critique of Political Economy*, is the outcome of a self-professed intellectual journey nurtured within the Althusserian-inspired work of Stephen Resnick and Richard Wolff and their *Rethinking Marxism* project (Gibson-Graham 1996). Through "the strategies of postmodern Marxism and poststructural feminism," Gibson-Graham set out to disrupt old "modernist" modes of theorizing and "re-imagine" capitalism. Indeed, they take the very power and historical durability of capitalism as an outcome of certain "discursive commitments" that include "organicist social conceptions, heroic historical narratives, evolutionary scenarios of social development, and essentialist, phallocentric, or binary patterns of thinking" (Gibson-Graham 1996: 4, 5).

For Gibson-Graham, the origin of such modernist sins[8] of theorizing lie in the seductiveness of metaphors that depict structured totalities "made up of hierarchically ordered parts [that are] energised by an immanent force" (1996: 97). In Gibson-Graham's reckonings with "totality" we see a familiar ontological shyness: the neo-Kantian's want to "de-ontologize" the world. Capitalism, we are told by Gibson-Graham, is to be seen as "an uncentered aggregate of practices" as this enables us to "step outside the discourse of Capitalism, to abjure its powers and transcend the limits it has placed on socialist activity" (1996: 255, 264). To assist with this nominalist project of cutting particulars from their universals, Althusser's idea of "overdetermination" is called upon "to forgo the ecstasy of rationalism and the arrogant security of determinant effects" (Gibson-Graham 1996: 119).

In an interesting attempt at freeing analysis from the "arrogant security" of generality, Gibson-Graham (1996: 192–205) offer the case of Broken Hill Proprietary Limited (BHP) where, in the 1980s, the "Big Australian" moved to internationalize its business interests and steel production. Faced with global competition, BHP was compelled – "on the pain of extinction" as Marx and Engels (1969: 112) put it in 1848 – to introduce new technologies, to restructure and sometimes close plant operations in order to achieve ever more efficient ways of extracting surplus value from labor. Gibson-Graham note that both corporate and "leftist" discourses of the time served to construct and reinforce universalist and essentialist accounts of BHP and surrounding events. In contrast, and following the "anti-essentialist" lead offered by fellow post-Marxists Resnick and Wolff (1987),[9] Gibson-Graham suggest, as an act of "epistemological terrorism," the construction of "an alternative vision of BHP as decentred, fluid, disorderly and racked with uncertainty" (1996: 201). However, they recognize that such an act brings with it some difficulties:

> there are limits upon such a tactic. To create a discourse of the enterprise as a dissipative system, as empty, as multiple, as the site of competing and exhaustive claims, as made up of individuals who are many things (including local community dwellers and family members, philanthropists and ruthless managers, staunch unionists, and misogynists), and as a constellation of dynamics (of profitability, conservatism, disaccumulation, philanthropy, competition and

protection, to name just a few, is almost too daunting in the face of an over-whelming scepticism born, perhaps, of a lack of desire for such a discourse.

(Gibson-Graham 1996: 201)

In Gibson-Graham's pessimistic assessment of their epistemological tactics, some now familiar themes re-emerge. Firstly, as in all anti-naturalist and anti-foundation-alist conventionalisms, Gibson-Graham's post-Marxism tends to methodological individualism. As we see in the above assessment, the "social" is taken as simply short-hand for various groups of individuals (e.g. philanthropists, managers, union-ists, etc.) who interact within a somewhat vague array of "dynamics." Indeed, this "tactic" of *social reductionism* is evident throughout their text. In relation to class, for example, it is straightforwardly described as "a group of individuals" brought together through "a process without essence" (Gibson-Graham 1996: 50, 55). Like Resnick and Wolff, who only allow class the status of an adjective (1987: 159), Gibson-Graham de-ontologize class and commit it to the Domain of the Actual where distinguishing between different events, experiences and concepts substitutes for differentiating mechanisms. This, the second of our familiar themes, is reflective of a neo-Kantian assumption of Humean causation and the subsequent reluctance to distinguish be-tween the transitive and intransitive dimensions of science.[10] With class understood as no more than an actual empirical process occurring alongside many other equally influential empirical processes, or "aspects of society" (Gibson-Graham 1996: 55), the idea of the transcendence of class becomes a nonsense. Indeed, class is something to be embraced and nurtured. As Gibson-Graham plainly put it: "Our political and theoretical interest is in creating alternative (and potentially emancipatory) economic futures in which class diversity can flourish" (1996: 52).

What we observe in the overdetermined theories of Gibson-Graham and Resnick and Wolff is the conflation of the abstract with the concrete where heuristic devices become "reality" (see Note 10). This move has political consequences. Without bringing specificity to the concrete – beyond its discursive content – the potency of theory to inform practice is diminished. For it is in the real-concrete world where transformative work and practice occurs. For Marx, revolutionary practice is theo-retically informed practice that entails abstracting from the "chaotic conception of the whole" to the "simplest determinations" only to return, not to chaotic conceptions, but the appropriation in thought of a "rich totality of many determinations." This movement is impossible for Gibson-Graham and Resnick and Wolff: they never leave the chaotic conception of the whole.

Furthermore, the off-hand, and out-of-hand, dismissal of critical realism by both Gibson-Graham and Resnick and Wolff reveals how strongly they are welded to their neo-Kantianism and a subsequent fear of the "universal" – expressed, for example, as reflection of anything deemed "determinist," "essentialist" or "teleological." This is un-fortunate – particularly for Gibson-Graham who search for an "emergent Marxism" (1996: 112) – because Bhaskar (like Marx) is not committed to "universality" but to "necessity." A serious engagement with Bhaskar's work, rather than a conviction by caricature (see Note 10), might have provided a vantage point from which to possibly see anew their epistemological, ontological *and* ideological commitments. As this chapter has shown, in realist (and historical materialist) terms, "necessity" refers to "natural necessity" that is expressed in the power of things: in deep-real mechanisms. In relation to emergent strata, power is structurally determined. However, in its horizontal engagement with other co-determining mechanisms, certain powers may be nullified and others amplified. How powers *actually* play out in different contexts and at other times is a matter for empirical work. There are no pre-determined guarantees. Equally, power is not an obscure mystery chaotically dispersed in a myriad of heterogenous happenings.

For instance, as a class, capitalists have power over workers because of their structurally instantiated ability to supervise labor, control investment, and purchase labor power. The relation between workers and capitalists is not a contingent one based on chance encounters. It is an enduring and *necessary* relation: one in which capitalists *need* the power of labor and workers *must* sell their labor power in order to survive. However, although workers are in a subordinate position they are not power-less. They have, for example, the capacity to withhold their labor. This capacity, of course, is highly contingent – shaped by local circumstances and historical struggle. Not the least of these are concessions won by the working class that have resulted in specific legislative arrangements around, for example, the length of the working day, conditions of employment, and the right to strike.

According to Marx, capitalism carries deep within it the triggers of its own destruction: "there are so many mines to explode it." But Marx recognized that this destruction will not occur on its own in "quiet metamorphosis" (Marx 1973: 159). A human future requires human intervention. Those potential flash-points – the deep-real contradictions at the very heart of capitalism – have to be actively and consciously exposed. But this exposure requires more than just "seeing" capitalist life as it appears or simply imaging things differently. While gross disparities in wealth and environmental destruction, for example, stare us in the face every day, grasping the essence of those absurdities is not a straightforward matter. Penetrating the surface appearance of capitalist social relations of production demands nothing less than deliberate teaching of Marxist critique to develop class consciousness beyond its *embryonic form* (Lenin 1902, Section 2.1).

Conclusion

This chapter points to the necessity of critique – for a socialist pedagogy – in the realization of a truly human future. The chapter's method has been to use critical realism to argue for a strong historical materialism that grasps class as the deep-real, essential feature of capitalism. This method – also an act of critique – follows Lenin's insistence that the realization of socialism is impossible without a revolutionary theory (1902, Section 2.1). Class struggle, in other words, includes theoretical struggle – or, we might say, a struggle for "vantage point." A socialist pedagogy then, whether it is developed and practiced in worker organizations, the halls of academia, homes, factories, churches or schools, is the deliberate working towards and active construction of vantage points that enable (1) a *stretching* across geo-space while simultaneously connecting past, present and future and (2) *reaching* into the ontologically deep thereby connecting the contradictory necessities of human beings (rooted in both the natural and social worlds) and capitalism.

While providing only the broad sketch of socialist pedagogy here, describing it as a struggle over vantage point is not to be interpreted as advocating a struggle simply over words or ideas. Class struggle is about real things and things that really matter, i.e. the world as it *is* and what it can *become*. This necessarily requires an engagement with the world through theoretically informed practice.

Notes

1 What follows in this chapter is the outcome of conversations with colleagues, comrades and critical friends for some time now around the general question: "Does Marxism really need critical realism?" Important among this group are Sam Sellar, Jenni Carter and Chris Davis (our "Writing Group") who always manage to push me in directions that continually surprise. I would also like to thank Rachel Sharp, Sean Creaven and Greg Martin who kindly took time to read and comment upon earlier drafts. And, in particular, I would like to express my indebtedness to Deb Kelsh for her generous support and encouragement through the process of preparing this work for publication. Her critique-al engagement with the ideas I attempt to develop within and her insightful feedback have, I believe, significantly strengthened the final result. In the end, of course, all errors that remain are mine.

2 Describing the base-superstructure relationship as a "metaphor" is not meant to convey the idea that it is simply a heuristic device or theoretical abstraction. Rather, it is to be taken to refer to the objects of Marxist scientific work: the stratified nature and broad causal relations of human societies. In critical realist terms, the "metaphor" belongs to the "intransitive" dimension of science rather than its epistemological, or "transitive," dimension (Bhaskar 1978). With this understanding, the descriptors of "metaphor" and "model" will be used throughout the chapter.

3 In this essay the adjective "classical" will at times precede the noun "Marxism." On such occasions the adjective will be placed within "scare quotes" to highlight one of two things. Firstly, it will be to indicate that such a descriptor is not unproblematic. Within the history of Marxism, scholars differ in their interpretations of what Marx and Engels actually meant to convey through their materialist theory of history. Some, like Cohen (1978) for example, draw largely from analytic philosophy to define and distinguish between ideas like "base" and "superstructure" or "relations of production" and "forces of production," while others interpret historical materialism from a dialectical tradition of internal relations (see Sayer 1987; Ollman 1993). On other occasions, "classical" will be employed to distinguish the above accounts from anti-, neo-, and post-Marxist positions that reject "old-fashioned" historical materialism as positivist, reductionist and historicist.

4 This is not an error to which Bhaskar considers Marx fell. As Hartwig (2007) notes, Bhaskar recognizes that the instransitive/transitive distinction "was probably first conceptualised (in effect) by Marx in distinguishing 'objectivity' as such from the 'objectification' ('objectivation') of human praxis" (264).

5 Marx employs the organic metaphor "metabolism" to indicate that the natural and social worlds are internally related and comprise a differentiated totality. Social metabolism as the "metamorphosis of commodities" occurring through the labor process (see Marx 1976: 198–209) and the circulation of capital (see Marx 1981, Chapter 19) rests in the deeper "metabolic interaction [*Stoffwechsel*] between man and nature [which is] the everlasting nature imposed condition of human existence" (Marx 1976: 290).

6 Unlike class, social "disadvantage" emerging from the likes of "race" and gender inequalities is superstructural. Their roots are not material. For instance, in relation to the idea of "race," Carter (2003) notes that "few contemporary social scientists would wish to defend ... race as a category describing significant genotypical or phenotypical variation among

human populations or ... aver a belief in the existence of biological races" (151). "Race," in other words, is a social invention: an "historical novelty," as Callinicos (1993) has described it, "characteristic of capitalist societies" (16). Likewise, gender is a superstructural mechanism. However, it is important to note that in realist approaches to sex and gender it is common to differentiate between the two. The latter, like "race," is a higher order emergent feature of specific social, cultural and economic arrangements. The former, on the other hand, refers to natural kinds (males and females). But, unlike class, "sexual difference has no political implications itself: those emerge from organisation at higher levels" (New 2005: 70).

7 J. K. Gibson-Graham is a writing identity comprising two persons: Katherine Gibson and Julie Graham. I will refer to the writing persona "Gibson-Graham" in the plural.

8 In a critique of post-Marxist accounts of historical materialism and class analysis, McLennan (1996) identifies "Four Sins" that "modernist" Marxist theorizing is claimed to commit: reductionism, functionalism, essentialism and universalism. McLennan argues that, in general, post-Marxist claims rest on constructed caricatures of what "classical" Marxism is presumed to represent.

9 Space does not permit a detailed consideration of this very interesting piece of work upon which Gibson-Graham draw heavily. For those interested in a powerful Marxist critique of Resnick and Wolff (1987) I recommend Kelsh (1998). However, attention must be brought to one claim made by Resnick and Wolff: that Bhaskarian critical realism is a form of philosophical rationalism. In their eagerness to dismiss "realism" – apparently in all its many and varied philosophical colors – as having any greater explanatory power than their own epistemological position, Resnick and Wolff tie the general idea of philosophical "realism" directly to the sinful "rationalist school" (see McLennan 1996). Then, noting that Bhaskar "seems to exercise the widest influence amongst the realists" (Resnick and Wolff 1987: 288), Bhaskar's entire body of work is discarded in one broad sweep of association. With none of Bhasker's work cited by Resnick and Wolff, there is no indication they have read, let alone engaged with, any critical realist ideas. This seems strange for social theorists who claim to be committed to openness, heterogeneity and a "desire to communicate" (Resnick and Wolff 1987: 1). As I have shown earlier in this chapter, Bhaskar argues clearly and strongly that rationalism falls into the epistemic fallacy: it fails to distinguish between the transitive and intransitive dimensions of science. It is worthwhile revisiting what Bhaskar (1978) actually said about this matter, in relation to the possibility of scientific knowledge, a decade prior to the publication of Resnick and Wolff's *Knowledge and Class*:

> For the transcendental realist, it is not a necessary condition for the existence of the world that science occurs. But it is a necessary condition for the occurrence of science that the world exists and is of a certain type. Thus the possibility of our knowledge is not an essential property, and so cannot be a defining characteristic, of the world.
>
> (38)

10 I suspect that Gibson-Graham would reject this association with empiricism. Resnick and Wolff do so explicitly (see, for example, 1987: 7–10). However, while correctly rejecting the certainty of observational and experiential knowledge of actual events and processes, Gibson-Graham (as well as Resnick and Wolff) abandon the possibility of any extra-discursive checks on knowledge. As we have seen, this move is facilitated by the adoption of a sentiment: "overdetermination." In the hands of both sets of knowledge workers this leads to a conflation of thought-object and real-object. Marx's distinction between essence and appearance explicitly rejects such essentializing conflation. Efforts to reject empiricism while still holding to a flat ontology result in "idealist contortions where the essential and the abstract are denied any reference to real objects and are reduced to heuristic devices for understanding the empirical" (Sayer 1998: 134).

Bibliography

Althusser, L. (1996) *For Marx*, London: Verso.

Archer, M. (1995) *Realist Social Theory: the morphogenic approach*, Cambridge: Cambridge University Press.

Bhaskar, R. (1978) *A Realist Theory of Science*, 2nd edn, Sussex: Harvester.

—— (1986) *Scientific Realism and Human Emancipation*, London: Verso.

—— (1989) *Reclaiming Reality: a critical introduction to contemporary philosophy*, London: Verso.

—— (1991) *Philosophy and the Idea of Freedom*, Oxford: Basil Blackwell.

—— (1994) *Plato etc.: the problems of philosophy and their resolution*, London: Verso.

—— (1998) *The Possibility of Naturalism*, 3rd edn, London: Routledge.

Bowles, S. and Gintis, H. (1976). *Schooling in Capitalist America: educational reform and the contradictions of economic life*, London: Routledge & Kegan Paul.

Callinicos, A. (1993) *Race and Class*, London: Bookmarks.

—— (1999) *Social Theory: a historical introduction*, Cambridge: Polity.

—— (2004) *Making History: agency, structure and change in social theory*, Oxford: Polity.

Carter, B. (2003) "What race means to realists," in J. Cruickshank (ed.) *Critical Realism: the difference it makes*, London: Routledge.

Cohen, G. (1978) *Karl Marx's Theory of History: a defense*, Princeton: Oxford University Press.

Collier, A. (1989) *Scientific Realism and Socialist Thought*, Hemel Hemsptead: Harvester Wheatsheaf.

Creaven, S. (2000) *Marxism and Realism: a materialistic application of realism in the social sciences*, London: Routledge.

Elliot, G. (2006) *Althusser: the detour of theory*, 2nd edn, Leiden: Brill.

Engels, F. (1969; 1878) *Anti-Dühring*, London: Lawrence and Wishart.

Foster, J. B. (2000) *Marx's Ecology: materialism and nature*, New York: Monthly Review Press.

Geras, N. (1978) "Althusser's Marxism: an assessment," in *New Left Review* (eds) *Western Marxism: a critical reader*, London: Verso.

Gibson-Graham, J. K. (1996) *The End of Capitalism (as we knew it): a feminist critique of political economy*, Cambridge: Blackwell.

Gramsci, A. (1971) *Selections from the Prison Notebooks*, London: Lawrence & Wishart.

Hartwig, M. (ed.) (2007) *Dictionary of Critical Realism*, London: Routledge.

Harvey, D. (2006) *The Limits to Capital*, London: Verso.

Hunt, I. (1998) "A dialectical interpretation and resurrection of historical materialism," *Poznań Studies in the Philosophy of the Sciences and the Humanities*, 60: 153–95.

Kelsh, D. (1998) "Desire and class: the knowledge industry in the wake of poststructuralism," *Cultural Logic*, 1, 2. Online. Available at http://clogic.eserver.org/1–2/kelsh.html (accessed March 30, 2007).

Kuhn, R. (1996) "Class analysis and the Left in Australian history," in R. Kuhn and T. O'Lincoln (eds), *Class and Class Conflict in Australia*, Melbourne: Longman.

Lebowitz, M. (1992) *Beyond Capital: Marx's political economy of the working class*, London: Macmillan.

Lenin, V. I. (1902) *What Is To Be Done?* Online. Available at http://marxists.org/archive/lenin/works/download/what-itd.pdf (accessed March 28, 2007).

McLennan, G. (1996) "Post-Marxism and the 'Four Sins' of modernist theorizing," *New Left Review*, 218: 53–74.

Mandel, E. (1976) "Introduction," in K. Marx *Capital: a critique of political economy, Vol. I*, London: Penguin.

Marx, K. (1969; 1852) "The Eighteenth Brumaire of Louis Bonaparte," in *Karl Marx and Frederick Engels: selected works, Vol. 1*, Moscow: Progress Publishers.

—— (1970; 1859) *A Contribution to the Critique of Political Economy*, Moscow: Progress Publishers.

—— (1973; 1857–8) *Grundrisse: foundations of the critique of political economy*, London: Penguin.

—— (1975; 1844) "Economic and philosophical manuscripts," in *Karl Marx: early writings*, London: Pelican Books.

—— (1976; 1867) *Capital: a critique of political economy, Vol. I*, London: Penguin.

—— (1977; 1877) "Letter to Mikhailovsky," in D. McLennan (ed.) *Karl Marx: selected writings*, Oxford: Oxford University Press.

—— (1978; 1843) "For a Ruthless Criticism of Everything Existing," in R. Tucker (ed.) *The Marx-Engels Reader*, 2nd edn, New York: Norton.

—— (1981; 1894) *Capital: a critique of political economy, Vol. III*, London: Penguin.

Marx, K. and Engels, F. (1969; 1848) "Manifesto of the Communist Party," in *Karl Marx and Frederick Engels: selected works, Vol. 1*, Moscow: Progress Publishers.

—— (1976) *The German Ideology*, Moscow: Progress Publishers.

New, C. (2005) "Sex and gender: A critical realist approach," *New Formations*, 56: 54–70.

Niiniluoto, I. (2002) *Critical Scientific Realism*, Oxford: Oxford University Press.

O'Connor, J. (1998) *Natural Causes: essays in ecological Marxism*, New York: Guilford.

Ollman, B. (1993) *Dialectical Investigations*, New York: Routledge.

Rees, J. (1998) *The Algebra of Revolution: the dialectic and the classical Marxist tradition*, London: Routledge.

Resnick, S. and Wolff, R. (1987) *Knowledge and Class: a Marxian critique of political economy*, Chicago: The University of Chicago Press.

Sayer, A. (1998) "Abstraction: a realist interpretation," in M. Archer, *et al.* (eds) *Critical Realism: essential readings*, London: Routledge.

Sayer, D. (1987) *The Violence of Abstraction: the analytic foundations of historical materialism*, Oxford: Basil Blackwell.

Thompson, E. P. (1978) *The Poverty of Theory and Other Essays*, London: Merlin Press.

Timpanaro, S. (1975) *On Materialism*, London: New Left Books.

7 Globalization, class, and the social studies curriculum

E. Wayne Ross and Greg Queen

Abstract

The study of what is now called "globalization" – roughly meaning global linkages, organization of social life on a global scale, and growth of a global consciousness – has always had a place in the social studies curriculum in North America. And while globalization has never been the major focus of the social studies curriculum, it has been given significant attention in recent decades under the broad rubric of "global education." The term globalization has become ubiquitous, yet its meaning is notoriously slippery and used in contradictory ways. Our aims in this chapter are twofold. First we examine the concept of globalization in an attempt to identify various ways in which the term is used as part of the school curriculum. We argue that globalization is a key concept, perhaps the most important concept, within the social studies curriculum. Secondly, and based on our examination of what globalization is, we illustrate how issues of class and capitalism are central to teaching not only about globalization, but for the entire social studies curriculum.

Introduction

The study of what is now usually referred to as "globalization" – roughly meaning global linkages, organization of social life on a global scale, and growth of a global consciousness – has always had a place in the social studies curriculum, even if globalization *per se* has never been the major focus of that curriculum in North America. Moreover, while in recent decades globalization has been given significant attention by researchers under the broad rubric of "global education," critical perspectives on it remain largely absent from social studies classrooms (Gaudelli 2003; Merryfield and Subedi 2006).

Our aims in this chapter are twofold. First, because "globalization" has become a ubiquitous catchphrase, yet its meaning is notoriously slippery, we examine this concept, analyzing and identifying various ways in which the term is used, and argue that teaching about globalization should not be de-coupled from a class-based analysis of capitalism. We argue that globalization is a key concept, perhaps the most important concept, within the social studies curriculum and briefly outline some imperatives for why class remains central to social studies in schools. Second, based on our examination of what globalization is, we provide an extended description of how class analysis has been used as the organizing principle in a high school social studies course centered on globalization.

What is globalization?

Despite its widespread usage, or perhaps because of it, globalization remains ill-defined, contested, and is often employed in ways that obfuscate rather than clarify circumstances. A Google search of "define: globalization" returns 27 definitions. Perhaps the most representative of the definitions is: "the increasing interconnectedness of different parts of the world through common processes of economic, environmental, political, and cultural change." As in the typical textbook glossary, this particular definition is an innocuous gloss that sheds little light on what exactly globalization is and how it affects people's everyday lives. Closer examination of how globalization is defined by different writers makes the complexity of the term more clear. Here are six definitions that Frank Lechner (n. d.) includes on "The Globalization Website":

> [T]he inexorable integration of markets, nation-states, and technologies to a degree never witnessed before – in a way that is enabling individuals, corporations and nation-states to reach around the world farther, faster, deeper and cheaper than ever before ... the spread of free-market capitalism to virtually every country in the world.
>
> (Friedman 1999: 7–8)

> The compression of the world and the intensification of consciousness of the world as a whole ... concrete global interdependence and consciousness of the global whole in the twentieth century.
>
> (Robertson 1992: 8)

> A social process in which the constraints of geography on social and cultural arrangements recede and in which people become increasingly aware that they are receding.
>
> (Waters 1995: 3)

> The historical transformation constituted by the sum of particular forms and instances of ... [m]aking or being made global (i) by the active dissemination of practices, values, technology and other human products throughout the globe (ii) when global practices and so on exercise an increasing influence over people's lives (iii) when the globe serves as a focus for, or a premise in shaping, human activities.
>
> (Albrow 1996: 88)

> Integration on the basis of a project pursuing "market rule on a global scale."
>
> (McMichael 2000: xxiii)

As experienced from below, the dominant form of globalization means a historical transformation: in the economy, of livelihoods and modes of existence; in politics, a loss in the degree of control exercised locally ... and in culture, a devaluation of a collectivity's achievements ... Globalization is emerging as a political response to the expansion of market power ... [It] is a domain of knowledge.

(Mittelman 2000: 149)

Scholte (2000) argues that conceptions of globalization can be placed into five broad categories: (1) *Globalization as internationalization* or simply "another adjective to describe cross-border relations between countries." This is perhaps the most common use of the term in the social studies curriculum, where the concept of interdependence, particularly economic interdependence as a function of international trade, is a primary focus of the historical grand narrative. (2) *Globalization as liberalization* or a "borderless" and de-regulated world economy, often referred to as neoliberalism. This is the dominant conception of globalization in mainstream political discourse. (3) *Globalization as universalization* or the process of spreading various objects and experiences to people everywhere (e.g. computing). (4) *Globalization as Westernization*, in which social structures of modernity (e.g. capitalism, industrialism, bureaucratism) are spread in a way that destroys pre-existing cultures and local self-determination in the process. (5) *Globalization as deterritorialization* or the reconfiguration of geography such that social spaces are no longer mapped in terms of territorial place but are shaped by events occurring far away (and vice versa).[1]

Smith and Smith (2002) note that the discourse on globalization is marked by four key themes. The first, which takes its lead from Scholte, is de-localization. Many activities that previously involved face-to-face interaction can now be, and often are, conducted at great distances (e.g. banking, retailing, and teaching). Nations, like individuals and neighborhood institutions, are also affected by de-localization as the power of governments to direct and influence their economies' declines in relation to the economic activity in other countries; the internationalization of financial markets; and the emergence of trans-national economic institutions such as the World Bank and the International Monetary Fund. In other words, globalization affects social relations among individuals and among countries.

Secondly, the "momentum and power" of change is cited as a particular feature of globalization, specifically developments in science and technology that have led to information technology innovations and the creation of a "knowledge economy" and its accompanying "risk society." The argument goes:

> Productivity and competitiveness are, by and large, a function of knowledge generation and information processing; firms and territories are organized in networks of production, management and distribution; the core economic activities are global – that is, they have the capacity to work as a unit in real time, or chosen time, on a planetary scale.

(Castells 2000: 52)

And, as new technologies are put to work in an effort to create profits, new levels of risk are created. For example, as Beck explains, "a universalization of hazards

accompanies industrial production, independent of the place where they are produced: food chains connect practically everyone on earth to everyone else. They dip
under borders" (Beck 2000: 39).[2]

The third theme of globalization identified by Smith and Smith (2002) is the
rise of multinational corporations, in particular their impact on local communities
through the exploitation of labor and resources; their constant search for new and
under-exploited markets (e.g. tobacco companies focus on youth markets in the
global South); the erosion of public space by corporate activities (e.g. privatization of
public space); and their significant influence on government policy making at local,
national, and international levels.

Capitalism and global free markets (and the instability and divisions they produce)
are identified as the fourth theme of globalization. Neoliberalism is the prevailing
political economic paradigm in the world today and the impetus behind the mainstream conception of globalization. Neoliberalism is an ideological monoculture, in
that when neoliberal policies are criticized a common response is that "there is no
alternative" (aka TINA). While the term neoliberalism is largely unused in public
discourse, it references something everyone is familiar with – policies and processes
that enable a relative handful of private interests to control as much as possible of
social life in order to maximize their personal profit. Politicians across the political
spectrum embrace neoliberalism, from right to left, enabling the interests of wealthy
investors and large corporations to define social and economic policy.

"Free markets," private enterprise, consumer choice, entrepreneurial initiative,
and the deleterious effects of government regulation are the tenets of neoliberalism.
Indeed, the corporate controlled media spin would have the public believe that the
economic consequences of neoliberal economic policy are good for everyone. There
is, however, no doubt that free market capitalism – and the neoliberal public policies
that have been put in place to sustain it – has produced dramatic inequalities (Ross
and Gibson 2007; Stiglitz 2002). Despite promises to the contrary, "the major tenet
of free market economics – that unregulated markets will of their own accord find
unimprovable results for all participants – proved to be nonsense. It does not hold in
theory. It is not true" (Hutton 1996: 237). As Branko Milanovic (2005), an econom-
ist at the World Bank, explains, "the hierarchy of the [world] regions [has] stayed
about the same since the time of Adam Smith, but income differences among them
[have] widened" (47); the richest nations have "been able to pull ahead of the rest,
and in only a few exceptional cases have non-Western countries been able to catch
up" (61). In 2006, according to the United Nations, the net transfer of capital from
poorer countries to rich ones was almost $800 billion, up from $229 billion in 2002,
making the poorest countries, like those in sub-Saharan Africa, money exporters to
rich countries (Rosenberg 2007).

Some critics of globalization target its deleterious effects, but do not challenge the
free market capitalism that produces those outcomes. For example, Smith and Smith
are critical of the inequalities created by globalization (e.g. widening gaps between the
rich and poor countries/individuals; erosion of democracy and local control), but do
not challenge the underlying logic of neoliberalism. They argue that these outcomes
are the result of a particular version of globalization that has been imposed by the

world's financial elites (e.g. government and corporate leaders and organizations such as the International Monetary Fund, the World Bank, the World Economic Forum), which can be remedied by reorganizing and reframing market-based approaches so more people can benefit. (One might call their position a critical version of TINA).

The key problem with many representations of globalization – even those offered from critical perspectives such as Smith and Smith's – is the idea that globalization is a break from capitalism. At the core of the Marxist critique of capitalism is the concept of class and the class struggle between the "two great classes directly facing each other: Bourgeoisie and Proletariat" (Marx and Engels 1986: 80). As a result of the perception that globalization represents a social order that is "post" capitalism, critical analysis of globalization is de-coupled from a class-based analysis of capitalism:

> Globalization in the sense of connectivity in economic and cultural life across the world, is of a different order to what has gone before. As we said at the start, the speed of communication and exchange, the complexity and size of the networks involved, and the sheer volume of trade, interaction and risk give what we now label as "globalization" a peculiar force.
>
> (Smith and Smith 2002: n. p.)

We certainly agree that struggles against the inequalities produced by globalization are important, indeed essential. However, we believe that the inequalities and the struggles against them must be understood, not in terms of shifts in culture (shifts in "the speed of communication and exchange") that have presumably moved society beyond capitalism, but rather in terms of capitalism itself as it develops new technologies and markets in order to raise the rate of profit. Shifts in culture are effects of capitalist development in pursuit of profit. Losing sight of this fundamental aim of capitalism results in even critical perspectives on globalization calling only for treatment of symptoms (economic inequalities) rather than abolition of the disease that produces them (the social relations of production at the core of which is class).

We argue, along the same lines as Bertell Ollman, that the developments described as globalization, which are all internally related, do not constitute a "peculiar force" beyond capitalism, but rather a new stage of capitalism, what Ollman (2001) calls "capitalism with the gloves off on a world wide scale" (9):

> If anything, with these changes our society is more thoroughly capitalist than ever before. After all, more and more of the world is privately owned, more and more wealth is devoted to maximizing profits rather than serving needs (and only serving needs in so far as they maximize profits), more and more people sell their labor power in order to live, more and more objects (ideational as well as material) carry price tags and can be bought in the market, and money and those who have a lot of it have more power and status than ever before. This is capitalism, capitalism with a vengeance, and that's globalization. Which means, too, that the problems associated with globalization cannot be solved – as so many liberals would like to do – without dealing with their roots in the capitalist system.
>
> (Ollman 2001: 93–4)

We are increasingly affected by the acceleration of inequities from economic, eco-logical, and technological dependence, and the repercussions of global imperialism, human conflict, poverty, and injustice. Achieving what we believe are central goals of social studies education (e.g. civic competence; creation of free, creative individuals) does not allow us to ignore these realities as they are produced by global capitalism (Ross 2006).

Why teach class?

We answer this question in two parts. First, class – and class-based analysis of capitalism/globalization – are clearly crucial topics to be included in the social stud-ies curriculum. The content, purposes, and pedagogy of social studies education in North American schools has always been contested and the key element in the disputes is the relative emphasis of "cultural transmission" versus "critical thought" in the classroom (Ross 2006). But, despite these historical (and ongoing debates), class issues are central to the content of social studies, even as it has been defined by the National Council for the Social Studies (NCSS):

> Social studies is the integrated study of the social sciences and humanities to promote civic competence. Within the school program, social studies provides coordinated, systematic study drawing upon such disciplines as anthropology, archaeology, economics, geography, history, law, philosophy, political science, psychology, religion, and sociology, as well as appropriate content from the humanities, mathematics, and natural sciences. The primary purpose of social studies is to help young people develop the ability to make informed and rea-soned decisions for the public good as citizens of a culturally diverse, democratic society in an interdependent world.
>
> (NCSS 1994: n. p.)

NCSS has also outlined 10 thematic strands that form the basis of the social studies curriculum standards. These strands are:

1 Culture
2 Time, Continuity, and Change
3 People, Places, and Environments
4 Individual Development and Identity
5 Individuals, Groups, and Institutions
6 Power, Authority, and Governance
7 Production, Distribution, and Consumption
8 Science, Technology, and Society
9 Global Connections
10 Civic Ideals and Practices

(NCSS 1994: n. p.)

Based upon the definition and curriculum strands presented by NCSS, there is no doubt that class should be a central curricular topic.

By "class," we do not mean categories that merely group people on the basis of income level or status. This understanding of class is fundamentally Weberian, that is, descriptive of groups of people (Kelsh 2001; Kelsh and Hill 2006). In contrast, Marx conceptualizes class as a relation to property: the capitalist class owns property, understood as the means of production, while the working class does not; it owns only its labor power, which it must sell to the capitalist in exchange for wages that are less than the value of the commodities that workers produce. The capitalist class pockets the difference as profit, which means capitalists can live off the labor power of others. As Marx and Engels (1986) argue, "The essential condition for the existence, and for the sway of the bourgeois class, is the formation and augmentation of capital; the condition for capital is wage labour" (93). In contrast to Weber, who uses class simply to describe groups of people, Marx's theory of class is explanatory: it explains why inequity exists, why social change occurs, as well as the functions of the state, political power, and ideology, all key ideas within the social studies curriculum. Marx's theory of class, based on the premise that the written "history of all hitherto existing society is the history of class struggles" (Marx and Engels 1986: 79), illustrates how class interests and the confrontations of power that they produce are the central determinants of social and historical processes. And, if one conceives of social studies as "the study of all human enterprise over time and space" (Stanley and Nelson 1994: 26), the centrality of class to the social studies curriculum becomes ineluctable.

Second, and more importantly, we should be teaching about class because inequality – internationally and nationally – is intensifying and is one of two dominant contemporary trends in the world's political economy (the other is slower economic growth) (Tabb 2006). As described above, the gap between the richest and poorest countries is widening. In his examination of the world economy, Landes (1999) calculated that the difference in income per person between the richest nation (Switzerland) and the poorest non-industrial country (Mozambique) as about 400 to 1. Two hundred and fifty years ago, the gap between richest and poorest was perhaps 5 to 1, and the difference between Europe and, say, East or South Asia (China or India) was around 1.5 or 2 to 1 (Landes 1999: xx).

In the United States, at least one in five children lives in poverty. From 1999 to 2005 the number of Americans in poverty rose from just over 30 million to nearly 40 million, approaching the highest levels in over 40 years. And, while in any given year 12–15 percent of the US population is "officially poor," over a 10-year period 40 percent of Americans experience poverty in at least one year because most cycle in and out of poverty (Zweig 2004). In 2001, the poverty rate for minors in the United States was the highest in the industrialized world, with 15 percent of all minors and 30 percent of African American minors living below the poverty threshold. Additionally, the standard of living for those in the bottom 10 percent was lower in the US than in any other developed nation except the United Kingdom, which had the lowest standard of living for impoverished children (Williams, *et al.* 2005).

At the time of writing, the latest figures from the Federal Reserve's Survey of Consumer Finances show that the rich are getting richer, the poor are getting poorer, and the racial divide is growing, as is wealth inequality:

- the wealthiest tenth saw their average net worth grow to three million dollars by 2004, up another 6 percent since 2001, and up 76 percent since 1995 (in 2004 dollars);
- the poorest quarter by net worth fell backwards from being $50 in the black in 2001 to being $1,400 in the red in 2004;
- from 1995 to 2004, white families' average net worth rose 82 percent after inflation, while that of families of color rose 61 percent;
- as of 2001, the top 1 percent owned 33 percent of US wealth, while the bottom 50 percent of the population owned 2.8 percent of wealth;
- from 1983–98, the net worth of the top 1 percent increased by 42 percent, while the net worth for the bottom 40 percent decreased by 76 percent.

(United for a Fair Economy 2006: n. p.)

The education system equalizes the opportunity of all citizens and the individual can achieve success through hard work, intelligence and creativity – or at least that is the rhetoric. Conservatives argue that inequality that results in an impoverished class is the result of the inferiority of the poor compared to the rest of society (Herrnstein and Murray 1994). The inequalities that do exist in our society are not the result of the social, economic and political institutions of society, they argue, but the result of free and fair competition, and those who succeed have more merit and deserve more social rewards than those who were unable to successfully compete. The children who are unable to rise up and fit into the upper classes of society suffer from cultural deprivations that they experienced in their impoverished childhood.

We reject the idea that inequality is a natural consequence of the genetic differences between humans. Rather, inequality is a result of the social relations of production of capitalism under which workers, beyond the wages they receive, do not have access to the social wealth they produce. Luttwak (1999) describes the contemporary global capitalist system as turbo-capitalism:

At present, almost all elite Americans, with corporate chiefs and fashionable economists in the lead, are utterly convinced that they have discovered the winning formula for economic success – the only formula – good for every country, rich or poor, good for all individuals willing and able to heed the message, and, of course, good for elite Americans: PRIVATIZATION + DEREGULATION + GLOBALIZATION = TURBO-CAPITALISM = PROSPERITY. Business people all over the world mostly agree with them – only a few, in a few countries, have some reservations ... Increasingly, political leaders almost everywhere also accept this simple formula for economic success, ensuring its ever wider application in one country after another.

(25)

Historically public education has used the capitalist/business model to assess the value of schools, teachers, students, communities in which the schools are located, and whole states. Standards Based Education Reform (SBER) – as embodied in the

No Child Left Behind Act – is the current approach used by capitalist interests to shape the nature and aims of public education (Vinson and Ross 2003). In SBER, school districts and teachers are to align their instruction with a set of state-regulated standards of knowledge and skills. Standardized high-stakes tests, tests that have "rewards" and "punishments" attached to the results, are regularly administered to determine the value of the implemented curriculum, teacher instruction, and student acquisition of the standard knowledge and skills. This model is based upon the idea that all children are vessels to be filled, that children are the same everywhere, and that education is apolitical. However, the reality is that children are creators of knowledge, are different, and education is a partisan activity. SBER is being used to justify and/or mask social inequalities that are not natural consequences, but rather the result of the economic, political and social institutions and decisions of the elites in society (e.g. those who work to advance capitalist interests and often benefit handsomely from doing so.)

It is important that educators, parents, children and community members recognize that the current education reform model is being used to increase elite control over society that inevitably leads to greater disparities in wealth and power. Students need to recognize their location in our class-based society to know when it is necessary to be an agent for change towards equality and democracy and a resister to inequality and authoritarianism. Secondly, it is necessary for teachers to read the social context in which they teach and question the content of their classroom to assess the political consequences implied in their curriculum organization and their methods of instruction and assessment. We believe that teaching in general, and teaching the social studies in particular, necessitates a Marxist critique of capitalism and how capitalism affects the socioeconomic structure of society and the school within it. An important part of social studies is helping students so they can understand the world, that things change, and that they can act upon the world to expand equality and democracy in the interest of the public and not the elite and the capitalist class.

Marx (1992), Perlman (1969), Debord (1994), and others have discussed fetishism of commodities and the reification of social relations. What are really changing and changeable relations between people (capitalist and worker) appear unchanging and unchangeable. As many of our students say, "that is just the way it is, always has been and always will be." Social studies, particularly history, can be and is frequently taught as a commodity, a concrete and already completed thing, evacuated of the capitalist social relations that produced it. That is, social studies can be taught as a set of circumstances that had to happen and that there was not much struggle over the outcomes being observed. Again, this is the result of teaching "history" in such a way that separates it – abstracts and reifies it – from the history of class struggle. In the former method, history is taught as a collection of observable facts that are to be consumed by students and reproduced for the teacher.

One of our goals as social studies educators is to engage students in such a manner that the fetishism and reification in their minds begin to break down, and they begin to look at things as a result of social relations where capitalists produce and use institutions to solidify their power over the working class for their own gain, that is, exploitation, and the working class, in a quest for equality and liberation, organizes themselves to resist and abolish the class structure that enables this power. In other words, we believe history should be taught as a study of the struggle between those who own the means of production and those who must sell or hand over their labor power to capitalists to survive.

Teaching history in this manner provides working-class students, the folks who have the most at stake in creating a more equal democratic society, a compass to give them direction, to help them focus their observations of the world. The assumption is that the working-class students we teach will know which side they are on, but of course it is not always that clear-cut, as you will see below.

Class as the organizing principle for the social studies curriculum: an example

In this section, Greg Queen, who is a social studies teacher at Fitzgerald High School in Warren, Michigan, describes how he has created a curriculum for his high school social studies classes that places issues of social relations of production and class front and center.

When organizing the curriculum for an American Studies class that examines US history from 1945 to the present (typically a required course in US schools), I have identified five themes that are interwoven throughout one semester and fit within the NCSS strands. The five themes are: inequality, capitalism, racism, globalization, and the war in Iraq. The themes interpenetrate each other, but students begin to realize that capitalism is the primary thread and when they understand this, the other themes make more sense for them. To introduce these themes to the students, I created an opening unit titled *What is History? Teaching about Inequality*.

On the first day of the semester, I open with a discussion of inequality by leading an activity called "Ten Chairs of Inequality" (Kellog 1998). This activity plays a central role in the curriculum and I refer back to it throughout the semester. The activity visually demonstrates the distribution of wealth in the United States. Ten students volunteer and each represents 10 percent of society. They each sit in their own desk that represents 10 percent of the nation's wealth. This shows students wealth that is equally distributed. Next, I explain that wealth is not equally distributed and in fact its distribution changes over time. By moving desks and students around, I show them that in 1976, 10 percent of the nation, one person, controlled 50 percent of the nation's wealth, five desks. Hence, four students needed to get out of their desks and sit on top of the five desks that remain with the other 90 percent. I tell them that today at least 70 percent of the nation's wealth is controlled by 10 percent of the population and the other 90 percent share the remaining 30 percent of the wealth.

One of the most important lessons within this activity is when I explain (simplistically) how the capitalist system works. I tell them that the working class wakes up and does their morning routines. Next they travel to the capitalist class's work sites. The working class stays there for eight hours, minimally. At the end of the day, the capitalists pay the workers. The workers travel back home to rest, eat, clean, etc. Next the working class goes to the stores (owned by the capitalists) and buys the products they made that day. The money the boss paid the workers goes back into the hands of the capitalists. I then ask – but how do the capitalists "make" money in this exchange? At this point I present the class with a cartoon strip (Figure 7.1) by Fred Wright (1975).[3]

At the end of the lesson, I ask various questions. For example, who are the super rich? Where do the super rich get their wealth? Why does wealth concentrate into the few hands of the super rich? What do the super rich tell others to justify their

Figure 7.1 Fred Wright cartoon, 'So Long Partner!'

wealth and the inequality that exists? When times are tough for workers (e.g. low wages, unemployment, increased work) who might the super rich blame for the tough times? Why might workers accept inequality? How can workers increase equality? This lesson dramatically brings forward many issues and creates more questions than answers.

The next class activity, also on the theme of inequality, is called "Give Me the Facts." In this activity, I use material from a book called *A Field Guide to the U.S. Economy* (Teller-Elsberg, *et al.* 2006; see Figure 7.2). Students examine charts and graphs displaying poverty statistics and illustrating the disparities of wealth and privilege in society. Various graphics show that many rich people are born into their wealth, that workers' paychecks are getting smaller, benefits are shrinking, more people per household work to make the same amount of income, taxes on business have decreased, social spending has decreased, and minorities are over-represented in the lower wage jobs.

I point out to students that the 1970s was a decade where major shifts began to occur in the standard of living of the working class; from the high standard of living enjoyed by many in the 1960s, largely owing to labor struggles in the 1930s and 1940s, the working class in the 1970s began to experience a decline in their standard of living. This fact is connected to the shift in wealth discussed in the "Ten Chairs of Inequality" activity. These two activities conclude the opening discussion of inequality and we move on to look at a Marxist critique of the processes of capitalism.

1.5   CEO Pay

THE AVERAGE RETAIL CLERK IN the U.S. would have to work for 419 years to earn what the average corporate chief executive officer (CEO) makes in a single year. That's a boost for CEOs, whose average pay is growing again after dipping in 2001 and 2002. Between 2003 and 2004, workers saw their earnings increase by an average of 2.2%, while CEOs received an average raise of 15%.

The best-paid employees are also company owners. Much of the compensation CEOs get includes stock options—the ability to purchase compa-

ny stock at better-than-market prices. The benefits are enormous. When Oracle CEO Lawrence Ellison exercised his stock options in 2001, he made over $700 million.

Are CEOs worth it? Higher pay does not guarantee superior performance; companies with the highest-paid CEOs often do worse than other firms. While Oracle was making Ellison a very, very rich man, the market value of the company fell 57% and nearly 1,300 workers were laid off.

R. JAY MAGILL

Average pay of
CEOs compared
to retail clerks
and medical doctors
in 2004

Retail clerk	$22,930
Medical doctor	$138,490
CEO	$9,600,000

Figure 7.2 'CEO Pay,' from *A Field Guide to the U.S. Economy* (Teller-Elsberg *et al.* 2006).

Teaching about capitalism

The presentations and discussions of capitalism are complex and some students do have difficulty digesting the material. I open by pointing out the similarities and differences among slavery, feudalism, and capitalism, comparing the master/slave, king/serf and capitalist/worker relations. Students read the chapter on capitalism from Mick Brooks' (1983) outline of historical materialism. Using three sets of questions, which I created, students work through this material.

In summary, the Brooks chapter explains that capitalists measure their wealth in money whereas other systems measured wealth in land or slaves. Unlike the slave system or feudalism, in capitalism, the capitalists must take a large portion of their wealth and put it back into production to increase the productivity of labor, or find ways to make the same amount of products in less time or make more products in the same amount of time. The reason that capitalists try to increase the productivity of labor is because the capitalists try to decrease the amount of time it takes to make a product. By saving time in the production of a commodity (including labor power), the capitalist creates wealth – capital – for herself/himself. The reason that the capitalist creates wealth is because s/he does not have to pay a worker for the time saved. If this capitalist does not improve the productivity of labor, another capitalist will. The latter capitalist will survive the competition and the former capitalist will not. This is why it is necessary for a capitalist to reinvest in the productivity of labor, creating the dynamic, or motor, of capitalism. The idea that labor power is similar to a product because it is bought and sold on the market is also explained. Labor power differs from other products because it has the ability to create value beyond the value paid the laborer (as described in Fred Wright's cartoon strip, Figure 7.1). It is because the worker is capable of producing more value than s/he is paid that the capitalist wants to buy the laborer's labor power and control the circumstances in which the laborer produces. By controlling the labor, the capitalist is better able to control the value created by the laborer. However, the capitalist and worker struggle daily – firings/strikes, speed ups/slow downs, etc. – over control of the value created by the laborer.

In class, we also discuss the similarities and differences between necessary and surplus labor (i.e. the labor that pays for the maintenance of the worker and the labor that yields unpaid surplus-value to the capitalist) and how the distinction between the two is obscured when combined into the single process of labor in the factory (as compared to feudal societies, where it was clearer when a serf or peasant was working for herself or himself and when she or he labored for her or his lord). We also discuss how capitalists attempt to extract more and more surplus-value from labor by increasing the amount of time worked per worker (i.e. absolute surplus value) and by decreasing wages or increasing productivity and intensity of work (i.e. relative surplus value). These are key ideas for students to understand because absolute and relative surplus labor (and workers' resistance to this exploitation) are at the core of the conflict between classes and are rarely, if ever, analyzed in the social studies curriculum.

I conclude the capitalism theme with a classroom discussion of various cartoon strips from Bertell Ollman's website (n. d.), which examines capitalism from different angles. These cartoons are excellent sources for provoking discussion and there are many "ah hah" moments when reading the cartoons because what students have studied is succinctly re-presented through the humor, irony, and paradox of the cartoons – all of which Ollman uses to foreground the contradictions of capitalism.

Teaching about racism

The third theme of the unit is the problem of racism, which is explored through two activities. First, we read Jonathan Kozol's "Where Ghetto Schools Fail" (1967). In this article, Kozol discusses the events that led to him being fired from his teaching job. Teaching in a predominantly African American school, he ventures away from the prescribed curriculum and begins to use items that are more relevant to the lives of the students. This ultimately brings him into conflict with some members of the community and then school administration. He gets fired. The questions I pose to the class include: Why is Kozol fired? Why are so many of the books in his classroom outdated? Why he is told to stop teaching content his students are interested in and to stick to the required curriculum? This article provokes thinking about the relationships among school, curriculum, power, and the role of standardized testing.

Secondly, we read and create skits to an article titled "At a Slaughterhouse, Some Things Never Die: Who Kills, Who Cuts, Who Bosses Can Depend on Race," which was published as part of *The New York Times* series on "How Race is Lived in America" in 2000 (LeDuff 2000). The main ideas of the article are as follows: The Smithfield Packing Co., in North Carolina, have seen their profits nearly double while wages have remained flat. So a lot of Americans there have quit, and a lot of Mexicans have been hired to take their places. But more than management, the workers see one another as the problem, and they "see the competition in skin tones." The intent of this article is to get students to see the relationship between race, class and power. Inevitably the notion that the Mexican workers are the cause of this situation comes up and the idea that the immigrants are responsible for the lower wages is difficult to challenge, but I push students to rethink that idea. The point that I try to drive home in using this article is that the capitalist boss makes wage and employment decisions, not the workers. Hence the capitalist class plays a major role in causing/reinforcing class and racial antagonisms.

Teaching about globalization

In the fourth theme in the unit, students watch and discuss two videos that deal with sweatshop labor (*Zoned for Slavery: the child behind the label* and *Global Village or Pillage?* [Bennett, *et al.* 1995; Brecher, *et al.* 2000]). These videos give students an opportunity to see how labor is controlled and how workers, particularly in poorer countries, are seriously exploited by capitalist global relations. The students identify with the videos because they dramatically illustrate how children their age in other parts of the world are laboring for nickels and dimes. These videos reinforce concepts developed earlier in the unit, such as inequality and capitalism. It becomes clear to the students that these sweatshops are exploitative and used to enrich capitalist bosses. Our study of globalization provides a bridge for the final unit topic, the war in Iraq, or in general, imperialist war.

Teaching about imperialist war

Two pieces that have proved to be very useful in teaching the concept of imperialist war are "A Warmonger Explains War to a Peacenik" (n. d.) and "Questions and Answers about Foreign Policy (and the U.S. Invasion of Iraq)" (Bunker 2003). I use these two pieces because most students have heard only the Bush administration's explanation for going to war, and these two pieces challenge widely accepted justifications for the war in a clear and accessible way. Both of the articles are dialogues between one person who supports the war and one who is skeptical or naïve. The skeptic/naïve person questions all the arguments given by the war supporter.

These readings create questions in the minds of students about the mainstream logic that supports the US invasion of Iraq, and they create in students a desire to learn about alternative explanations for the war. In addition to the dialogues, I use a video of an ABC News Nightline episode, "In the National Interest: Dividends from the War on Terrorism" (Sievers 2002), which argues that the war on terrorism is intersecting with the needs of the oil giants and other elite who depend upon cheap oil. Nightline host Ted Koppel contends that whoever controls access to oil will have significant power in the global economy. The final lesson on the theme of war involves an examination of a portion of George W. Bush's March 6, 2003 press conference. In this press conference, President Bush answers many questions regarding the US "war on terror" and the then impending invasion of Iraq. It appears to be a legitimate media interaction until somebody acts as if they have been called on by Bush. Bush responds with "We'll be there in a minute. King, John King. This is a scripted – (laughter)." Bush then smirks (President George Bush Discusses Iraq in National Press Conference 2003). Students become very skeptical of what they hear and see after viewing the press conference. This is a very powerful lesson for students to learn.

Near the end of the unit, I present students with a series of "Master/Slave" questions (Gibson n. d.):

What does the Master want?
What does the Slave want?

What must the Master do?
What must the Slaves do?

How do Masters rule?
How do Slaves resist?

What does the Master want the Slaves to know?
What do the Slaves want the Master to know?

What does the Master want the Slaves to believe?
What does the Slave want the Master to believe?

Is truth the same for the Master as it is for the Slaves?
Who has the greater interest in the more profound truths?

(n. p.)

Students inevitably ask, "should we just be applying these to the time when there were slaves and masters or can we apply it to the capitalist/worker relationship?" This question reveals significant and relevant learning. As a result, students now have a new sense or understanding of freedom and unfreedom. In my experience, after this point students begin to see the world from a "class perspective" and more readily recognize their own class position.

Inequality, capitalism, racism, globalization, and war in the social studies curriculum

Each of these themes is spiraled throughout subsequent units of the American Studies class. Some units emphasize one theme more than another and some are whole units in themselves. However, the dominant approach throughout the semester is placing historical moments in the context of the needs of capitalism. Titles of the subsequent units are: "From World War Two to the Cold War," "Civil Rights," "Vietnam," "Under Control," and "War in Iraq." The main idea of the unit "From World War Two to the Cold War" is to show that, although the US declared it was fighting against militarism, totalitarianism, racism and imperialism, the US government and US corporations were acting in ways during and after World War II that reinforced militarism, totalitarianism, racism and imperialism within the US and around the world.

In the "Civil Rights" unit, we examine the idea that the elite divide the working class and weaken their unity using racism. As a result, the working class is easier to exploit (although resistance and opposition still occur), which helps secure elite control. Secondly, we look at how the local, state and national governments have been used by the elite to enforce segregation both in the North and the South. Most importantly, students see how violent racial oppression was during the Civil Rights Era. In my diverse classroom, this is powerful for all students. The minority students feel a sense of pride in their history and the white students form an appreciation and deeper understanding of the struggles endured by their classmates' parents and grandparents.

In the unit on Vietnam, the US war on Vietnam is taught as an imperialist war. I use part of the Public Broadcasting System (PBS) *Vietnam: a television history* video series (Ellison, *et al.* 1996). This series has important footage that speaks from the point of view of those resisting US aggression. In the unit titled "Under Control," we focus on how the elite thought there was an "excess of democracy" in the US during the 1960s and felt they needed to check the power of the people. The primary focus is on how the ruling class manages to paint the fall of Nixon, the illegal actions of the Central Intelligence Agency (CIA) and the Federal Bureau of Investigation (FBI) as anomalies of the system rather than the norm. In addition, we trace how the ruling class manages to dismantle social programs by scapegoating the beneficiaries while maintaining the military industrial complex. When I teach the unit titled "War in

Iraq," the Vietnam unit is important because students can apply the knowledge and analytic skills gleaned from that historical event to the War in Iraq. The "Under Control" unit is important because it provides an opportunity for students to make connections between a decline in social programs and the need for increased militarization of the US budget to engage in imperial wars. The theme of globalization is emphasized in the "World War Two to the Cold War" unit and the "Vietnam War" unit.

I work to build a classroom ethos that has a deep respect for differences of opinion, knowing that the content students will be studying contains contrasting perspectives that elicit a variety of opinions. My personal pedagogical goal is to allow students to challenge authoritative voices (including my own). Most students are uncomfortable or unfamiliar with challenging the ideas of their teacher, at least initially. When I see students whisper to each other after another student or I make a comment, I encourage them to share their perspective. Most times, it is something in opposition to what was just spoken, and by sharing it, the lesson deepens. Many, if not most, teachers practice a banking concept of teaching – as Paulo Freire (1970) called it – where students are to absorb the content and reproduce it. The student who can most accurately reproduce the content gains highest marks. However, I do not think any opinion stated in class should just go unchallenged. Many times, the opinions and perspectives of students are based upon half-truths or incorrect information (as is typical of what Otero [2006] refers to as "experience-based concepts" [249]). I do not believe unexamined beliefs, ideas, or perspectives should be allowed to stand in the classroom, no matter what their source.

There are risks to "being political" in the classroom. I would not advise teachers being too outspoken until they have developed the trust and support of the community. I have been teaching for over 10 years within the district. Students appreciate my "voice" in the classroom. They communicate this to their parents and I have had many parents call regarding concerns over the content of the classroom and I do not take these concerns lightly. From my experience, parents are often afraid their children are being indoctrinated because they are being taught a "one-sided" curriculum. (Interestingly, these parents do not complain about other teachers who teach only the textbook point of view.) I tell parents that I struggle very hard to create space in the classroom for discussion and a variety of perspectives, and they are usually satisfied.

However, there have been times when parents take their complaints to higher authorities (Dueweke 2004; Wowk 2004). Recently, during the 2004 election, when I taught the dialogue titled *Daddy Why Did We Have To Invade Iraq* (Bunker 2003), a parent disagreed with the content of this dialogue and of the class. His initial claim was that the author of the piece had a website that, if children went to it, they might see or read things which were inappropriate for their age. I did not know the website existed because the piece was popular enough to have appeared on at least 30 different websites and was sent to me as an attachment via a list serve. The parent was also upset with the Master/Slave questions I assigned the students. After a conference between the parent, my immediate supervisor, and myself, the parent appealed to the district Board of Education. Prior to the Board of Education meeting, someone informed the local media. The event appeared on a local news broadcast, and in both a metro-wide newspaper and a local tabloid. Despite having a discipline letter in my personnel file for one year for allegedly "not being balanced in my teaching," the administration was "supportive." The building principal advised staff members to support the Board of Education president and me, and said that, although at times I may be outspoken, I was still a good teacher.

How do students respond to the material? First, students develop a richer sense of history. Students see history less often as an object but more as something that was contested. Second, students begin to see the world through the prism of class struggle. They begin to recognize themselves as part of the working class. Even the skeptical students show signs that they do not include themselves with the elite. Third, it becomes clear that students are asked to think and not just absorb information, unlike their other history classes.

Below are a few examples of student responses from their final exam, for which they were asked to write a 400 word reflection essay and instructed they could write whatever they wanted, or they could respond to all or some of the following question: "How has this class helped you to understand your life better, to understand how history/society changes, to understand the role that the individual and/or groups play in the making of history, and/or to see the world differently?"

> I did not know how important it was for the working class to come together. The capitalists divide us by blaming it on others of different skin. They blame low wages on immigrants when in fact they are the ones paying the working class. If the working class would open their eyes, identify the lies and unite our world would or could rather become a much better place.

> This class has definitely made me see the world differently. It has made me see that even though we think that we all have equal opportunities, this isn't actually true. That is why I will try to make a stand like others have done before and start to make a difference in this world.

> My outlook on our world today has developed over the past semester. Throughout my life I was taught one side of the story. You taught us the other half. Putting both pieces of knowledge together I have discovered by own belief system. If I hadn't taken this class I would never have understood the pitfalls of the capitalist economic structure. Our current government is not perfect by any means. In the one hour a day you are given, you teach us to highlight those downsides and make change towards what we should have and not to live with what we are given.

> I have learned more about the other side of capitalism in your class. How it's bad, what should be done with it and so on. But the right way for capitalism is the good way of it. The way you never showed or taught it — the other side ... Now this American Studies class has be one sided. Nothing in this class has approved or agreed with anything about capitalism or anything on that side of

the agenda. Nothing has been said good or nice about how capitalism can really work. I personally really do not care about the Bush statements. This class in the beginning really bothered me to the sense that I should just walk out of the class. But now, it's just boring and being repeated over and over again. All this talk about capitalism is really only hurting our society. Thank you for the time you took to show me the other side. I probably won't use this but it's good to learn about something you totally disagree with.

Conclusion

In 1997 John Cassidy's article "The Return of Karl Marx" created a minor sensation, but not because it offered any new or important insights about Marx or Marxism. What was remarkable about the article was where it was published, the venerable *New Yorker* magazine. Cassidy reported a conversation with an investment banker in which the financier said:

> The longer I spend on Wall Street, the more convinced I am that Marx was right. I'm absolutely convinced that Marx's approach was the best way to look at capitalism. There is a Nobel Prize waiting for the economist who resurrects Marx and puts it all together.
>
> (258)

This comment inspired Cassidy to read Marx, and then tell the readers of the *New Yorker* what he found:

> riveting passages about globalization, inequality, political corruption, monopolization, technical progress, the decline of high culture, the enervating nature of modern existence – issues that economists are now confronting anew, sometimes without realizing that they are walking in Marx's footsteps.
>
> (258)

We believe that "riveting passages about globalization, inequality, political corruption, monopolization, technical progress, the decline of high culture, the enervating nature of modern existence" have a place in the social studies curriculum too. And we agree with Cassidy that, as long as capitalism is around, Marx's work and the thought and analysis it inspires will remain relevant, particularly in social studies classrooms.

Notes

1 Scholte argues that it is only the fifth of these approaches to defining globalization that adds new insights; all the others, he argues, are compatible with territorialism.
2 A recent, and dramatic, example of this particular risk is the safety of China's food industry, which was put in the international spotlight after wheat gluten and rice protein containing melamine scrap was exported and mixed into pet food, resulting in the death of dogs and cats in Canada and the United States. In May 2007 Zheng Xiaoyu, former head of China's State Food and Drug Administration was convicted on charges of bribery

and dereliction of duty in relation to the deaths of dozens of Chinese citizens from fake or bad drugs and food products, as well as the melamine scandal (Barboza 2007).

3 Fred Wright (1907–84) was one of the most widely admired American labor cartoonists of the twentieth century, and for much of his career was associated with the United Electrical, Radio and Machine Workers of America (UE). View the cartoon online at http://www.iamawlodge1426.org/toonville3.htm

Bibliography

A Warmonger Explains War to a Peacenik (n. d.) Online. Available at http://www.morepeace.org/warmonger_explains_war.htm (accessed June 28, 2007).

Albrow, M. (1996) *The Global Age*, Stanford: Stanford University Press.

Barboza, A. (2007) "Ex-chief of China Food and Drug Unit Sentenced to Death for Graft," *The New York Times* (May 30). Online. Available at http://www.nytimes.com/2007/05/30/world/asia/30china.html?ex=1183262400&en=679682275c1530bd&ei=5070# (accessed June 29, 2007).

Beck, U. (2000) "Living your life in a runaway world: individualization, globalization and politics," in W. Hutton and A. Giddens (eds) *On the Edge: living with global capitalism*, London: Vintage.

Bennett, J., Belle, D., Kean, K., Stern, R. and Kernighan, C. (1995) *Zoned for Slavery: the child behind the label* [video], New York: Crowing Rooster Arts.

Brecher, J., Costello, T. and Smith, B. (2000) *Global Village or Global Pillage?* [DVD], Lanham, MD: National Film Network.

Brooks, M. (1983) "Historical Materialism," *Inqaba ya Basebenzi* (November). Online. Available at http://www.newyouth.com/archives/theory/historical_materialism.html (accessed June 1, 2007).

Bunker, A. (2003) *Questions and Answers about Foreign Policy (and the U.S. invasion of Iraq)*. Online. Available at http://www.geocities.com/anarchiebunker/foreignpolicy.htm (accessed June 28, 2007).

Cassidy, J. (1997) "The Return of Karl Marx," *New Yorker* (October 20–7): 248–59.

Castells, M. (2000) *The Rise of the Networked Society*, Oxford: Blackwell.

Debord, G. (1994) *The Society of the Spectacle*, New York: Zone Books.

Dueweke, C. (2004) "Parent questions materials used in government class," *Warren Weekly* (October 20): 7A, 14A. Online. Available at http://www.detroitnews.com/2004/macomb/0410/07c05–296230.htm (accessed June 2, 2007).

Ellison, R., Vecchione, J. and Lyman, W. (1996) *Vietnam: a television history*, Boston, MA: WGBH Boston Video.

Freire, P. (1970) *Pedagogy of the Oppressed*, New York: Continuum.

Friedman, T. L. (1999) *The Lexus and the Olive Tree: understanding globalization*, New York: Farrar, Straus Giroux.

Gaudelli, W. (2003) *World Class Teaching and Learning in Global Times*, Mahwah, NJ: Lawrence Erlbaum Associates.

Gibson, R. (n. d.). "Master/Slave Questions." Online. Available at http://www.pipeline.com/~rgibson/masterslave.htm (accessed June 2, 2007).

Herrnstein, R. J., and Murray, C. A. (1994) *The Bell Curve: intelligence and class structure in American life*, New York: Free Press.

Hutton, W. (1996) *The State We're In*, London: Vintage.

Kellog, P. (1998) "Ten chairs of inequality," *Rethinking Schools* 12, 3. Online. Available at http://www.rethinkingschools.org/archive/12_03/wealth.shtml (accessed June 1, 2007).

Kelsh, D. (2001) "(D)evolutionary socialism and the containment of class: for a red theory of class," *Red Critique* 1, 1: 9–13. Online. Available at http://www.redcritique.org/spring2001/devolutionarysocialism.htm (accessed July 6, 2007).

Kelsh, D., and Hill, D. (2006) "The culturalization of class and the occluding of class consciousness: the knowledge industry in/of education," *Journal for Critical Education Policy Studies* 4, 1. Online. Available at http://www.jceps.com/index.php?pageID=article&articleID=59 (accessed July 7, 2007).

Kozol, J. (1967) "Where ghetto schools fail," *Atlantic Monthly* 220, 4: 107–10.

Landes, D. (1999) *The Wealth and Poverty of Nations*, New York: W. W. Norton.

Lechner, F. (n. d.) *The Globalization Website.* Online. Available at http://www.sociology.emory.edu/globalization/index.html (accessed June 28, 2007).

LeDuff, C. (2000) "At a Slaughterhouse, Some Things Never Die: Who Kills, Who Cuts, Who Bosses Can Depend on Race," *The New York Times* (June 16). Online. Available at http://partners.nytimes.com/library/national/race/061600leduff-meat.html (accessed June 1, 2007).

Luttwak, E. (1999) *Turbo-capitalism: winners and losers in the global economy*, New York: HarperCollins.

McMichael, P. (2000) *Development and Social Change: a global perspective*, Thousand Oaks, CA: Pine Forge Press.

Marx, K. (1992) *Capital: a critique of political economy (Volume 1)*, New York: Penguin.

—— and Engels, F. (1986) *The Communist Manifesto*, New York: Penguin.

Merryfield, M. M. and Subedi, B. (2006) "Decolonizing the mind for world-centered global education," in E. W. Ross, (ed.) *The Social Studies Curriculum: purposes, problems, and possibilities*, 3rd edn, Albany: State University of New York Press.

Mittelman, J. H. (2000). *The Globalization Syndrome*, Princeton, NJ: Princeton University Press.

Milanovic, B. (2005). *Worlds Apart: measuring international and global inequality*, Princeton, NJ: Princeton University Press.

National Council for the Social Studies (NCSS) (1994) *Curriculum Standards for Social Studies.* Online. Available at http://www.socialstudies.org/standards/introduction/ (accessed June 29, 2007).

Ollman, B. (2001) *How to Take an Exam – and remake the world*, Montreal: Black Rose Books.

Ollman, B. (n. d.) "Dialectical Marxism: the writings of Bertell Ollman." Online. Available at http://www.nyu.edu/projects/ollman/index.php (accessed June 28, 2007).

Otero, V. K. (2006) "Moving beyond the 'get it or don't' conception of formative assessment," *Journal of Teacher Education*, 57, 3: 247–55.

Perlman, F. (1969) *The Reproduction of Daily Life*, Detroit: Black & Red.

President George Bush Discusses Iraq in National Press Conference (2003). Online. Available at http://www.whitehouse.gov/news/releases/2003/03/20030306–8.html# (accessed June 2, 2007).

Robertson, R. (1992) *Globalization: social theory and global culture*, Thousand Oaks, CA: Sage.

Rosenberg, T. (2007) "Reverse foreign aid," *New York Times Magazine* (May 27). Online. Available at http://www.nytimes.com/pages/magazine/index.html (accessed June 1, 2007).

Ross, E. W. (ed.) (2006) *The Social Studies Curriculum: purposes, problems and possibilities*, 3rd edn, Albany: State University of New York Press.

Ross, E. W. and Gibson, R. (eds) (2007) *Neoliberalism and Education Reform*, Cresskill, NJ: Hampton Press.

Scholte, J. A. (2000) *Globalization: a critical introduction*, London: Palgrave.

Sievers, L. (Executive Producer) (2002) *Nightline: in the national interest: dividends from the war on terrorism* (Parts 1 and 2; April 25–6) [Television broadcast], New York: ABC News. Online. Available at http://www.thedossier.ukonline.co.uk/video_september11.htm (accessed June 29, 2007).

Stiglitz, J. E. (2002) *Globalization and its Discontents*, New York: W. W. Norton.

Smith, M. K. and Smith, M. (2002) "Globalisation." *The Encyclopedia of Informal Education.* Online. Available at http://www.infed.org/biblio/globalization.htm (accessed May 30, 2007).

Stanley, W. B. and Nelson, J. L. (1994) "The foundations of social education in historical context," in R. Martusewicz and W. Reynolds (eds), *Inside/Out: contemporary critical perspectives in education*, New York: St. Martin's.

Tabb, W. K. (2006) "The power of the rich," *Monthly Review*, 58, 3: 6–17.

Teller-Elsberg, J., Folbre, N., Heintz, J. and the Center for Popular Economics (2006) *A Field Guide to the U.S. Economy Revised and Updated*, New York: New Press.

United for a Fair Economy (2006) *New Data: the wealth divide widens.* Online. Available at http://www.faireconomy.org/press/2006/wealth_divide_widens.html (accessed October 22, 2004).

Vinson, K. D. and Ross, E. W. (2003) *Image and Education: teaching in the face of the new disciplinarity*, New York: Peter Lang.

Waters, M. (1995) *Globalization*, New York: Routledge.

Williams, B., Sawyer, S. C. and Wahlstrom, C. M. (2005) *Marriages, Families & Intimate Relationships*, Boston, MA: Pearson.

Wowk, M. (2004) "Father irked by son's anti-Bush lesson," *The Detroit News* (October 7). Online. Available at http://www.detroitnews.com/2004/macomb/0410/07c05–296230.htm (accessed October 22, 2004).

Wright, F. (1975) "So Long Partner!" New York: United Electrical, Radio and Machine Workers of America.

Zweig, M. (ed.) (2004) *What's Class Got to Do With It?: American society in the twenty-first century*, Ithaca, NY: Cornell University Press.

8   Class: the base of all reading[1]

Robert Faivre

Abstract

This chapter argues that while reading repeatedly reappears as a site of cultural crisis, this apparent crisis is an effect of shifts in production and not only a cultural matter. Through an extended critique of contemporary theories of reading – ranging from Alberto Manguel's *A History of Reading*, which privatizes and personalizes all reading, to John Berger's classic *Ways of Seeing*, which demythologizes reading and surfaces the political economy of culture in capitalism – the chapter develops a materialist theory of reading through which to intervene in the dominant theories of reading. The chapter argues that, contrary to the dominant theories, class is the base of all reading and that the resolution of the "crisis" is to be found in the development of class-conscious reading: comprehensive, conceptual reading that takes the side of working people in the struggle for a just society.

Introduction: reading in crisis?

In the US today, reading is in crisis. Or, so it seems according to two reports (in 2004 and 2007) by the US National Endowment for the Arts (NEA), chaired by Dana Gioia. In the "Preface" to *Reading at Risk* (US NEA: 2004), Gioia reported that the past two decades have seen "accelerating declines in literary reading among all demographic groups of American adults," declines correlating with "increased participation in a variety of electronic media" and indicating "an erosion in cultural and civic participation" (xii–xiii). In the course of reiterating that "There is a general decline in reading among teenage and adult Americans" (5) – and in particular "literary reading" (reading for pleasure: 10, 7–10) – Gioia, in the "Preface" to the 2007 report *To Read or Not To Read: a question of national consequence*, suggests that this trend has "more than literary importance": it has "demonstrable social, economic, cultural, and civic implications" insofar as "poor reading skills correlate heavily with lack of employment, lower wages, and fewer opportunities for advancement," as well as lower levels of participation in "civic and cultural life, most notably in volunteerism and voting" (US NEA: 5). Careful to note that "the data ... do not necessarily show cause and effect" (5), Gioia (US NEA 2007) nevertheless states that "the cold statistics confirm" that "books change lives for the better," and that "Whatever the benefits of new electronic media, they provide no measurable substitute for the intellectual and personal development initiated and sustained by frequent reading" (6).

In response to these reports, many public commentators have asserted the need to reinstate a common culture via the practice of "reading for pleasure." George Will, responding to the 2004 report, suggests that the decline in reading is not caused by the turn to electronic media for entertainment but merely aggravated by it. Rather, what has put the nation at risk in "today's new age of barbarism," by which he means terrorism, is the loss of "a common culture of shared reading" (A29), the reinstatement of which E. D. Hirsch argues for in *The Knowledge Deficit* (2006). Similarly, Caleb Crain (2007) worries that a decline in reading print may rob individuals of "the boldness to act" and that, therefore, "Such a habit might be quite dangerous for a democracy to lose" (n. p.). Andrew Solomon (2004) also sees the decline in "reading for pleasure" as a crisis in the health, politics, and education of the nation, and indeed a threat to civilization itself. Reading is "the essence of civilization" in that we need to read to live. For Solomon reading is fundamental to "community" and "democracy" (n. p.).

While according to these commentators from both right and left our very humanity is at stake in the crisis of reading, others on the left, such as Steven Johnson (2008), see "cause for celebration" rather than "national alarm," noting that the 2007 NEA report "completely excludes reading done on computers" (n. p.). Johnson, champion of popular culture (*Everything Bad is Good for You: how today's popular culture is actually making us smarter* 2005), dismisses the "crisis" in reading through a turn to pragmatics. He concedes that "literary" reading ("books") may be slipping statistically. But, foregrounding the reading practices of "digital natives" who have grown up engaging in "text-based interactive media," Johnson contends that "the only reason the intellectual benefits" of these reading practices provide, in Gioia's words, "no measurable substitute" for ("literary") reading (US NEA 2007: 6) is simple: "they haven't been measured yet" (Johnson 2008: n. p.). Also in favor of embracing digital literacies, which he sees as adding to literary reading ("reading for depth") the dimension of "lateral reading," is Matthew Kirschenbaum (2007: n. p.). He is critical of the NEA report insofar as it is "curiously devoid of historical awareness" of a wide variety of modalities of reading, past and present, including a variety of contemporary types of screen reading that participate in what he calls "the remaking of reading," where "reading is both reimagined and re-engineered, made over creatively as well as technologically" (n. p.). In his view, both computer users and "the stereotypical bookworm" share "the same aura of deep concentration and immersion" (n. p.).

Despite the political differences of the commentators, however, the responses to the reports are remarkably the same. What links these accounts is that they isolate reading from the underlying class relations that shape it. Their local differences – whether there is a "crisis" in reading or "cause for celebration," whether screen literacies are understood as opposing or as extending "literary" (humanist) reading – represent only an index of the various consciousness ("reading") skills that are mere surface registers of, and made necessary by, what all of these commentators put out of sight: the regime of wage labor (without which capital cannot exist) and the shifts that repeatedly occur in that regime as capital pursues ever higher profits. With wage labor out of sight, these commentators represent the current "crisis" of reading either as a moral failure or an out-of-date and out-of-touch judgment made by traditionalists (humanists) whose focus on literary reading blocks them from recognizing the value of the new literacies required by new media. But in either case, they valorize reading as a private act that participates in and contributes to the constitution of common (sub)cultures, represented as spaces that, at once, transcend and offer sustenance to carry on with the grind of everyday life. "Relief" from the everyday, they suggest, can be available to all, and for pennies, if not nothing – if only there could be success in the renewal of a "personal" interest in reading.

Exemplary of this approach is the recent anthology of personal accounts of reading, *I Hear America Reading*, edited by Jim Burke, a teacher in California. Burke's anthology, which intersperses letters with literary quotations about "reading," is presented by its back-cover blurb (taken from his 1993 letter to the *San Francisco Chronicle* that resulted in the letters that constitute the book) as a response to a national crisis in "an era of decreasing commitment to literacy," and as a register of the hope and inspiration to be found in "the full spectrum of humanity." Literacy across social difference is represented here as a potential resolution to the literacy crisis and, indeed, as the purpose of reading: to hear the stories that are told and to appreciate in them "our story, the one we never tire of hearing" (5). What is this story? To judge by the anthology's contents, it is a pluralist story of singular experiences. It is a story of people overcoming obstacles in order to live as fully as possible within the limits of a reality that they cannot change: a prison inmate who appreciates "escaping" to exotic places by reading *National Geographic*, regretful adults who disliked reading when young and now urge students to discover the joys of reading and thus avoid their mistake, earnest professionals who offer maxims drawn from their reading such as "We are all 'different' and capable of much love" and "Life is a joy! It depends how you look at it" (Burke 1999: 80, 79).

But, as I argue in this essay, "how you look at it" is not simply a personal matter, despite the suggestion of Burke's editor.

My point, to be clear, is to explain that all reading practices and theories of reading are historical. By historical I mean that reading is shaped by labor and the labor relations in which it takes place. For instance, what unites all readers is that they are determined by the relationship between work and leisure, which is determined by the division of labor in society, which is itself determined by the mode of production. Reading today, in short, is determined by capitalism, and it is the labor of reading – the level of skill and the reason one reads in the first place – that all dominant discussion of reading has banned. The reasons are not surprising. Re-reading reading in terms of labor not only situates reading as a social practice with its roots in underlying social structures; it also draws attention to the fact that the problems of reading today are the problems of reading in class society. They are not, in other words, transcendental problems of reading as such. Reading (and its "crises") always reflects the priorities of the societies in which reading occurs. Reading in a society based on exploited labor will reflect the priorities of profit; in a society which puts meeting the needs of all at the forefront of society, reading will reflect very different priorities. Not talking about the labor and labor relations of reading is a way of not talking about the fundamentally unjust priorities of class society. And not talking about the historical nature of class society is a way of not talking about why the existing class relations can and should be transformed.

My argument, in other words, is that the dominant theories of reading as a cultural and "personal" matter are ideological theories of reading that reinforce the existing relations of exploitation and the inequalities produced by these relations. They cover over the fault-lines of class through an exclusive focus on the personal isolated from the structures which shape the cultural, and thus the personal and the individual. Reading, on these terms, is an occasion to meditate on (the joys of) singularity and sensuousness, rather than an inquiry into the underlying social relations which condition all reading. Such affective theories of reading, I believe, not only privatize reading, thus erasing the labor relations which make it possible, but, as a result, produce readers who are increasingly vulnerable to, and accepting of, the commodification of life under capitalism and the consequent concomitant deepening of exploitation and social inequality. And this is, in the end, precisely the effect of Gioia's (2007) dream of a common culture, a cultural space for reading and creative action which he presents as a space of value(s) transcending the market and its system of prices, yet also compatible with the "free market" which Gioia celebrates as the basis for a prosperous society. Gioia's cultural vision is contradictory in that it accepts the market as the space of freedom while it reacts against commodification, which it attributes to the market.

In order to make reading socially relevant and enable readers to be effective participants in the struggle for social justice, I argue that reading needs to be connected to the material conditions in which reading takes place. Thus, in contrast to the privatized theories of reading that have become immensely popular in the US, I argue for a materialist theory of reading. Reading, on these terms, conceptualizes social relations in their totality. Instead of accepting the empirical realities of daily life as given and autonomous in our "experience" of them, it seeks to unearth the structures that shape our experience, so as to advance new relations based on economic equality and the abolition of relations of exploitation.

To more fully examine the relation between the dominant mode of reading and the materialist theory of reading I am arguing for, I re-read, in what follows, two classic texts on reading, which are themselves situated on the fault-line of the social contradiction of class: the first is Alberto Manguel's *A History of Reading* (1996), which exemplifies affective reading, and the second is John Berger's *Ways of Seeing* (1972), which is a useful starting point for theorizing the ways in which reading is structured by the social. After establishing the relationship of these two statements on reading, I return to the current debates over the "crisis" of reading in order to begin to foreground its material dimensions.

Private reading is de-reading

Manguel's *A History of Reading* is a vast thematic catalog of literary anecdote, memoir, and cultured trivia of reading. Advancing the view that reading is simultaneously "common to us all" and at the same time deeply personal and singular, the book is structured in two main sections – "Acts of Reading" and "Powers of the Reader" – within which various themes are traced. These themes, which are presented as the almost obvious features of reading, are indicated by the chapter headings: "Learning to Read," "Picture Reading," "Being Read To," etc. They are supposed to stand as trans-historical scenes of reading, instantly recognizable and capable of supporting a density of details, those of one's own experience and of others'. As a catalog, Manguel's book does not build a comprehensive historical analysis of reading, but rather assembles its "history" as an almost accidental exploratory documentation of one reader's appreciation of reading. History, for an accidental reader like Manguel, is an open book from which to sample and savor the rich tapestry of the world's cultures through a deliberately unstudied approach. Thus, all knowledge is local, personal, felt, and above all, pleasurable. Such affective knowledge of reading and history becomes a sampling suggestive of endless and ongoing readings that lack any determinate connections.

Manguel focuses on details in order to locate the personal there. He cites his own reading in great detail, as well as that of his mentor Jorge Luis Borges, alongside many accounts and reports from his reading of cultural history. For example, in the chapter "Stealing Books," Manguel writes that

> The act of reading establishes an intimate, physical relationship in which all the senses have a part: the eyes drawing the words from the page, the ears echoing the sounds being read, the nose inhaling the familiar scent of paper, glue, ink, cardboard or leather, the touch caressing the rough or soft page, the smooth or hard binding; even the taste, at times when the reader's fingers are lifted to the tongue (which is how the murderer poisons his victims in Umberto Eco's *The Name of the Rose*). All this, many readers are unwilling to share – and if the book they wish to read is in someone else's possession, the laws of property are as hard to uphold as those of faithfulness in love. Also, physical ownership becomes at times synonymous with a sense of intellectual apprehension. We come to feel that the books that we own are the books we know, as if possession were, in libraries as in courts, nine-tenths of the law; that to glance at the spines of the books we call ours, obediently standing guard along the walls of our room, willing to speak to us and us alone at the mere flick of a page, allows us to say, "All this is mine," as if their presence alone fills us with their wisdom, without our actually having to labour through their contents.
>
> (244–5)

Here, reading is presented as a highly intimate, physical, sensuous, and above all, private activity. To read on Manguel's terms is to undergo a quasi-religious experience, a virtual communion with the presence of meaning contained in the book, which is absorbed through the senses. What counts when one reads is not the ideas or "content" of the book, or the frameworks of intelligibility through which one makes sense of the book, but the reader's sensory experience of reading. The "encounter" of a book is always a "singular" and rapturous experience. In other words, Manguel substitutes "perception" (the private experience of reading) for "conceptuality" (the social logic through which one abstracts and makes connections). The "ecstatic reading" promulgated by Manguel empties reading of its conceptual content and re-situates reading on an experiential plane. To situate individuals in their larger social relations is for him a violent, not to mention uninspired, act that restricts subjective agency. Social agency is found instead in the excessive details of private property ("books").

Manguel makes this quite clear when he states that, because any account claiming to be definitive is a false imposition and a violent totalization, he can only write a singular history of reading and not *the* definitive history of reading. Reading's "chronology," Manguel writes, "cannot be that of political history," because reading is life, life goes on, and neither is to be totalized as politics (22–3). According to this logic, to reduce the universally practiced and wholly individualized activity of reading to politics – that is, to a matter of the structuring of experience by the social relations between people – is an ignorant and indecent intrusion on what is an all but indefinable activity. Reading as a political act is made into a strategy aligned with those in positions of authority and power. To be true to reading, and to resist reigning power structures, then, is to bear witness to the great diversity of readings, without claiming the authority of a grand narrative of social justice.

Thus, following Borges, Manguel repeatedly refers to the idea of reading as "rescue." That is, just as reading itself is not to be totalized, so too are texts themselves to be left open for future readings and not pigeonholed in arbitrary categories of understanding. Instead reading, like the reader, is to be rescued from classifications.

> Categories are exclusive; reading is not – or should not be. Whatever classifications have been chosen, every library tyrannizes the act of reading, and forces the reader – the curious reader, the alert reader – to rescue the book from the category to which it has been condemned.
>
> (199)

Reading for Manguel, like writing for Derrida, is the space of "dissemination": it is continually opening out in its uncontainable intertextuality, fixed only by the violent boundaries imposed by totalizing epistemologies. The reader, then, is not to function as a follower of established authorities' concepts or categories, nor to impose an authoritative claim on what is read (although a possessive claim of ownership is abided), but rather to read for oneself, as if outside any categories of reading, experience, knowledge, ... Such a reader, then, will be a reading subject who focuses on the singularities and differences of a reading experience, not on the structures that make such experience possible. That is, such a reader will focus on that which appears as one's "private" possession (or that which has taken "possession" of one while reading), and not on the social relations in which "possession" (property) has become a trope.

By denying any determinate connections and situating all reading as personal, Manguel ultimately reduces all knowledge to autobiography. "Autobiography," to cite Stuart Hall (1996), another popularizer of de-totalizing experience, is essentially all that remains of knowledge in the wake of the collapse of the "grand narratives" of cultural and social theory – and this is of course for him and for Manguel a sign of an optimistic shift away from notions of collectivity and solidarity and toward a new sense of "personal" power (with a lowercase "p") and authority (with a lowercase "a"). In his discussion of how new developments in cultural studies and its history should be understood, Hall tellingly writes:

Autobiography is usually thought of as seizing the authority of authenticity. But in order not to be authoritative, I've got to speak autobiographically. I'm going to tell you about my own take on certain theoretical legacies and moments in cultural studies, not because it is the truth or the only way of telling the history. I myself have told it many other ways before; and I intend to tell it in a different way later. But just at this moment, for this conjecture, I want to take a position in relation to the "grand narrative" of cultural studies for the purposes of opening up some reflections on cultural studies as a practice.

(262–3)

This displacement of history and knowledge of social totality with autobiography and provisional understanding of a moment in a moving series of moments has the effect of dismissing any attempt to understand reading, society, and history as structured. Although represented as a means of intervening into hegemonic frameworks and dominant relations of power, it actually disenables reading subjects, since the unequal relations Hall wants to make available to critique are dispersed in a fog of contingencies. What kind of critical understanding of social relations can be developed if there are no determinate relations between any events? If no analysis is any more true than any other? If the "story" one tells is determined only by the local exigencies of the moment? One is hard pressed to find an approach to reading the social that is more legitimating of the operations of the powerful. This is, after all, precisely the logic that the Bush administration deployed to justify its onslaught on the Iraqi people: telling one story after another (from the existence of "weapons of mass destruction," to Saddam Hussein's "intent" to use weapons, to his "gassing of his own people," etc.) to serve the administration's private purposes, regardless of the reality. And in the same way that the Bush administration rejected as sympathetic to terror and tyranny all those who have sought to explain the conflict in Iraq on larger, historical terms, the attempt to develop comprehensive and coherent knowledge is dismissed, in countless texts of "left" writers such as Hall, Lyotard and Manguel, as "authoritarian" (not only "authoritative"), "totalitarian" and "terroristic" (not merely "totalizing"); that is, as "violent" impositions on an open, living process.

What is at stake here is, in short, the understanding produced by reading: "understanding" is presented as an always incomplete grasp of what one can privately experience. What distinguishes "private" experiences of reading, however, is not subjective difference but class. Differences in experience are the effects not simply of being discrete "individuals," but rather of the structuring of subjective experience by the objective conditions of life. We can see this, for instance, even in Manguel's own supposedly "provisional" above-class reading of reading. Manguel's text – which he presents as being free from the "impositions" and "exclusions" (the violence of categories) that "good reading" should avoid – is, far from being "above class," premised on a series of political and economic assumptions about the conditions of life. For instance, in claiming reading as common to us all, Manguel describes and assumes a very uncommon reading experience; in celebrating individual difference, he projects his own class privilege onto others. To be more specific, Manguel's appreciation of reading takes for granted the private library, leisure time for reading, advanced education, world travel, etc. His argument proceeds as if these were the conditions in which all people read, rather than the conditions of a very privileged global elite. But to mark the personal as the space of freedom when most of the world's people experience a profound lack of freedom in their personal lives is to advance a reading of the personal which denies economic and social inequality. Thus Manguel, who claims that totalizing readings are unreliable and inadequate for understanding the complexities of "personal" reading, in fact bases his argument on the silent assumption of a totalizing reading. In closing off what he does not want reading to be (political, economic, social-historical, etc.), Manguel sums up reading within the inexhaustible wholeness of the "individual" and the "singular," putting out of sight that which does not fit his definition.

Consequently, Manguel's text produces a reader who is transported from her social existence to an enraptured private experience, focusing on the seemingly singular while displacing the relation between the "singular" and the social totality. This is a reader, in other words, who is not only unable to make connections between her experiences and those of others, but "delights" in the apparent lack of structural connections. It is not surprising that in the dominant common sense of the US, Manguel's history of reading has been widely embraced as a "subtle" and "sensuous" expression rather than a violent celebration of private property and the subjective pleasures it provides the few. It is embraced as "subtle," however, not because it represents the "truth" of "universal" reading, but because, by fostering the illusions of individual freedom and autonomy that are so useful to the bourgeoisie insofar as they obscure the (changeable) structures that produce the haves and the have-nots, it represents the dominant interests of the existing class arrangements.

Manguel and other theorists of affective, private reading, then, ultimately de-conceptualize reading to make comprehension safe for the continuation of exploitative social structures. Contemporary theories of reading, to put this differently, are really modes of what I call "de-reading." Through the detour of situating reading on the plane of the experiential, de-reading is a means of inculcating a conceptualization of social relations as personal, affective or functional matters. The effect of de-reading is to conceptually de-link social issues and phenomena from each other and from the social totality of which they are a part. De-reading thus de-structures cultural practices, and makes them appear as free-floating, self-determining "personal" practices without any necessary conditions, interrelations or implications. In effect, it also de-"activates" readers. By masking in the cloak of the personal their subject position in the social relations of production, de-reading also makes them significantly less effective participants in the struggle to bring about economic and social equality. It makes them consenting reading subjects.

Yet, contradictorily, one of the consequences of "de-reading" is that in the name of privileging "personal" differences, one of the most fundamental aspects of a person's life – his or her class position – becomes entirely invisible or else is turned into a matter that appears to have nothing at all to do with class. In contrast to Manguel, I argue that any examination of people's "personal" reading practices that does not address the conditions in which they live and work, which are the effects of their position in the division of labor, misses the very dimensions of their lives that shape their practices and give different meanings to different practices. The "differences" in reading practices between a wage-worker on the night shift who reads to escape an impoverished reality and a CEO who reads to learn better strategies for lowering the cost of labor power to increase profits (which leads to growing prison populations) – are not simply cultural or free-floating differences. They are differences made possible by the division of labor in capitalist society.

De-reading is one side of reading in class society: it is ideological reading. But contrary to the common sense, ideology is not simply ideas that are "misinformed" or ideas that correspond to particular political programs. Rather, ideology, in the materialist sense, refers to ideas that justify unequal class relations. More specifically, ideology under capitalism, as Marx (1996) theorizes in *Capital*, is a direct effect of the exploitation that occurs in the wage-labor exchange.

Since the concept of "ideology" has been so emptied of its economic content in contemporary theory (when it is not being outright banned from use), it is neces- sary to take some time here to clarify its relation to wage-labor and the working day, and its significance for the question of reading. In the context of wage-labor, Marx (1996) explains, it appears that people are free to sell their labor (or not), and that in going to work and receiving a wage, workers receive fair compensation. Yet the actual relations that make this exchange possible contradict its appearance. Not only is the worker not free to sell her labor power – she is economically compelled to because she does not own the means of production – but the apparently equal exchange is actually based on the theft from the worker that occurs during the working day. The working day, Marx explains, is divided into two parts. One part of the working day involves the expenditure of the worker's labor-power which is necessary to reproduce the worker (that is, necessary labor, or labor which produces the use-values which meet the worker's needs, whether these are the minimal basic needs for survival or more complex needs), while the other part of the working day involves the excess expenditure of labor-power (surplus labor) in order to produce surplus value, which is claimed by the capitalist as profit. But this division, Marx emphasizes, "is not evident on the surface" (1996: 245). Whereas under feudalism, that part of the time spent working for the lord (the "*corvée*") and that time spent producing the serf's own means of subsistence was clearly established and violently enforced, under capitalism there is no such visible distinction. While "surplus labor in the corvée has an inde- pendent and immediately palpable form" (244), the appropriation of surplus labor is not directly available to experience (perception), since it is concealed beneath a veil of equivalence (wages), and requires a more complex, conceptual understanding of what takes place during the working day. Thus, although it appears that in going to work and receiving a wage, the worker receives fair compensation (the full value of what she produces), she is actually, as Marx puts it, being "robbed" by the capitalist. The entire basis of capitalist profit is the surplus value stolen by capitalists from the working class. It is precisely because all profits – indeed, all forms of capital – are based on surplus value, and because it is the goal of capitalists to constantly expand their rate of profit, that capital seeks to extend the time workers spend producing surplus value relative to that spent reproducing themselves and their families. The actuality of the working day in capitalism (exploitation), in short, is what explains why a seemingly equal exchange results in the greater and greater impoverishment of workers and the concentration of wealth into fewer hands.

Working people thus have an interest not only in reclaiming the fruits of their labor and taking control of the conditions of labor, but abolishing exploitation and establishing their collective ownership of the means of production. However, as it is in the interest of the ruling minority to maintain the existing relations, the capitalists' private interest in remaining free to purchase and thereby exploit the labor power of others is presented as the general interest, which is the reading that ideology is always aimed at producing. In other words, the ability to represent the particular interests of a privileged class as the interests of all, a move which Manguel repeats when he projects his class circumstances onto others, is not a moral matter, but an effect of the class relations of capitalism. "The ideas of the ruling class," Marx and Engels (1976) argue in *The German Ideology*, "are in every epoch the ruling ideas: i.e., the class which is the ruling *material* force of society, is at the same time its ruling *intellectual* force" (59). Thus those subject to the ruling class in the division of labor are also subject to the ruling class's ideas.

Like Manguel, Gioia's texts are exemplary instances of these class ideas. For Gioia (2008), culture in crisis is articulated in its relation to the market, but the market is presented as a space of exchange separated from its basis in exploitation. "The role of culture ... must go beyond economics," Gioia writes (19). His view is deeply contradictory. On the one hand, while culture fails when it gives into the market-place's "profit-driven commercialization of cultural values," culture succeeds when it provides access to values beyond price and thus helps people to value being "active citizens" rather than "passive consumers" of commodity culture (21). On the other hand, Gioia "love[s] the free market" and states that "The productivity and efficiency of the free market is beyond dispute" (19). In other words, Gioia openly accepts and celebrates the market and implicitly accepts its basis in the global exploitation of labor. He calls for a broad and inclusive culture, but he limits his attention to the visible surfaces of capitalism: media culture, the literary margin, and the market as a stand-in for the whole of the economic structure.

The effect of this reading of the relation of culture to a flattened economic surface is a separation of price and value, and thus the production of a cultural space which appears to exceed market relations (or at least the character of the market and its crude value system of "prices"). For Gioia, our culture is either going to continue to be influenced by the market at a human cost or it is going to return to an imagined former state, in which culture and reading were above the market. Such a reading is already a separation of market from production, a familiar reduction of the economic sphere to one of equal exchange, which puts exploitation out of view. Gioia seeks to (re)establish a common culture so that those who are unwittingly influenced by the market in their cultural practices can recover a culture of transcendent values (without price). This is a culture of personal choice; however, making such choices appear to transcend the market, actually recasts a core idea of the market – choice – as a universal value.

What persons exercise such choice? Far from understanding persons as divided by the determining relation to property – owning or not owning property capable of extracting profit through exploitation – Gioia (2008) sees the "population" as divided into "passive and active citizens," and the "defining difference" between the two "isn't income, geography, or even education. It depends on whether they read for pleasure and participate in the arts" (21). In other words, the difference is experience.

What is central to re-understanding reading in general, and this theory of reading advanced by Manguel and Gioia, is that the role of ideology is to legitimate "appearance" (free exchange) as "essence" (exploitation). It takes what is "directly visible" in capitalism (i.e. the "freedom" and "fairness" of the exchange of wages for labor power) as the "root explanation" of life under capitalism. Affective theories of reading such as Manguel's and Gioia's serve ideological ends in that they take for granted the apparently equitable, unstructured and undetermined relations between people who are apparently free and autonomous social beings. This appearance of capitalist society (which is quite at odds with actuality) is, in fact, the starting point of such an analysis. It is the fundamental, though unspoken, premise of such a history of reading, in which reading emerges as a purely personal and private matter without any social determinations.

Such theories of reading, in fact, simply "describe" or "repeat," at the level of theory and culture, capital's need to update the consciousness skills required for the new technologies within the framework of the old production relations. Manguel's representation of social structures as a morass of appearances without any determinate connections or causes, for instance, is really a more mediated embrace of global capital's most recent needs for a labor force skilled in the use of new cybertechnologies, which are less linear and structured. These technologies require readers with an even more fragmented consciousness: subjects with hypertextual intelligibilities. This state of consciousness is represented in the cultural common sense as the height of subjective "freedom" and theoretical "subtlety." For example, Kirschenbaum's (2007) praise of the "lateral reading" of the new digital literacies is exemplary of the celebration of reading the "deep" surfaces of class culture without showing and explaining cultural appearances in terms of their material basis in the determinative structures of production. In actuality, such surface reading – whether presented as literary or digital or in other terms – represents the deepening exploitation and subjective unfreedom of the working class worldwide. Surface reading is de-reading; it includes many modes of reading, which have the effect of resolving not simply cultural crises, but of perpetually maintaining a general unconsciousness about the basic social contradiction which periodically produces a crisis for the interests of the ruling class. Specifically, the real crisis that produces the apparent crises of culture is produced by developments which bring the forces of production into increased contradiction with the relations of production. As the material basis for transformation of the social relations is developed, so that transformation is not only necessary but possible, given the state of development of the productive forces, the contradiction between the forces and relations of production increases and becomes more and more difficult to deny as a determinative structure This is why right and left are mentioning class in their theories; it is also why they mention it in order to contain it to culture and the market, thereby effectually rewriting class as one surface feature among others. The calls for a common culture and for individual freedoms and flexibility have the effect of temporarily managing on the surface the historical crisis in the sharpening class contradiction in the base. The surface reading produced by Manguel, Gioia and others is reading as crisis management.

What I call transformative reading is, by contrast, situated at the boundaries of contemporary social relations, since it seeks to advance the conditions that will bring about the end of exploitation. It therefore insists on the necessity of concepts that enable reading to grasp the "particular" and the "personal" in relation to the global. The necessity and the possibility of such explanatory concepts which persistently relate the "visible" realities of everyday life to their "invisible" structures is a core aspect of any science. Science does not accept the surface appearances, but always seeks to explain them in their basic relations, even as ruling class ideas of science emphasize the uncertainty of reliable explanations. Transformative reading is the science of the advancing productive forces that make possible a just society.

Reading as de-mystification

To clarify what I mean by transformative reading, I turn now to a discussion of another foundational text on reading, John Berger's *Ways of Seeing* (1972). *Ways of Seeing* has long been regarded as a classic in reading visual culture. But what I want to argue is that we can understand *Ways of Seeing* as a theorization of reading more generally: a theorization of reading that begins not from the appearances of daily life under capitalism (although it spends a great deal of time addressing these experiences), but from the material relations that shape all appearances and our readings of them.

The main argument of the book is that "perception" – that is, our sensory impressions of the world around us, other beings, things, as well as images and other representations of these in art and media – is not individual, but always is constituted by socially derived "ways of seeing." In other words, our ways of seeing are historically developed ways of conceptualizing both what we experience and the social totality in which our experience occurs. The focus of *Ways of Seeing* is on the ways of seeing that have developed in capitalist society, beginning with an emphasis on the conventions of representation in art, specifically oil painting, and building to a discussion of how these same conventions inform "publicity" (his term for advertisement and related media imagery). By making this argument, Berger aims to show readers how and why certain ways of seeing have emerged in capitalism, and with what consequences, so that they might gain a greater metacognitive awareness over how they see, understand, and act on the world. In short, *Ways of Seeing* not only shows that the "personal" is structured by the social relations of class, but begins to advance a mode of reading that develops conceptual explanations of appearances (the visible, the sensually perceptible) in class society in light of the material relations (the invisible or the imperceptible that must be abstracted and represented as concepts) of class.

By now, works of high art (oil painting, sculpture, etc.) and the everyday texts of commodity culture (ads, television, popular films, etc.) hardly represent new objects of study. The field of cultural studies, which was emerging when *Ways of Seeing* was first published (1972), has long established that all cultural production, not just "high art," is worthy of study and needs to be situated in the context of the kinds of subjectivities they require for their production and consumption. What is significant about Berger's text is that it is located in the early years of the debates over "high" and "popular" culture and that it puts forward at this early juncture a class analysis of diverse cultural forms. In other words, in focusing on analysis of art and advertisement, Berger is responding to the conservative cultural critics of his day who produced an ideological above-class reading of culture which elevated art over other forms of cultural production in order to separate aesthetic value from market value. For example, *Ways of Seeing*, as both a television series and book, has been characterized as a "polemical riposte" to Kenneth Clark's 1969 television series and book *Civilisation*, which sought to (re)establish the traditional canon as the main body of shared culture and the common values of society (Fuller 1992: xviii). In demonstrating that all cultural value is in the end an articulation of market values, and arguing that claims to the contrary are anti-democratic, class-interested mystifications of the material relations, Berger is taking part in one of the main debates of the past century over the value of culture and the nature of cultural critique. What is at stake, in other words, is the determination of what should be "read," how, why, and with what consequences – not only for reading as a cultural practice but for the possibility of democracy and the improvement of people's lives. This point, so central to the emergence of cultural studies, bears repeating at a time when much of cultural studies has "forgotten" about the material relations of exploitation and focuses instead on the "materiality" of appearances. (See, for instance, Michael Berubé's *Aesthetics and Cultural Studies*, Stuart Hall's *Representations*, Jean Baudrillard's *Simulacra and Simulations*, and Elizabeth Edwards and Janice Hart's *Photographs/Objects/Histories: on the materiality of images*.)

To address these questions – what, how, why, wherefore? – *Ways of Seeing* begins by explaining the relationship of seeing (perception) and knowing (conception). Berger states that "The relation between what we see and what we know is never settled" (1972: 7). In other words, sensuous perception, which is often assumed to precede conceptualization, is able to grasp only the immediate (as in Berger's opening example: "The child looks and recognizes before it can speak" [7]), while conceptualization is a mediation of what is perceived that connects visible appearances to the often invisible social structures. What we see or perceive has a kind of felt immediacy, but this perception of immediacy (and its attendant sense of naturalness) is itself an experience which is constituted by the social relations. What appears to be natural (or not) can only ever be the product of a way of seeing that has been made possible by the given social situation. There is, in short, a dialectical relation between perception and conception that is always mediated by class.

Berger addresses this disconnect between appearance and the conditions of possibility that give rise to the appearance by examining the image and the conventions of image-making in capitalism. Any image, he argues, is not a natural occurrence but a reproduction of a particular way of seeing and thus of a reading of both what the image depicts and its relation to those to whom it is presented. Berger's brief discussion of the development of the artistic convention of "perspective" is particularly useful in demonstrating the historicity of seeing/reading. Perspective – a method for creating a proportional image that suggests dimensions and therefore seems "real" – emerged as an aesthetic convention as the bourgeois class emerged as an economic and political power. Its emergence is not a coincidence or accident, but rather an articulation of the values of the economic field in the cultural field. In perspective, all lines converge on a single horizon or vanishing point which is the projection of the single eye of the centered viewer. Berger writes

> Perspective makes the single eye the centre of the visible world. Everything converges on to the eye as to the vanishing point of infinity. The visible world is arranged for the spectator as the universe was once thought to be arranged for God.
>
> (16)

Perspective can thus be regarded as a way of "organizing the visual field" (18) — in other words, as a particular way of reading the world, which locates the spectator as the center of the world, the center of meaning. Berger shows that this way of seeing — which produces the centered, private subject who sees all that can be seen/known — is a class-interested way of seeing in that it reproduces in the visual/aesthetic field what is being advanced by emerging interests in the economic and political fields: namely, that the "individual" is the rightful center of understanding, meaning, and value. Berger's discussion of perspective, in other words, emphasizes that "seeing" is historical, rather than "natural." Perspective "proposed to the spectator that he was the unique centre of the world" (18). This is an idea central to the development of the subjects of wage-labor. So that capital can accumulate "freely" (that is, legally and fairly), wage-labor, unlike *corvée* labor in feudal relations, must be understood by the subject of wage-labor as labor "voluntarily" undertaken as a "free" "individual." In other words, the actual, historical material circumstances of wage-labor — that it is undertaken by people who have been expropriated of the means of production, who therefore own nothing but their labor power, and who therefore are compelled, in order to live, to agree to the fundamentally unequal exchange constituting the regime of wage-labor — must be mystified. Further, the mystification must naturalize the subject as a "free" "individual." Insofar, then, as all spectators are situated by the convention of perspective to see the same (omniscient) view (when clearly they are not only not omniscient but not of a common class either), perspective covers over the actual material relations in which some are able to accumulate capital freely, while others are forced to engage in "free" labor to survive. Perspective organizes the visible around the individual as the center of meaning and directs attention to the appearances of freedom and self-determination and away from the material relations, thereby (re)producing the subject of wage-labor as a "free" "individual."

It is in the context of the analysis of appearances and their material conditions that Berger's contribution to a materialist theory of reading needs to be situated. He is working to explain the ways in which appearances under private property relations simultaneously reflect and obscure material conditions, a contradictory social phenomenon that requires not simple affirmation but critique of appearances under capital. It is for this reason he is particularly concerned with explaining the mystifications of class that are articulated in oil paintings and publicity (advertising), which for him offer exemplary opportunities to unpack the complex relations of class. The critical spectator or reader – that is, the reading subject that *Ways of Seeing* is aimed at producing – brings concepts to bear to show that the singular appearance of the painting (or the ad, or of any text) is actually divided, conflicted, contradictory. This is not a mere matter of textual deconstruction – drawing out the supposed inherent internal undoing of any text. It is instead a matter of showing that ideological closures of meaning are never aimed at explaining but at *explaining away* the contradictory nature of capitalism.

Take, for instance, Berger's discussion of a painting by Thomas Gainsborough (*c.*1750), *Mr and Mrs Andrews*, which can be readily viewed on the website of the British National Gallery (http://www.nationalgallery.org.uk). The painting depicts a well-dressed eighteenth century couple under a tree. A pastoral landscape behind them stretches to the hills and clouds in the distance; they look toward us. Berger tells us that Kenneth Clark had written in *Landscape into Art* (1949) that the picture shows us a couple who in the spirit of Enlightenment are appreciating real nature – a real place that they know and love, as opposed to some idealized space invented by the artist. Berger counters that this is indeed the way of seeing that the painting aims to establish, but that study of the painting as a commissioned artwork shows that it is a depiction of bourgeois property-holders whose "proprietary attitudes" toward a "recognizable landscape" is "visible in their stance and their expressions" (106–7). What Berger suggests here is that when we study the "stance" and "expression" of the figures depicted, rather than reflect on them only in terms of their own (aesthetic) qualities or their relation to an abstract ideal (i.e. Nature), we need to ask: what are the material conditions that give meaning to such stances and expressions? What are the class relations that make not just the stances but also the commission of the painting possible in the first place? Berger's reading is rejected by the critic Lawrence Gowing (quoted in Berger: 107), who – in a move echoed by Manguel – declares Berger's class reading to be an interposition of Berger's own political reading between the artwork and its viewer, who will see the picture better by considering that the Andrews couple are depicted not owning the land but appreciating it. In response to Gowing's reading, which takes for granted the historical conditions in which such a couple can come to be in the position to "appreciate" their land, Berger brings to our attention what makes possible such a relation to the land in the first place. Possession of the land, he argues, is a precondition of such appreciation and enjoyment (107–8), and possession of the land by individuals is a historical development, not a trans-historical or universal situation. Berger argues that the property relations, which the critics obscure in their insistence that the picture shows something exceeding mere property, are at the heart of the meaning of the picture.

What Berger's reading reveals is the mystification of the material relations, which other critics produce by focusing on the cultural surfaces and marginalizing – or indeed denying – the relations that determine culture. "Mystification" – to explain Berger's term – is the imposition of the subjectivity (the way of seeing) of the class of property-owners and decision makers on the working class. In his own words, mysti-fication "is the process of explaining away what might otherwise be evident" (15–16). In this he is critiquing those modes of reading which isolate images from their material conditions, rendering them apparently autonomous (self-evident). Critical reading, by contrast, re-connects images to their material reality. Mystification, as a version of ideology, substitutes experiential sense for conceptual causal explanation. In other words, what is important to emphasize is that for Berger, reading (like seeing) is, in the most fundamental sense, a mode of conceptualizing the totality of social relations. It is a process by which one comes to know the inter-relations of the world, its complex history, and one's position in that world in relation to others. Thus, what one reads and how one reads is historical – and by "historical" Berger does not mean "accidental." Rather what and how one reads is shaped by the social relations of labor, which serve as the foundation of daily practices, and without knowledge of which it becomes impossible to develop a comprehensive understanding of "reading." To read critically in capitalism therefore means, not to disregard or dismiss the forms and appearances of culture, but to unearth the structures that remain hidden beneath the surface of daily life, which are not graspable in their totality by "perception" but only through *conceptual* understanding. In *Ways of Seeing*, Berger aims to get at the class content of images by reading what appears to the eye in relation to what is invisible but for concepts.

In working to develop such a reading, Berger addresses the reader as a social subject, especially as a class subject and a gendered subject. Having developed this reading through an engagement with various genres of oil painting, Berger closes with a discussion of the ubiquitous imagery of advertisements ("publicity") in contemporary culture. He writes,

> Does the language of publicity have anything in common with that of oil painting which, until the invention of the camera, dominated the European way of seeing during four centuries? It is one of those questions which simply needs to be asked for the answer to become clear. There is a direct continuity.
>
> (134)

The language of oil painting was mainly directed toward the bourgeois "spectator-owners" as a means of confirming the rightness of their place in the world; the purpose of publicity, which, as Berger shows, "speaks" the same "language," is to show the class of the "spectator-buyers" that their place in the world can be improved through consumption. That is, in his reading of ads for soap, clothes, home furnishings, alcohol, travel, credit, etc., Berger shows how these images work to get social subjects, the producers of value in class society, to define themselves as private subjects, as individual consumers, to whom certain ideas of pleasure are made visible while the actual conditions which undermine the ideals of democracy and equality become invisible.

Berger writes that the images and claims of publicity form "a kind of philosophical system" which "interprets the world," and that, through this systematic re-interpretation of the world, "Publicity turns consumption into a substitute for democracy" (149). Thus, the spectator-buyer's consciousness of "what one is" and "what one would like to be" are cast in private terms by publicity, and one's dissatisfaction with the current conditions of one's life are rewritten in ways that deny access to the idea that what needs to change is not something about oneself but rather the entire social structure (private property).

Berger's aim is to help the reader cut through the commodified surfaces of daily life and see that she is not an individual in a unique situation but that she is part of a social collective – the working class, or the "masses," as he puts it – whose class interest (in changing the existing relations) it is the role of the culture industry to deny. And this denial is justified (and thus hidden from the reader) by a massive media apparatus which systematically substitutes private, temporarily pleasurable experiences of consumption for real freedom (from exploitation and oppression). In his conclusion, Berger writes that "without publicity capitalism could not survive," and that in fact "Capitalism survives by forcing the majority, whom it exploits, to define their own interests as narrowly as possible" (154). Berger's goal in linking publicity – capitalism's commodity culture – to traditions in art history is to show the continuity of conflicting class interests and thus to enable the contemporary reader to begin to see through the appearances to the structure and thus – perhaps – to think and act differently, that is, to think and act in her class interest in a just society.

In short, the kind of reader which Berger's theory of reading produces is one who connects cultural practices to their material conditions, for instance, by showing how the conceptual framework of a particular image, text, practice, and so forth articulates a particular class-interested view of the social relations. Berger seeks to enable a reader who is not "fooled" by capital, but who sees and understands how particular ways of framing the issues either mystify or reveal the underlying structures. One of Berger's fundamental assumptions, in other words, seems to be that knowledge of the underlying structures can help people to be more effective actors in transforming their material conditions.

Yet Berger's text is not without limits. Berger's aim in *Ways of Seeing* is, as I have suggested, to de-mystify the appearances of commodity culture and thus to provide an opening onto a critical reading, not only of appearances but of their function within the class relations. But whether this opening is sufficient to enable social transformation is a different matter. For at the same time as Berger emphasizes the need for structural change (not just change at the level of ideas), his text also opens on to a movement to disconnect the workings of culture and ideology from the economic relations of wage-labor – a movement that both has been commandeered by cultural studies today and is especially explicit in Berger's more recent writings.

However, unlike other critiques of Berger, mine is not that he is "outdated" or too "reductive." Rather my argument is that he is not reductive enough. For instance, although he appeals to ideology and the need for ideology critique, the economic basis of ideology – the relations of exploitation that necessitate it – is never addressed in his text. As a result, we are left with a political theory of ideology and ideological reading that does not, in the end, get to its roots, though it gestures towards them. Having left unseen the roots, which are, as I have argued, transformable, it is not surprising that Berger tends toward a fatalist view of capitalism. For example, while Berger suggests that "full consciousness of the contradiction and its causes" is possible, and thus that one might "join the political struggle for full democracy" (1972: 48), he presents publicity as "the life of this culture" (154) which almost totally quashes all hopes, so that what is most likely to enable some kind of change is "our moral sense" (153). The limit here is that it is not clear how a "moral sense" which is not already subsumed by the culture that produces it is developed; that is, even while Berger begins to develop concepts that are "outside" the cultural common sense, he does not explain what makes such transformative concepts possible, and thus turns to a moralism that both accepts a fatalist view of capitalism and posits an outside sense that is not explained. In fact, in arguing for morality, he posits an "outside" that is really part of the "inside" of capitalist relations: an argument for simply reforming (updating) capital rather than transforming its exploitative relations. This is further confirmed in a much more recent interview (Bonaventura 1996), in which Berger states, "I can't accept human liberation as some thing that can finally be gained. [...] I think it's something that has to be constantly and eternally struggled for" (n. p.). Following a much more postmodern line of argument relative to his earlier work, Berger here suggests that the goal of struggle, as he puts it, is not to actually "achieve" liberation but to "preserv[e] human dignity in the present" (Bonaventura 1996: n. p.). It seems that Berger, like many others on the left, has retreated from the kinds of arguments for social change he more forcefully defended in his earlier work, even as many on the right have found it necessary to engage issues of class and inequality. To read in order to "preserve human dignity in the present" is quite different than to read as part of a practice of achieving the liberation of the exploited from the relations of exploitation – to end the relations that cause "indignity." Such reading not only sounds a lot like the calls for a common culture of transcendent values made by Clark and Gioia, but reflects a (privileged) acceptance of social inequality.

Reading the root of crisis (or transformative reading)

Even on the left, then, acquiescence to capital is increasingly the rule of the day. Returning to the contemporary debates over the reading "crisis," the effects of such acquiescence can be seen in the position on the reading crisis taken by Charles Taylor (2004). In an editorial on Salon.com, Taylor equates reading with "a visual experience" and reduces much of the commentary on the reading crisis, specifically the position taken by Solomon and Will, to "high-brow" snobbery. In short, he argues that Solomon, *et al.* are overly concerned with "traditional literacy," which is believed to be connected to Culture, intellectual development and critical citizenship, none of which are the reality of "reading" for the average person. As opposed to Solomon, *et al.*, Taylor argues that it is "mistaken" to see a division between "literacy and illiteracy," and that "the real contrast ... is between different models of literacy." In particular, Taylor believes that the traditionalists overlook that "visual literacy" is more complex and necessary today than "traditional" or "conceptual" literacy (n. p.).

While Taylor assumes that his view is more "in touch" with reality, he (like Johnson and Kirschenbaum) is really producing a view of reading and literacy that is just as much an ideological obfuscation as are the views of privatized reading put forth by Will and Solomon. First, in reducing reading to "a visual experience," even one which "enriches other experiences" (2004: n. p.), Taylor denies that reading is a conceptual practice – visual or otherwise. What such a theorization of reading does is prevent the examination of the conceptual assumptions behind "spontaneous" or "private" reading, while it also dismantles the means which students need to understand the social totality. Reading is once again rendered as a personal experience rather than a social practice. Second, the crisis over reading reflects changes in capital that have brought about new needs in the workforce – more pragmatic information skills that are tied to cyberliteracy, among other things. On the one hand, the right wants to go back to times when education was "well-rounded" and steeped in the traditional values. But this is a nostalgic view that romanticizes and mystifies capital's earlier needs, including the marginalized position of women and people of color in the workforce. The left, on the other hand, responds more favorably to new needs of capital. Their embrace of the fragmentary and the singular is a reflection of capital's need for new working-class subjectivities that do not require conceptual learning but easily replaceable skills that benefit corporations. Right and left quarrel over the moral surface features of the "crisis," but they do not grasp it by the roots; consequently, they produce readings and theories of reading which enable the existing relations of inequality to continue and to deepen.

Because of this, not only does privatized reading erase the material structures that compel the majority of the world's people to sell their labor power because the means of production have been privatized. Like all other forms of ideology, privatized reading also obscures what the forces of production have made possible under capitalism, namely new relations of production based on collective ownership. By substituting affective, experiential knowledge for concepts that would enable readers to understand the complex determining relations that constitute social structures, privatized reading keeps "invisible" the growing contradiction between the forces and relations of production. While production has become increasingly global and capable of meeting the needs of *all* people, what is ideologically fostered among the working class is that the privatization and commodification of life (which in fact benefits a very tiny transnational class of capitalists) is the most "democratic" way for all to live, even while the left accepts that democracy "doesn't offer any guarantees" (Taylor 2004: n. p.). Ideology "disappears" the objective contradictions of capitalism in order to present what is (what "appears") as what will always be. It turns capitalism into the transcendental signifier of human life itself in order to maintain increasingly outdated private relations.

Reading, as it has developed within capitalism, develops in order to serve the needs of capital for an exploitable workforce with skills corporations require. While the material conditions exist for the development of full critical literacy for all, the social relations between the classes are such that this development occurs only inasmuch as it enables the dominant class to meet its need for new ways to accumulate capital. This contradiction of education and literacy in capitalism means that reading is always in crisis; the crisis appears today to be a crisis of people not reading as they once did, or as they need to in order to be employed in the new technical industries, or as they need to in order to serve the national interest, ... But reading in class society is *always* contradictory; that is, it articulates the dominant class interests of its moment: the ruling class has an interest in developing certain aspects of knowledge (such as technical knowledge) in the working class, while at the same time blocking the development of other aspects of knowledge (such as knowledge of the social relations, which can guide transformative practices).

The reading "crisis," in short, is an effect of a shift in production; it is a reflection of the development of the cyber-skills of the new technologies and the new humanities. It represents a shift in what capital finds necessary for the new generation of workers to know, to facilitate capital's further globalization. The solution is not in some moral resolution of the crisis within capitalist relations, but rather in the transformation of these relations to equal ones, that is, in the end of exploitation and the development of new relations between people in production and all other aspects of social life. The resolution of the "crisis" is not to be found in a re-instatement of "literature," but rather in the development of class conscious reading: comprehensive, conceptual reading that takes the side of working people in the struggle for a just society.

I have been arguing that reading which does not read the appearances in relation to their root relations is ideological reading. Thus, I am claiming that *either* the crisis of reading is going to be resolved in the imaginary through ideology, an always partial and defensive resolution that will constantly need to be updated, or it is going to be resolved in actual material reality by revealing what is ideological, explaining its necessity, making visible the causes of the reading crisis, and making intelligible the possibility of a society of free and equal subjects whose reading develops as a comprehension of the perceptual in relation to the conceptual. Such reading is reading that is transformative; it is transformative reading because it shows that the current social structure is transformable, and because, armed with this knowledge, the working class can make a revolution and transform society.

Reading is not the answer to social problems, but it is a social practice at the center of any attempt to understand or change society. Transformative reading explains the class contradictions, and thus not only opens up the possibility of developing the knowledge necessary for transforming the social relations, but in fact is a necessary precondition for such social practice. Transformative reading is the science of the advancing productive forces, reading the world not only to interpret it, but to change it.

Note

1   Portions of this chapter are drawn from Faivre (2005).

Bibliography

Baudrillard, J. (1994) *Simulacra and Simulations*, Ann Arbor: University of Michigan Press.
Berger, J. (1972) *Ways of Seeing*, London: BBC / Penguin.
Berubé, M. (2005) *Aesthetics and Cultural Studies*, Oxford: Blackwell.
Bonaventura, P. (1996) "Master of diversity," *New Statesman*. Online. Available at http://www. newstatesman.com/200111120032 (accessed July 14, 2004).
Burke, J. (1999). *I Hear America Reading: why we read — what we read*, Portsmouth NH: Heinemann.
Clark, K. (1969) *Civilisation: a personal view*, London: BBC.
—— (1949) *Landscape into Art*, London: J. Murray.

Crain, C. (2007) "Twilight of the books,' *The New Yorker* (December 24). Online. Available at http://www.newyorker.com/arts/critics/atlarge/2007/12/24/071224crat_atlarge_crain (accessed February 15, 2008).

Edwards, E. and Hart, J. (2004) *Photographs/objects/histories: on the materiality of images*, New York: Routledge

Faivre, R. (2005) "Reading and Its Cultural Politics," *The Red Critique*, 10. Online. Available at http://www.redcritique.org/WinterSpring2005/readinganditsculturalpolitics.htm (accessed July 10, 2007).

Fuller, P. (1992) "Philistines anonymous," *New Statesman & Society* 5, 228 (13 November): xviii+.

Gainsborough, T. (*c.*1750) *Mr and Mrs Andrews*, London: The National Gallery. Online. Available at http://www.nationalgallery.org.uk (accessed June 27, 2007).

Gioia, D. (2008) "The transformative power of art," *Liberal Education* 94, 1: 18–21. Online. Available at http://www.aacu.org/liberaleducation/le-wi08/le-wi08_power_art.cfm (accessed February 15, 2008).

Hall, S. (1996) "Cultural studies and its theoretical legacies," in D. Morley and K.-H. Chen (eds) *Stuart Hall: critical dialogues in cultural studies*, New York: Routledge.

—— (ed.) (1997) *Representation: cultural representations and signifying practices*, London: Sage Publications.

Hirsch, E. D. (2006) *The Knowledge Deficit*, Boston: Houghton Mifflin Company.

Johnson, S. (2008) "Dawn of the digital natives," *The Guardian*. Online. Available at http://www.guardian.co.uk (accessed February 15, 2008).

Kirschenbaum, M. (2007) "How reading is being reimagined," *The Chronicle Review*, 54, 15 (December 7): B20.

Manguel, A. (1996) *A History of Reading*, New York: Viking.

Marx, K. (1996) *Capital*, Vol. 1, in *Collected Works* 35, New York: International Publishers.

—— and Engels, F. (1976) *The German Ideology*, in *Collected Works* 5, New York: International Publishers.

Solomon, A. (2004) "The closing of the American book," *International Herald Tribune*. Online. Available at http://www.iht.com (accessed July 17, 2004).

Taylor, Charles. (2004) "Let's save literature from the literati." *Salon.com* Online. Available at http://www.salon.com (accessed July 14, 2004).

United States National Endowment for the Arts (US NEA) (2004) *Reading at Risk: a survey of literary reading in America*. Research Report #46. Online. Available at http://www.arts.gov (accessed June 30, 2004).

—— (2007) *To Read or Not to Read: a question of national consequence*. Research Report #47. Online. Available at http://www.arts.gov (accessed December 1, 2007).

Will, George F. (2004) "Readers' block." *Washington Post* (July 23): A29.

Afterword

The contradictions of class and the praxis of becoming

Peter McLaren

At this ferociously ambivalent juncture in world history, with the flames of finance neoliberalism scourging the ideologists of capital that have found themselves strapped to the smoldering stake of global investment, it has never been more urgent to approach the question of social class from a Marxist perspective. This book does just that, arising from the ashes of capital's disgrace.

In today's world, imperialism has chosen to hide behind "humanitarian" military interventions into rogue states in the name of bringing about democracy and free trade. Social justice has resolved that it is acceptable to have inequality as long as it is not the product of racial or gender discrimination – in other words, as long as it confines itself purely to capitalist social relations. The intensification of capitalism's two primal axes of reproduction – deregulation and privatization – has impacted the conditions of possibility for barbarism to appear and wreak havoc in new and horrific ways that do not escape the precincts of education and the politics of knowledge production. Sadly, in the academy, and especially in institutions of graduate education, the challenge to capitalism has not taken place in the realm of material life, but rather in the arena of discourse and the politics of representation. The reason-centered subject of colonial power that subjugates subaltern peoples of the periphery (semi-feudal peripheral social relations) is not challenged directly by revolutionary praxis, but is now "decentered" as a text by way of a critique of Enlightenment humanism and by challenging the doxa of institutional disciplinary regimes. Such theoretical maneuvering serves as little more than an official apologetics for neoliberal capital and imperial power. It has a long history of use by a lineage of pedigreed scholars long on independent thought but short on political backbone whose protagonistic agency is more a frowzy affectation than a political obligation. Such a state of affairs sends a chilling horripilation through cadres of sincere social justice educators.

Class, critique, and social transformation

As I have indicated elsewhere (Aguirre 2001), the Marxist concept of class is not only a concept necessary for understanding capitalism. It is a concept necessary to the critique of class itself. Class as Marx theorized it is a central tool for the exploration of the constitution of capitalism that is premised upon a project for the abolition of class. It provides, in other words, a theory *against* capitalist society, and not just a theory *of* it. Class theory is therefore concerned with the *abolition* of class (Marx's position) and the opening up of human history from the desolation of its pre-history.

As all of the essays in this volume point out, however, the Marxist theory of class has largely been dismissed around the globe and over the last several decades, supplanted by culturalist versions of class, what Deborah Kelsh here calls "cultureclass." Versions of cultureclass favor a focus on exploring the decentering seen to be an effect of systems of representation operating within apparatuses of power-knowledge delinked from class and the exploitation of labor power. As a consequence, cultural differences are understood in terms of hybrid and continually shifting "in-between-spaces" in culture, that is, as effects of culture. Dismissed is any understanding of cultural differences as differences that are sustained, exacerbated, and (re)produced by the totality of social relations of production, kept in play only as long as they are useful to capital in its thirsty search for more and more profit.

Marx argued that society is a totality of relations that cannot be separated from the class relations of material production:

> the social relations within which individuals produce, the social relations of production, are altered, transformed, with the change and development of the material means of production, of the forces of production. The relations of production in their totality constitute what is called the social relations, society, and, moreover, a society at a definite state of historic development ...
>
> (1933: 28–9)

Changing society means changing the social relations of production in their totality, and for this to occur, it is necessary for the proletariat to have knowledge of the totality of social relations; it is this knowledge that is central to the development of revolutionary class consciousness that enables universal liberation of all people from the capitalist regime of exploitation. And while it is important to recognize, with Gramsci, that consciousness can be "contradictory" (1971: 333), the struggle for social justice cannot be successfully engaged through the perpetual and local parsing of the ambivalence inherent in power-knowledge relations, or through the repeated rupturing of a signifying chain, but through the revolutionary praxis of the oppressed, forged in sustained and principled class struggle, that aims to end class society. Knowledge workers can contribute to that revolutionary struggle by struggling at the level of knowledges to reveal the role dominant knowledges play in maintaining capitalism by hiding the social relations of production in their totality. It is important to emphasize this: historical materialist critique of the dominant knowledges is socially necessary labor for the abolition of capitalism.

In line with Marx, proponents of critical pedagogy hold that ideas must be situated in history and experience, as fallible generalizations that need to be ideologically unveiled by means of the praxis of historical materialist critique, which, because it aims to develop knowledge of social totality, is a necessary (though not sufficient) praxis in the class struggle to transform existing social relations. The development of this praxis takes on a special urgency today, when obeisance to the capitalist class remains an unspoken given, when capitalism's capacity to integrate the working class through their incorporation in financial markets and through the internationalization of the neoliberal market economy remains steady, and when expectations that neoliberal capitalism can be superseded by a better form of organizing social and economic life – such as socialism (or even Keynesian capitalism) – have been repeatedly renounced and undermined by political elites who act as the agents for the capitalist class (and are handsomely rewarded for their ideological services).

Central to the development of the praxis of historical materialist critique is the development of knowledge of internal relations, but not in terms of (cultural) relations of difference whose interactions are indeterminate, spontaneous, and hybridizing, and therefore unknowable and unchangeable. Rather, internal relations need to be understood as dialectical contradictions, a unity in which the relation of opposition is necessary for the constitution and existence of each of the two elements, whose relations unfold and shift in terms of a logic of movement that is rooted in material class practices and therefore knowable and changeable.

Internal relations and dialectical contradiction

Marx understood social life as shaped by dialectical contradiction, specifically the historically produced internal relations of capital and labor that constitute capital/ism. We participate in these relations, which permeate and shape our everyday lives, from where we live and how we die, to the level and type of anxiety we may or may not experience, to the amount and kind of nutrients we ingest to reproduce our individual existences. They, too, shape our thinking into forms of dichotomized thinking (Allman 2007). Dichotomized thinking is a thinking that arises from and reproduces the fragmented and partial consciousness of social totality, and consequently blocks revolutionary class consciousness. Part of the legacy of bourgeois consciousness and its "class morality," disseminated by academic thinking and in everyday discourse, dichomotized thinking can be traced to the principles, norms and rules that are carried into practice by the ruling class and that reflect and work to enable it to achieve its basic economic interests. Dichotomized thinking yields understanding that is distorted because it fails to perceive the components of dialectical contradictions as related, and internally so. Consequently, we experience and simultaneously make sense of related opposites (such as capital versus labor) as if they are discrete or separate from each other – a circumstance that serves the interests of the capitalist class. In order to struggle against such fractured and partial thinking, it is necessary to learn to grasp the fundamental relations of social life as dialectical – a whole constituted by opposing elements that cannot be changed without affecting the terms themselves between which the relation holds (Allman 2007). A philosophy of internal relations helps us develop a historical and developmental way of conceptualizing social life, a way of comprehending how the opposing elements of social life are related over time and reshaped by their own dialectical laws of motion.

With internal relations, one element of the relation cannot exist without the other. If the internally related opposites cease to exist, this occurs only because the entire relation has been abolished. All dialectical contradictions are internal relations, a relation of two opposing entities that could not exist, continue to exist, or have come into existence in the absence of their other (Allman, *et al.* 2005). The opposites could not be what they are or what they are to become outside of this relation.

A dialectical contradiction – the fundamental one of capitalism is capital-labor – an internal relation that is an antagonistic relation: the existence of each opposite is variously constrained or hampered by the fact that it is in a necessary internal relation with its opposite, and both are attempting to occupy the same space. However, one of the opposites, despite these limitations, actually benefits from the relation. It is in the interest of this opposite – often referred to as the positive – to maintain the relation. In terms of the capital-labor relation, it is in the interest of capital to maintain the relation. The other opposite – the negative – although it can better its circumstances temporarily within the relation, is severely limited by its relation to its opposite because the positive continually uses it to its own advantage, to the point of near devastation (although for the positive to continue to exist, it cannot follow through with the abolition of the negative). Labor is the negative pole in the capital-labor relation. It is in the interests of the negative pole to abolish the capital-labor relation (Allman, *et al.* 2005). The negative opposite does not cease to exist, but it does cease to exist in the position of the negative, the inferior, opposite due to its existence within an internal relation/dialectical contradiction.

Drawing on Hegel, Marx refers to the abolition of the contradictory opposites as the "negation of negation":

> The capitalist mode of appropriation, the result of the capitalist mode of production, produces capitalist private property. This is the first negation of individual property, as founded on the labour of the proprietor. But capitalist production begets, with the inexorability of a law of Nature, its own negation. It is the negation of negation. This does not re-establish private property for the producer, but gives him individual property based on the acquisitions of the capitalist era: *i.e.*, on co-operation and the possession in common of the land and of the means of production.
>
> (1967: 763)

Capital takes away individual property and substitutes for it private property; to transform capitalism into socialism, labor takes away private property and gives the individual property based on common ownership of land and the means of production.

Practical revolutionary activity – activities such as historical materialist critique, protests, and strikes – is mediating activity: it is activity that, by producing knowledge of the social totality and acting to change it, moves toward negation of the negation and simultaneously produces class consciousness activity. The mediating movement of the negation of the negation, in other words, contributes to a process of becoming.

Understanding internal relations in terms of dialectical contradictions helps us understand revolutionary praxis not as some arche-strategy of political performance undertaken by academic mountebanks in the semiotics seminar room, but instead in terms of humans grasping the social totality as it is changing, and acting as it changes in order to open spaces for greater understanding that in turn enable more effective and unified action. It is through such dialectical activity that we develop our capacities and capabilities. We change society by changing ourselves and we change ourselves in our struggle to change society. The act of knowing is always a knowing act. It troubles and disturbs the universe of objects and beings, because it cannot exist outside of them; it is interactive, dialogical. We learn about reality not by reflecting on it but by changing it. Paying attention to the social totality and its changes, struggling to grasp them, and intervening in them to create a new integrated world view founded upon a new social matrix is the hallmark of the public scholar and educator. It is Marx's form of revolutionary praxis.

We need to grasp what absolute negation as a new beginning means for today. In the face of intensified class contradiction that provides new contexts of being and becoming, critical pedagogy faces the test of being reconstructed anew, in and through historical materialist critique grounded in the Marxist theory of class. And this reconstruction stipulates that we need to start to define, through a critique of what is, the characteristics of a world outside of capital's value form. We need, in other words, to start constructing a post-capitalist society that is a socialist society. Armed with the Marxist theory of class and a theory of internal relations informing a critical/revolutionary pedagogy, this possibility can become a reality.

In closing and toward beginning

This book engages in the socially necessary labor of historical materialist critique that reveals the internal relations of class. It is a powerful intervention into existing left revisionist discourses in education that, believing there is no alternative to capitalism, dismiss the Marxist concept of class. In doing so, these revisionist discourses rob the proletariat of the concept of class as Marx theorized it. Yet Marx's concept of class is necessary in the struggle to end exploitation by ending the class society in which "capital" is the "dead labor" of workers, dead labor that, as the property of the capitalist class, is converted into capital and made "vampire-like": capital "only lives by sucking living labor, and lives the more, the more labor it sucks" (Marx 1967: 233). Marx's concept of class is a necessary concept for explaining the internal relation between capital and labor and the role of social relations in fashioning the subject, following Marx's assertion of the priority of social being over individual consciousness. This book provides new concepts – cultureclass (Deborah Kelsh), hypohumanities (Teresa L. Ebert and Mas'ud Zavarzadeh), de-reading and transformative reading (Robert Faivre) – and advances existing ones – the state (Ravi Kumar; Enver Motala and Salim Vally), xeno-racialization (Mike Cole and Alpesh Maisuria), globalization and the social studies curriculum (E. Wayne Ross and Greg Queen), strong historical materialism (Grant Banfield) – that are all useful in deepening our knowledge of internal relations and thus in pointing to a new beginning – a socialist beginning. This important work provides us with the relational, contextual and historicist thinking absent from most anti-totalizing and banalizing leftist work in education that now represents the entrenched orthodoxies, institutionally consecrated touchstones and canonical handbooks of the progressive tradition. It is a book that has the potential to revolutionize how educators understand and employ the concept of class in their work and their everyday praxis. As such, it is a book that surely will provoke the kind of debate and discussion needed to break us free from the prehistory of humanity and take us into the future where history can finally be written.

Bibliography

Aguirre, L. C. (2001) "The role of critical pedagogy in the globalization era and the aftermath of September 11, 2001. Interview with Peter McLaren." *Revista Electrónica de Investigación Educativa*, 3 (2). Online. Available at http://redie.uabc.mx/vol3no2/contents-coral.html (accessed September 8, 2008).

Allman, P. (2007) *On Marx: an introduction to the revolutionary intellect of Karl Marx*, Rotterdam, The Netherlands: Sense Publishers.

Allman, P., McLaren, P. and Rikowski, G. (2005) "After the Box People: the labor-capital relation as class constitution and its consequences for Marxist educational theory and human resistance," in P. McLaren, *Capitalists and Conquerors: a critical pedagogy against empire*, Lanham, MD: Rowman & Littlefield.

Gramsci, A. (1971) *Selections from the Prison Notebooks*, New York: International Publishers.

Marx, K. (1967) *Capital: Volume 1*, trans. S. Moore and E. Aveling, ed. F. Engels, New York: International Publishers.

—— (1933) *Wage-labour and Capital*, New York: International Publishers.

Index of names

Related titles from Routledge

The Developing World and State Education
Edited by Dave Hill and Ellen Rosskam
ISBN: 978-0-415-95776-2

Global Neoliberalism and Education and its Consequences
Edited by Dave Hill and Ravi Kumar
ISBN: 978-0-415-95774-8

The Rich World and the Impoverishment of Education
Edited by Dave Hill
ISBN: 978-0-415-95775-5

Contesting Neoliberal Education
Edited by Dave Hill
ISBN: 978-0-415-95777-9